A GUIDE TO THE
MANNERS, ETIQUETTE,
AND DEPORTMENT
OF THE MOST REFINED SOCIETY

A Guide to the
MANNERS, ETIQUETTE,
AND DEPORTMENT
of the Most Refined Society

COMPILED FROM THE LATEST RELIABLE AUTHORITIES

JOHN H. YOUNG, A. M.

R EVISED, ENLARGED, AND ILLUSTRATED

THE LYONS PRESS

Originally published in 1879 by W. C. King & Co.,
Publishers as *Our Deportment, or the Manners, Conduct
and Dress of the Most Refined Society; Including Forms for
Letters, Invitations, Etc., Etc., Also Valuable Suggestions
for Home Culture and Training.*
Revised, Enlarged, and Illustrated 1881 and 1883.

First Lyons Press Edition, March 2001

Printed in the United States of America

2   4   6   8   10   9   7   5   3   1

Library of Congress Cataloging-in-Publication Data
is available on file.

Preface.

O one subject is of more importance to people generally than a knowledge of the rules, usages and ceremonies of good society, which are commonly expressed by the word "Etiquette." Its necessity is felt wherever men and women associate together, whether in the city, village, or country town, at home or abroad. To acquire a thorough knowledge of these matters, and to put that knowledge into practice with perfect ease and self-complacency, is what people call good breeding. To display an ignorance of them, is to subject the offender to the opprobrium of being ill-bred.

In the compilation of this work, the object has been to present the usages and rules which govern the most refined American society, and to impart that information which will enable any one, in whatever circumstances of life to acquire the perfect ease of a gentleman, or the gentle manners and graceful deportment of a well-bred lady, whose presence will be sought for, and who, by their graceful deportment will learn the art of being at home in any good society.

The work is so arranged, that every subject is conveniently classified and subdivided; it is thus an easy matter to refer at once to any given subject. It has been the aim of the compiler to give minutely all points that are properly embraced in a work on etiquette, even upon matters of seemingly trivial importance. Upon some hitherto disputed points, those rules are given, which are sustained by the best authorities and endorsed by good sense.

As the work is not the authorship of any one individual, and as no individual, whatever may be his acquirements, could have the presumption to dictate rules for the conduct of society in general, it is therefore only claimed that it is a careful compilation from all the best and latest authorities upon the subject of etiquette and kindred matters, while such additional material has been embraced within its pages, as, it is hoped, will be found of benefit and interest to every American household.

J. H. Y.

Contents.

CHAPTER I.

CHAPTER II.

MANNERS.

CHAPTER III.

INTRODUCTIONS.

CHAPTER IV.

SALUTATIONS.

6 CONTENTS.

CHAPTER V.

ETIQUETTE ON CALLS.

CHAPTER VI.

ETIQUETTE ON VISITING.

CHAPTER VII.

ETIQUETTE OF CARDS.

CHAPTER VIII.

CONVERSATION.

CHAPTER IX.

DINNER PARTIES.

CHAPTER X.

TABLE ETIQUETTE.

CHAPTER XI.

RECEPTIONS, PARTIES AND BALLS.

CHAPTER XII.

STREET ETIQUETTE.

CHAPTER XIII.

ETIQUETTE OF PUBLIC PLACES.

CHAPTER XIV.

TRAVELING ETIQUETTE.

CHAPTER XV.

RIDING AND DRIVING.

CHAPTER XVI.

COURTSHIP.

CHAPTER XVII.

WEDDING ETIQUETTE.

CHAPTER XVIII.

HOME LIFE AND ETIQUETTE.

CHAPTER XIX.

HOME TRAINING.

CHAPTER XX.

HOME CULTURE.

CHAPTER XXI.

WOMAN'S HIGHER EDUCATION.

CHAPTER XXII.

THE LETTER WRITER.

CHAPTER XXIII.

GENERAL RULES TO GOVERN CONDUCT.

CHAPTER XXIV.

ANNIVERSARY WEDDINGS.

CHAPTER XXV.

BIRTHS AND CHRISTENINGS.

CHAPTER XXVI.

FUNERALS.

CHAPTER XXVII.

ETIQUETTE AT WASHINGTON.

CHAPTER XXVIII.

ETIQUETTE OF FOREIGN COURTS.

CHAPTER XXIX.

BUSINESS.

CHAPTER XXX.

DRESS.

CHAPTER I.

Introductory.

"Ingenious Art with her expressive face,
Steps forth to fashion and refine the race."—COWPER.

KNOWLEDGE of etiquette has been defined to be a knowledge of the rules of society at its best. These rules have been the outgrowth of centuries of civilization, had their foundation in friendship and love of man for his fellow man—the vital principles of Christianity—and are most powerful agents for promoting peace, harmony and good will among all people who are enjoying the blessings of more advanced civilized government. In all civilized countries the influence of the best society is of great importance to the welfare and prosperity of the nation, but in no country is the good influence of the most refined society more powerfully felt than in our own, "the land of the future, where mankind may plant, essay, and resolve all social problems." These rules make social intercourse more agreeable, and facilitate hospitalities, when all

(13)

members of society hold them as binding rules and faithfully regard their observance. They are to society what our laws are to the people as a political body, and to disregard them will give rise to constant misunderstandings, engender ill-will, and beget bad morals and bad manners.

Says an eminent English writer: "On manners, refinement, rules of good breeding, and even the forms of etiquette, we are forever talking, judging our neighbors severely by the breach of traditionary and unwritten laws, and choosing our society and even our friends by the touchstone of courtesy." The Marchioness de Lambert expressed opinions which will be endorsed by the best bred people everywhere when she wrote to her son: "Nothing is more shameful than a voluntary rudeness. Men have found it necessary as well as agreeable to unite for the common good; they have made laws to restrain the wicked; they have agreed among themselves as to the duties of society, and have annexed an honorable character to the practice of those duties. He is the honest man who observes them with the most exactness, and the instances of them multiply in proportion to the degree of nicety of a person's honor."

Originally a gentleman was defined to be one who, without any title of nobility, wore a coat of arms. And the descendants of many of the early colonists preserve with much pride and care the old armorial bearings which their ancestors brought with them from their homes in the mother country. Although despising titles and ignoring the rights of kings, they still clung to the "grand old name of gentleman." But race is no longer the only requisite for a gentleman, nor will race united with learning and wealth make a man a gentleman, unless there are present the kind and gentle qualities of the heart, which find expression in the principles of the Golden Rule. Nor will race, education and wealth combined make a woman a true lady if she shows a want of refinement and consideration of the feelings of others.

Good manners are only acquired by education and observation, followed up by habitual practice at home and in society, and good manners reveal to us the lady and the gentleman. He who does not possess them, though he bear the highest title of nobility, cannot expect to be called a gentleman; nor can a woman, without good manners, aspire to be considered a lady by ladies. Manners and morals are indissolubly allied, and no society can be good where they are bad. It is the duty of American women to exercise their influence to form so high a standard of morals and manners that the tendency of society will be continually upwards, seeking to make it the best society of any nation.

As culture is the first requirement of good society, so self-improvement should be the aim of each and all of its members. Manners will improve with the cultivation of the mind, until the pleasure and harmony of social intercourse are no longer marred by the introduction of discordant elements, and they only will be excluded from the best society whose lack of education and whose rude manners will totally unfit them for its enjoyments and appreciation. Good manners are even more essential to harmony in society than a good education, and may be considered as valuable an acquisition as knowledge in any form.

The principles of the Golden Rule, "whatsoever ye would that men should do to you, do ye even so to them," is the basis of all true politeness—principles which teach us to forget ourselves, to be kind to our neighbors, and to be civil even to our enemies. The appearance of so being and doing is what society demands as good manners, and the man or woman trained to this mode of life is regarded as well-bred. The people, thus trained, are easy to get along with, for they are as quick to make an apology when they have been at fault, as they are to accept one when it is made. "The noble-hearted only understand the noble-hearted."

In a society where the majority are rude from the thoughtfulness of ignorance, or remiss from the insolence of bad breeding, the iron rule, "Do unto others, as they do unto you," is more often put into practice than the golden one. The savages know nothing of the virtues of forgiveness, and regard those who are not revengeful as wanting in spirit; so the ill-bred do not understand undeserved civilities extended to promote the general interests of society, and to carry out the injunction of the Scriptures to strive after the things that make for peace.

Society is divided into sets, according to their breeding. One set may be said to have no breeding at all, another to have a little, another more, and another enough; and between the first and last of these, there are more shades than in the rainbow. Good manners are the same in essence everywhere—at courts, in fashionable society, in literary circles, in domestic life— they never change, but social observances, customs and points of etiquette, vary with the age and with the people.

A French writer has said: "To be truly polite, it is necessary to be, at the same time, good, just, and generous. True politeness is the outward visible sign of those inward spiritual graces called modesty, unselfishness and generosity. The manners of a gentleman are the index of his soul. His speech is innocent, because his life is pure; his thoughts are right, because his actions are upright; his bearing is gentle, because his feelings, his impulses, and his training are gentle also. A gentleman is entirely free from every kind of pretence. He avoids homage, instead of exacting it. Mere ceremonies have no attraction for him. He seeks not to say any civil things, but to do them. His hospitality, though hearty and sincere, will be strictly regulated by his means. His friends will be chosen for their good qualities and good manners; his servants for their truthfulness and honesty; his occupations for their usefulness, their gracefulness or their elevating tendencies, whether moral, mental or political."

In the same general tone does Ruskin describe a gentleman, when he says: "A gentleman's first char-

acteristic is that fineness of structure in the body
which renders it capable of the most delicate sensation,
and of that structure in the mind which renders it
capable of the most delicate sympathies—one may say,
simply, ' fineness of nature.' This is, of course, compati-
ble with the heroic bodily strength and mental firmness;
in fact, heroic strength is not conceivable without such
delicacy. Elephantine strength may drive its way
through a forest and feel no touch of the boughs, but
the white skin of Homer's Atrides would have felt a
bent rose-leaf, yet subdue its feelings in the glow of
battle and behave itself like iron. I do not mean to call
an elephant a vulgar animal; but if you think about
him carefully, you will find that his non-vulgarity consists in such gentleness as is possible to elephantine
nature—not in his insensitive hide nor in his clumsy
foot, but in the way he will lift his foot if a child lies
in his way, and in his sensitive trunk and still more
sensitive mind and capability of pique on points of
honor. Hence it will follow that one of the probable
signs of high breeding in men generally, will be their
kindness and mercifulness, these always indicating
more or less firmness of make in the mind."

Can any one fancy what our society might be, if all
its members were perfect gentlemen and true ladies, if
all the inhabitants of the earth were kind-hearted; if,
instead of contending with the faults of our fellows we
were each to wage war against our own faults ? Every
one needs to guard constantly against the evil from

within as well as from without, for as has been truly said, "a man's greatest foe dwells in his own heart."

A recent English writer says: "Etiquette may be defined as the minor morality of life. No observances, however minute, that tend to spare the feelings of others, can be classed under the head of trivialities; and politeness, which is but another name for general amiability, will oil the creaking wheels of life more effectually than any of those unguents supplied by mere wealth and station." While the social observances, customs and rules which have grown up are numerous, and some perhaps considered trivial, they are all grounded upon principles of kindness to one another, and spring from the impulses of a good heart and from friendly feelings. The truly polite man acts from the highest and noblest ideas of what is right.

Lord Chesterfield declared good breeding to be "the result of much good sense, some good nature and a little self-denial for the sake of others, and with a view to obtain the same indulgence from them." Again he says: "Good sense and good nature suggest civility in general, but in good breeding there are a thousand little delicacies which are established only by custom."

CHAPTER II.

Our Manners.

N O one quality of the mind and heart is more important as an element conducive to worldly success than civility—that feeling of kindness and love for our fellow-beings which is expressed in pleasing manners. Yet how many of our young men, with an affected contempt for the forms and conventionalities of life, assume to despise those delicate attentions, that exquisite tenderness of thought and manner, that mark the true gentleman.

MANNERS AS AN ELEMENT OF SUCCESS.

History repeats, over and over again, examples showing that it is the bearing of a man toward his fellowmen which, more than any other one quality of his nature, promotes or retards his advancement in life. The success or failure of one's plans have often turned upon the address and manner of the man. Though there are a few people who can look beyond the rough husk or shell of a fellow-being to the finer qualities hidden within, yet the vast majority, not so keen-visaged nor tolerant, judge a person by his appearance and demeanor, more than by his substantial character. Experience of every day life teaches us, if we would but learn, that civility is not only one of the essentials of high success, but that it is almost a fortune of itself, and that he who has this quality in perfection, though a blockhead, is almost sure to succeed where, without it, even men of good ability fail.

A good manner is the best letter of recommendation among strangers. Civility, refinement and gentleness are passports to hearts and homes, while awkwardness, coarseness and gruffness are met with locked doors and closed hearts. Emerson says: "Give a boy address and accomplishments, and you give him the mastery of palaces and fortunes wherever he goes; he has not the trouble of earning or owning them; they solicit him to enter and possess."

In every class of life, in all professions and occupations, good manners are necessary to success. The business man has no stock-in-trade that pays him better than a good address. If the retail dealer wears his hat on his head in the presence of ladies who come to buy of him, if he does not see that the heavy door of his shop is opened and closed for them, if he seats himself in their presence, if he smokes a pipe or cigar, or has a chew of tobacco in his mouth, while talking with them, or is guilty of any of the small incivilities of life, they will not be apt to make his shop a rendezvous, no matter how attractive the goods he displays.

A telling preacher in his opening remarks gains the good will of his hearers, and makes them feel both that he has something to say, and that he can say it, by his manner. The successful medical man inspires in his patients belief in his sympathy, and confidence in his skill, by his manner. The lawyer, in pleading a case before a jury, and remembering that the passions and prejudices of the jurymen govern them to as great an extent as pure reason, must not be forgetful of his manner, if he would bring them to his own way of thinking. And how often does the motto, "Manners make the man," govern both parties in matters of courtship, the lady giving preference to him whose manners indicate a true nobility of the soul, and the gentleman preferring her who displays in her manner a gentleness of spirit.

MANNER AN INDEX OF CHARACTER.

A rude person, though well meaning, is avoided by all. Manners, in fact, are minor morals; and a rude person is often assumed to be a bad person. The manner in which a person says or does a thing, furnishes a better index of his character than what he does or says, for it is by the incidental expression given to his thoughts and feelings, by his looks, tones and gestures, rather than by his words and deeds, that we prefer to judge him, for the reason that the former are involuntary. The manner in which a favor is granted or a kindness done, often affects us more than the deed itself. The deed may have been prompted by vanity, pride, or some selfish motive or interest; the warmth or coldness with which the person who has done it speaks to you, or grasps your hand, is less likely to deceive. The manner of doing any thing, it has been truly said, is that which stamps its life and character on any action. A favor may be performed so grudgingly as to prevent any feeling of obligation, or it may be refused so courteously as to awaken more kindly feelings than if it had been ungraciously granted.

THE TRUE GENTLEMAN.

Politeness is benevolence in small things. A true gentleman must regard the rights and feelings of others, even in matters the most trivial. He respects the individuality of others, just as he wishes others to respect his own. In society he is quiet, easy, unobtrusive, putting on no airs, nor hinting by word or manner that he deems himself better, or wiser, or richer than any one about him. He never boasts of his achievements, or fishes for compliments by affecting to underrate what he has done. He is distinguished, above all things, by his deep insight and sympathy, his quick perception of, and prompt attention to, those small and apparently insignificant things that may cause pleasure or pain to others. In giving his opinions he does not dogmatize; he listens patiently and respectfully to other men, and, if compelled to dissent from their opinions, acknowledges his fallibility and asserts his own views in such a manner as to command the respect of all who hear him. Frankness and cordiality mark all his intercourse with his fellows, and, however high his station, the humblest man feels instantly at ease in his presence.

THE TRUE LADY.

Calvert says: "Ladyhood is an emanation from the heart subtilized by culture;" giving as two requisites for the highest breeding, transmitted qualities and the culture of good training. He continues: "Of the higher type of ladyhood may always be said what Steele said of Lady Elizabeth Hastings, 'that unaffected freedom and conscious innocence gave her the attendance of the graces in all her actions.' At its highest, ladyhood implies a spirituality made manifest in poetic grace. From the lady there exhales a subtle magnetism. Unconsciously she encircles herself with an atmosphere of unruffled strength, which, to those who come into it, gives confidence and repose. Within her influence the diffident grow self-possessed, the impudent are checked, the inconsiderate are admonished; even the rude are constrained to be mannerly, and the refined are perfected; all spelled, unawares, by the flexible dignity, the commanding gentleness, the thorough womanliness of her look, speech and demeanor. A sway is this, purely spiritual. Every sway, every legitimate, every enduring sway is spiritual; a regnancy of light over obscurity, of right over brutality. The only real gains ever made are spiritual gains—a further subjection of the gross to the incorporeal, of body to soul, of the animal to the human. The finest and most characteristic acts of a lady involve a spiritual ascension, a growing out of herself. In her being and bearing, patience, generosity, benignity are the graces that give shape to the virtues of truthfulness."

Here is the test of true ladyhood. Whenever the young find themselves in the company of those who do not make them feel at ease, they should know that they are not in the society of true ladies and true gentlemen, but of pretenders; that well-bred men and women can only feel at home in the society of the well-bred.

THE IMPORTANCE OF TRIFLES.

Some people are wont to depreciate these kind and tender qualities as trifles; but trifles, it must be remembered, make up the aggregate of human life. The petty incivilities, slight rudenesses and neglects of which men are guilty, without thought, or from lack of foresight or sympathy, are often remembered, while the great acts performed by the same persons are often forgotten. There is no society where smiles, pleasant looks and animal spirits are not welcomed and deemed of more importance than sallies of wit, or refinements of understanding. The little civilities, which form the small change of life may appear separately of little moment, but, like the spare pennies which amount to such large fortunes in a lifetime, they owe their importance to repetition and accumulation.

VALUE OF PLEASING MANNERS.

The man who succeeds in any calling in life is almost invariably he who has shown a willingness to please and to be pleased, who has responded heartily to the advan-

ces of others, through nature and habit, while his rival
has sniffed and frowned and snubbed away every help-
ing hand. "The charming manners of the Duke of
Marlborough," it is said, "often changed an enemy to a
friend, and to be denied a favor by him was more pleasing than to receive one from another. It was these personal graces that made him both rich and great. His
address was so exquisitely fascinating as to dissolve
fierce jealousies and animosities, lull suspicion and
beguile the subtlest diplomacy of its arts. His fascinating smile and winning tongue, equally with his sharp
sword, swayed the destinies of empires." The gracious
manners of Charles James Fox preserved him from personal dislike, even when he had gambled away his last
shilling, and politically, was the most unpopular man in
England.

MANNERS AND PERSONAL APPEARANCE.

A charming manner not only enhances personal
beauty, but even hides ugliness and makes plainness
agreeable. An ill-favored countenance is not necessarily a stumbling-block, at the outset, to its owner,
which cannot be surmounted, for who does not know
how much a happy manner often does to neutralize the
ill effects of forbidding looks? The fascination of the
demagogue Wilkes's manner triumphed over both physical and moral deformity, rendering even his ugliness
agreeable; and he boasted to Lord Townsend, one of the
handsomest men in Great Britain, that "with half an
hour's start he would get ahead of his lordship in the

affections of any woman in the kingdom." The ugliest
Frenchman, perhaps, that ever lived was Mirabeau; yet
such was the witchery of his manner, that the belt of no
gay Lothario was hung with a greater number of bleeding female hearts than this "thunderer of the tribune,"
whose looks were so hideous that he was compared to a
tiger pitted with the small-pox.

FORTUNES MADE BY PLEASING MANNERS.

Pleasing manners have made the fortunes of men in
all professions and in every walk of life—of lawyers,
doctors, clergymen, merchants, clerks and mechanics—
and instances of this are so numerous that they may be
recalled by almost any person. The politician who has
the advantage of a courteous, graceful and pleasing manner finds himself an easy winner in the race with rival
candidates, for every voter with whom he speaks becomes
instantly his friend. Civility is to a man what beauty is
to a woman. It creates an instantaneous impression in
his behalf, while gruffness or coarseness excites as quick
a prejudice against him. It is an ornament, worth more
as a means of winning favor than the finest clothes
and jewels ever worn. Lord Chesterfield said the art of
pleasing is, in truth, the art of rising, of distinguishing
one's self, of making a figure and a fortune in the world.
Some years ago a drygoods salesman in a London shop
had acquired such a reputation for courtesy and exhaust-
less patience, that it was said to be impossible to provoke from him any expression of irritability, or the
smallest symptom of vexation. A lady of rank learning

of his wonderful equanimity, determined to put it to the test by all the annoyances with which a veteran shop-visitor knows how to tease a shopman. She failed in her attempt to vex or irritate him, and thereupon set him up in business. He rose to eminence in trade, and the main spring of his later, as of his earlier career, was politeness. Hundreds of men, like this salesman, have owed their start in life wholly to their pleasing address and manners.

CULTIVATION OF GOOD MANNERS.

The cultivation of pleasing, affable manners should be an important part of the education of every person of whatever calling or station in life. Many people think that if they have only the substance, the form is of little consequence. But manners are a compound of spirit and form—spirit acted into form. The first law of good manners, which epitomizes all the rest is, "Thou shalt love thy neighbor as thyself." True courtesy is simply the application of this golden rule to all our social conduct, or, as it has been happily defined, "real kindness, kindly expressed." It may be met in the hut of the Arab, in the courtyard of the Turk, in the hovel of the freedman, and the cottage of the Irishman. Even Christian men sometimes fail in courtesy, deeming it a mark of weakness, or neglecting it from mere thoughtlessness. Yet when we find this added to the other virtues of the Christian, it will be noted that his influence for good upon others has been powerfully increased, for it was by this that he obtained access to the hearts of others. An old English writer said reverently of our Saviour: "He was the first true gentleman that ever lived." The influence of many good men would be more than doubled if they could manage to be less stiff and more elastic. Gentleness in society, it has been truly said, "is like the silent influence of light which gives color to all nature; it is far more powerful than loudness or force, and far more fruitful. It pushes its way silently and persistently like the tiniest daffodil in spring, which raises the clod and thrusts it aside by the simple persistence of growing."

POLITENESS.

Politeness is kindness of manner. This is the outgrowth of kindness of heart, of nobleness, and of courage. But in some persons we find an abundance of courage, nobleness and kindness of heart, without kindness of manner, and we can only think and speak of them as not only impolite, but even rude and gruff. Such a man was Dr. Johnson, whose rudeness secured for him the nickname of Ursa Major, and of whom Goldsmith truthfully remarked, "No man alive has a more tender heart; he has nothing of the bear about him but his skin." To acquire that ease and grace of manners which is possessed by and which distinguishes every well-bred person, one must think of others rather than of himself, and study to please them even at his own inconvenience. "Do unto others as you would that others should do unto you"—the golden rule of life—is also the law of politeness, and such politeness implies self-sacrifice, many struggles and conflicts. It is an art and tact, rather than an instinct and inspiration. An eminent divine has said: "A noble and attractive every-day bearing comes of goodness, of sincerity, of refinement. And these are bred in years, not moments. The principle that rules our life is the sure posture-master. Sir Philip Sidney was the pattern to all England of a perfect gentleman; but then he was the hero that, on the field of Zutphen, pushed away the cup of cold water from his own fevered and parched lips, and held it out to the dying soldier at his side." A Christian by the very conditions of his creed, and the obligations of his faith is, of necessity, in mind and soul —and therefore in word and act—a gentleman, but a man may be polite without being a Christian.

CHAPTER III.

Introductions.

N acquaintanceship or friendship usually begins by means of introtions, though it is by no means uncommon that when it has taken place under other circumstances—without introduction—it has been a great advantage to both parties; nor can it be said that it is improper to begin an acquaintance in this way. The formal introduction has been called the highway to the beginning of friendship, and the "scraped" acquaintance the by-path.

PROMISCUOUS INTRODUCTION.

There is a large class of people who introduce friends and acquaintances to everybody they meet, whether at home or abroad, while walking or riding out. Such promiscuous introductions are neither necessary, desirable, nor at all times agreeable.

AN INTRODUCTION A SOCIAL ENDORSEMENT.

It is to be remembered that an introduction is regarded as a social endorsement of the person introduced, **and** that, under certain circumstances, it would be wrong to introduce to our friends casual acquaintances, of whom we know nothing, and who may afterwards prove to be anything but desirable persons to know. Care should be taken, therefore, in introducing two individuals, that the introduction be mutually agreeable. Whenever it is practicable, it is best to settle the point by inquiring beforehand. When this is inexpedient from any cause, a thorough acquaintance with both parties will warrant the introducer to judge of the point for him or herself.

UNIVERSAL INTRODUCTIONS.

While the habit of universal introductions is a bad one, there are many men in cities and villages who are not at all particular whom they introduce to each other. As a general rule, a man should be as careful about the character of the person he introduces to his friends, as he is of him whose notes he would endorse.

THE INTRODUCTION OF A GENTLEMAN TO A LADY.

A gentleman should not be introduced to a lady, unless her permission has been previously obtained, and no one should ever be introduced into the house of a friend, except permission is first granted. Such introductions, however, are frequent, but they are improper, for a person cannot know that an introduction of this kind will be agreeable. If a person asks you to introduce him to another, or a gentleman asks to be introduced to a lady, and you find the introduction would not be agreeable to the other party, you may decline on the grounds that you are not sufficiently intimate to take that liberty.

When a gentleman is introduced to a lady, both bow slightly, and the gentleman opens conversation. It is the place of the one who is introduced to make the first remark.

INFORMAL INTRODUCTION.

It is not strictly necessary that acquaintanceship should wait a formal introduction. Persons meeting at the house of a common friend may consider that fact a sufficient warrant for the preliminaries of acquaintance-ship, if there appears to be a mutual inclination toward such acquaintanceship. The presence of a person in a friend's house is a sufficient guaranty for his or her re-spectability. Gentlemen and ladies may form acquaint-ances in traveling, on a steamboat, in a railway car, or a stage-coach, without the formality of an introduction. Such acquaintanceship should be conducted with a cer-tain amount of reserve, and need not be prolonged be-yond the time of casual meeting. The slightest ap-proach to disrespect or familiarity should be checked by dignified silence. A young lady, however, is not accorded the same privilege of forming acquaintances as is a married or elderly lady, and should be careful about doing so.

INTRODUCTIONS AT A BALL.

It is the part of the host and hostess at a ball to introduce their guests, though guests may, with perfect propriety, introduce each other, or, as already intimated, may converse with one another without the ceremony of a formal introduction. A gentleman, before introducing his friends to ladies, should obtain permission of the latter to do so, unless he is perfectly sure, from his knowledge of the ladies, that the introductions will be agreeable. The ladies should always grant such permission, unless there is a strong reason for refusing. The French, and to some extent the English, dispense with introductions at a private ball. The fact that they have been invited to meet each other is regarded as a guaranty that they are fit to be mutually acquainted, and is a sufficient warrant for self-introduction. At a public ball partners must be introduced to each other. Special introducing may be made with propriety by the master of ceremonies. At public balls it is well for ladies to dance only, or for the most part, with gentlemen of their own party, or those with whom they have had a previous acquaintance.

THE MANNER OF INTRODUCTION.

The proper form of introduction is to present the gentleman to the lady, the younger to the older, the inferior in social standing to the superior. In introducing, you bow to the lady and say, "Miss C., allow me to introduce to you Mr. D. Mr. D., Miss C." It is the duty of Mr. D. upon bowing to say, "It gives me great pleasure to form your acquaintance, Miss C.," or a remark of this nature.

If gentlemen are to be introduced to one another, the

form is, " Col. Blank, permit me to introduce to you Mr. Cole. Mr. Cole, Col. Blank." The exact words of an introduction are immaterial, so long as the proper form and order is preserved.

The word "present " is often used in place of " introduce." While it is customary to repeat the names of the two parties introduced at the close of the introduction, it is often omitted as a useless formality. It is of the utmost importance that each name should be spoken distinctly. If either of the parties does not distinctly hear the name of the other he should say at once, without hesitation or embarrassment, before making the bow, " I beg your pardon; I did not catch (or understand) the name," when it may be repeated to him.

If several persons are to be introduced to one individual, mention the name of the single individual first, and then call the others in succession, bowing slightly as each name is pronounced.

It is the part of true politeness, after introductions, to explain to each person introduced something of the business or residence of each, as they will assist in opening conversation. Or, if one party has recently returned from a foreign trip, it is courteous to say so.

CASUAL INTRODUCTIONS.

While it is not necessary to introduce people who chance to meet in your house during a morning call; yet, if there is no reason for supposing that such an introduction will be objectionable to either party, it seems better to give it, as it sets both parties at ease in conversation. Acquaintanceship may or may not follow such an introduction, at the option of the parties. People who meet at the house of a mutual friend need not recognize each other as acquaintances if they meet again elsewhere, unless they choose to do so.

INTRODUCING RELATIVES.

In introducing members of your own family, be careful not only to specify the degree of relationship, but to give the name also. It is awkward to a stranger to be introduced to "My brother Tom," or "My sister Carrie." When either the introducer or the introduced is a married lady, the name of the party introduced can only be guessed at.

BESTOWING OF TITLES.

In introducing a person give him his appropriate title. If he is a clergyman, say "The Rev. Mr. Clark." If a doctor of divinity, say "The Rev. Dr. Clark." If he is a member of Congress, call him "Honorable," and specify to which branch of Congress he belongs. If he is governor of a State, mention what State. If he is a man of any celebrity in the world of art or letters, it is well to mention the fact something after this manner: "Mr. Fish, the artist, whose pictures you have frequently seen," or "Mr. Hart, author of 'Our Future State,' which you so greatly admired."

OBLIGATORY INTRODUCTIONS.

A friend visiting at your house must be introduced to all callers, and courtesy requires the latter to cultivate the acquaintance while your visitor remains with you. If you are the caller introduced, you must show the same attention to the friend of your friend that you wish shown your own friends under the same circumstances. Persons meeting at public places need not introduce each other to the strangers who may chance to be with them; and, even if the introduction does take place, the acquaintance need not be continued unless desired.

THE OBLIGATION OF AN INTRODUCTION.

Two persons who have been properly introduced have in future certain claims upon one another's acquaintance which should be recognized, unless there are sufficient reasons for overlooking them. Even in that case good manners require the formal bow of recognition upon meeting, which, of itself, encourages no familiarity. Only a very ill-bred person will meet another with a stare.

THE SALUTATION AFTER INTRODUCTION.

A slight bow is all that is required by courtesy, after an introduction. Shaking hands is optional, and it should rest with the older, or the superior in social standing to make the advances. It is often an act of kindness on their part, and as such to be commended. It is a common practice among gentlemen, when introduced to one another, to shake hands, and as it evinces more cordiality than a mere bow, is generally to be preferred. An unmarried lady should not shake hands with gentlemen indiscriminately.

THE FIRST TO RECOGNIZE.

It is the privilege of the lady to determine whether she will recognize a gentleman after an introduction, and he is bound to return the bow. In bowing to a lady on the street, it is not enough that a gentleman should touch his hat, he should lift it from his head.

THE "CUT DIRECT."

The "cut direct," which is given by a prolonged stare at a person, if justified at all, can only be in case of extraordinary and notoriously bad conduct on the part of the individual "cut," and is very seldom called for. If any one wishes to avoid a bowing acquaintance with another, it can be done by looking aside or dropping the eyes. It is an invariable rule of good society, that a gentleman cannot "cut" a lady under any circumstances, but circumstrances may arise when he may be excused for persisting in not meeting her eyes, for if their eyes meet, he must bow.

MEETING IN THE STREET.

If, while walking with one friend, in the street, you meet another and stop a moment to speak with the latter, it is not necessary to introduce the two who are strangers to one another; but, when you separate, the friend who accompanies you gives a parting salutation, the same as yourself. The same rule applies if the friend you meet chances to be a lady.

INTRODUCING YOURSELF.

If, on entering a drawing-room to pay a visit, you are not recognized, mention your name immediately. If you know but one member of the family and you find others only in the room, introduce yourself to them. Unless this is done, much awkwardness may be occasioned.

ABOUT SHAKING HANDS.

When a lady is introduced to a gentleman, she should merely bow but not give her hand, unless the gentleman is a well known friend of some member of the family. In that case she may do so if she pleases, as a mark of esteem or respect. A gentleman must not offer to shake hands with a lady until she has made the first movement.

A married lady should extend her hand upon being introduced to a stranger brought to her house by her husband, or by a common friend, as an evidence of her cordial welcome.

LETTERS OF INTRODUCTION.

Friendly letters of introduction should only be given to personal friends, introducing them, and only addressed to those with whom the writer has a strong personal friendship. It is not only foolish, but positively dangerous to give such a letter to a person with whom the writer is but slightly acquainted, as you may thus give your countenance and endorsement to a person who will take advantage of your carelessness to bring you into embarrassing and mortifying positions. Again, you should never address a letter of introduction to any but an intimate friend of long standing, and even then it should not be done, unless you are perfectly satisfied that the person you are to introduce will be an agreeable and congenial person for your friend to meet, as it would be very annoying to send to your friend a visitor who would prove to him disagreeable. Even amongst friends of long standing such letters should be given very cautiously and sparingly.

The form of letters of introduction is given in the chapter on "Letter-writing."

DELIVERING A LETTER OF INTRODUCTION.

It is not necessary to deliver a friendly letter of introduction to a person who resides in another town. It is better to send it to the person to whom it is directed, on your arrival, accompanied by your card of address. If he wishes to comply with the request of his friend he will call upon you, and give you an invitation to visit him; circumstances, however, might render it exceedingly inconvenient, or impossible for the person to whom the letter is addressed, to call upon you; consequently a neglect to call need not be considered a mark of ill-breeding, though by some people it is so considered. The person addressed must consult his own feelings in the matter, and while aiming to do what is right, he is not bound to sacrifice business or other important mat·ters to attend to the entertainment of a friend's friend. In such a case he may send his own card to the address of the person bearing the letter of introduction, and the latter is at liberty to call upon him at his leisure.

THE DUTY OF THE PERSON ADDRESSED.

In Europe it is the custom for a person with a letter of introduction to make the first call, but in this country we think that a stranger should never be made to feel that he is begging our attention, and that it is indelicate for him to intrude until he is positive that his company would be agreeable. Consequently, if it is your wish and in your power to welcome any one recommended to you by letter from a friend, or to show your regard for your friend's friend, you must call upon him with all possible dispatch, after you receive his letter of introduction, and give him as hospitable a reception and entertainment as it is possible to give, and such as you would be pleased to receive were you in his place.

LETTERS OF INTRODUCTION FOR BUSINESS PURPOSES.

Letters of introduction to and from business men may be delivered by the bearers in person, and etiquette does not require the receiver to entertain the person introduced as a friend of the writer. It is entirely optional with the person to whom the latter is introduced how he welcomes him, or whether he entertains him or not, though his courtesy would be apt to suggest that some kind attentions should be paid him.

CHAPTER IV.

Salutations.

CARLYLE says: "What we call 'formulas' are not in their origin bad; they are indisputably good. Formula is method, habitude; found wherever man is found. Formulas fashion themselves as paths do, as beaten highways leading toward some sacred, high object, whither many men are bent. Consider it: One man full of heartfelt, earnest impulse finds out a way of doing something—were it uttering his soul's reverence for the Highest, *were it but of fitly saluting his fellow-man*. An inventor was needed to do that, a poet; he has articulated the dim, struggling thought that dwelt in his own and many hearts. This is the way of doing that. These are his footsteps, the beginning of a 'path.' And now see the second man travels naturally in the footsteps of his foregoer; it is the easiest method. In the footsteps of his foregoer, yet with his improvements, with changes where such seem good; at all events with enlargements, the path ever widening itself as more travel it, till at last there is a broad highway, whereon the whole world may travel and drive."

SALUTATION ORIGINALLY AN ACT OF WORSHIP.

A lady writer of distinction says of salutations: "It would seem that good manners were originally the expression of submission from the weaker to the stronger. In a rude state of society every salutation is to this day an act of worship. Hence the commonest acts, phrases and signs of courtesy with which we are now familiar, date from those earlier stages when the strong hand ruled and the inferior demonstrated his allegiance by studied servility. Let us take, for example, the words 'sir' and 'madam.' 'Sir' is derived from seigneur, sieur, and originally meant lord, king, ruler and, in its patriarchal sense, father. The title of sire was last borne by some of the ancient feudal families of France, who, as Selden has said, 'affected rather to be styled by the name of sire than baron, as *Le Sire de Montmorenci* and the like.' 'Madam' or 'madame,' corrupted by servants into 'ma'am,' and by Mrs. Gamp and her tribe into 'mum,' is in substance equivalent to 'your exalted,' or 'your highness,' *madame* originally meaning high-born, or stately, and being applied only to ladies of the highest rank.

"To turn to our every-day forms of salutation. We take off our hats on visiting an acquaintance. We bow on being introduced to strangers. We rise when visitors enter our drawing-room. We wave our hand to our friend as he passes the window or drives away from our door. The Oriental, in like manner, leaves his shoes on the threshold when he pays a visit. The natives of the Tonga Islands kiss the soles of a chieftain's feet. The Siberian peasant grovels in the dust before a Russian noble. Each of these acts has a primary, an historical significance. The very word 'salutation,' in the first place, derived as it is from *salutatio*, the daily homage paid by a Roman client to his patron, suggests in itself a history of manners.

"To bare the head was originally an act of submission to gods and rulers. A bow is a modified prostration. A lady's courtesy is a modified genuflection. Rising and standing are acts of homage; and when we wave our hand to a friend on the opposite side of the street, we are unconsciously imitating the Romans, who, as Selden tells us, used to stand 'somewhat off before the images of their gods, solemnly moving the right hand to the lips and casting it, as if they had cast kisses.' Again, men remove the glove when they shake hands with a lady—a custom evidently of feudal origin. The knight removed his iron gauntlet, the pressure of which would have been all too harsh for the palm of a fair *chatelaine ;* and the custom, which began in necessity, has traveled down to us as a point of etiquette."

SALUTATIONS OF DIFFERENT NATIONS.

Each nation has its own method of salutation. In Southern Africa it is the custom to rub toes. In Lapland your friend rubs his nose against yours. The Turk folds his arms upon his breast and bends his head very low. The Moors of Morocco have a somewhat startling mode of salutation. They ride at a gallop toward a stranger, as though they would unhorse him, and when close at hand suddenly check their horse and fire a pistol over the person's head. The Egyptian solicitously asks you, "How do you perspire?" and lets his hand fall to the knee. The Chinese bows low and inquires, "Have you eaten?" The Spaniard says, "God be with you, sir," or, "How do you stand?" And the Neapolitan piously remarks, "Grow in holiness." The German asks, "How goes it with you?" The Frenchman bows profoundly and inquires, "How do you carry yourself."

Foreigners are given to embracing. In France and Germany the parent kisses his grown-up son on the forehead, men throw their arms around the necks of their friends, and brothers embrace like lovers. It is a curious sight to Americans, with their natural prejudices against publicity in kissing.

In England and America there are three modes of salutation—the bow, the hand-shaking and the kiss.

THE BOW.

It is said: "A bow is a note drawn at sight. You are bound to acknowledge it immediately, and to the full amount." It should be respectful, cordial, civil or familiar, according to circumstances. Between gentlemen, an inclination of the head, a gesture of the hand, or the mere touching of the hat is sufficient; but in bowing to a lady, the hat must be lifted from the head. If you know people slightly, you recognize them slightly; if you know them well, you bow with more familiarity. The body is not bent at all in bowing; the inclination of the head is all that is necessary.

If the gentleman is smoking, he withdraws his cigar from his mouth before lifting his hat to a lady, or if he should happen to have his hand in his pocket he removes it.

At the moment of the first meeting of the eyes of an acquaintance you bow. Any one who has been introduced to you, or any one to whom you have been introduced, is entitled to this mark of respect.

The bow is the touchstone of good breeding, and to neglect it, even to one with whom you may have a trifling difference, shows deficiency in cultivation and in the instincts of refinement. A bow does not entail a calling acquaintance. Its entire neglect reveals the character and training of the person; the manner of its observance reveals the very shades of breeding that exist between the ill-bred and the well-bred.

RETURNING A BOW.

A gentleman walking with a lady returns a bow made to her, whether by a lady or gentleman (lifting his hat not too far from his head), although the one bowing is an entire stranger to him.

It is civility to return a bow, although you do not know the one who is bowing to you. Either the one who bows, knows you, or has mistaken you for some one else. In either case you should return the bow, and probably the mistake will be discovered to have occurred for want of quick recognition on your own part, or from some resemblance that you bear to another.

THE MANNER OF BOWING.

The manner in which the salutation of recognition is made, may be regarded as an unerring test of the breeding, training, or culture of a person. It should be prompt as soon as the eyes meet, whether on the street or in a room. The intercourse need go no further, but that bow must be made. There are but few laws which have better reasons for their observance than this. This rule holds good under all circumstances, whether within doors or without. Those who abstain from bowing at one time, and bow at another, should not be surprised to find that the person whom they have neglected, has avoided the continuation of their acquaintance.

DUTIES OF YOUNG TO OLDER PEOPLE.

Having once had an introduction that entitles to recognition, it is the duty of the person to recall himself or herself to the recollection of the older person, if there is much difference in age, by bowing each time of meeting, until the recognition becomes mutual. As persons advance in life, they look for these attentions upon the part of the young. Persons who have large circles of acquaintance, often confuse the faces of the young whom they know with the familiar faces which they meet and do not know, and from frequent errors of this kind, they get into the habit of waiting to catch some look or gesture of recognition.

HOW TO AVOID RECOGNITION.

If a person desires to avoid a bowing acquaintance with a person who has been properly introduced, he may do so by looking aside, or dropping the eyes as the person approaches, for, if the eyes meet, there is no alternative, bow he must.

ON PUBLIC PROMENADES.

Bowing once to a person upon a public promenade or drive is all that civility requires. If the person is a friend, it is in better form, the second and subsequent passings, should you catch his or her eye, to smile slightly instead of bowing repeatedly. If an acquaintance, it is best to avert the eyes.

A SMILING BOW.

A bow should never be accompanied by a broad smile, even when you are well acquainted, and yet a high authority well says: "You should never speak to an acquaintance without a smile in your eyes."

DEFERENCE TO ELDERLY PEOPLE.

A young lady should show the same deference to an elderly lady that a gentleman does to a lady. It may also be said that a young man should show proper deference to elderly gentlemen.

WORDS OF SALUTATION.

The words commonly used in saluting a person are "Good Morning," "Good Afternoon," "Good Evening,"

"How do you do" (sometimes contracted into "Howdy" and "How dye do,") and "How are you." The three former are most appropriate, as it seems somewhat absurd to ask after a person's health, unless you stop to receive an answer. A respectful bow should accompany the words.

SHAKING HANDS.

Among friends the shaking of the hand is the most genuine and cordial expression of good-will. It is not necessary, though in certain cases it is not forbidden, upon introduction; but when acquaintanceship has reached any degree of intimacy, it is perfectly proper.

ETIQUETTE OF HANDSHAKING.

An authority upon this subject says: "The etiquette of handshaking is simple. A man has no right to take a lady's hand until it is offered. He has even less right to pinch or retain it. Two young ladies shake hands gently and softly. A young lady gives her hand, but does not shake a gentleman's unless she is his friend. A lady should always rise to give her hand; a gentleman, of course, never dares to do so seated. On introduction in a room, a married lady generally offers her hand; a young lady, not. In a ballroom, where the introduction is to dancing, not to friendship, you never shake hands; and as a general rule, an introduction is not followed by shaking hands, only by a bow. It may perhaps be laid down that the more public the place of introduction, the less handshaking takes place. But if the introduction be particular, if it be accompanied by personal recom-

4

mendation, such as, 'I want you to know my friend Jones,' or if Jones comes with a letter of presentation, then you give Jones your hand, and warmly, too. Lastly, it is the privilege of a superior to offer or withhold his or her hand, so that an inferior should never put his forward first."

When a lady so far puts aside her reserve as to shake hands at all, she should give her hand with frankness and cordiality. There should be equal frankness and cordiality on the gentleman's part, and even more warmth, though a careful avoidance of anything like offensive familiarity or that which might be mistaken as such.

In shaking hands, the right hand should always be offered, unless it be so engaged as to make it impossible, and then an excuse should be offered. The French give the left hand, as nearest the heart.

The mistress of a household should offer her hand to every guest invited to her house.

A gentleman must not shake hands with a lady until she has made the first move in that direction. It is a mark of rudeness not to give his hand instantly, should she extend her own. A married lady should always extend her hand to a stranger brought to her house by a common friend, as an evidence of her cordial welcome. Where an introduction is for dancing there is no shaking of hands.

THE KISS.

This is the most affectionate form of salutation, and is only proper among near relations and dear friends.

THE KISS OF FRIENDSHIP.

The kiss of friendship and relationship is on the cheeks and forehead. In this country this act of affection is generally excluded from public eyes, and in the case of parents and children and near relations, it is perhaps unnecessarily so.

KISSING IN PUBLIC.

The custom which has become quite prevalent of women kissing each other whenever they meet in public, is regarded as vulgar, and by ladies of delicacy and refinement is entirely avoided.

THE KISS OF RESPECT.

The kiss of respect—almost obsolete in this country—is made on the hand. The custom is retained in Germany and among gentlemen of the most courtly manners in England.

CHAPTER V.

Etiquette of Calls.

THERE are calls of ceremony, of condolence, of congratulation and of friendship. All but the latter are usually of short duration. The call of friendship is usually of less formality and may be of some length.

MORNING CALLS.

"Morning calls," as they are termed, should not be made earlier than 12 M., nor later than 5 P. M.

A morning call should not exceed half an hour in length. From ten to twenty minutes is ordinarily quite long enough. If other visitors come in, the visit should terminate as speedily as possible. Upon leaving, bow slightly to the strangers.

In making a call be careful to avoid the luncheon and dinner hour of your friends. From two until five is ordinarily the most convenient time for morning calls.

EVENING CALLS.

It is sometimes more convenient for both the caller and those called upon that the call should be made in the evening. An evening call should never be made later than nine o'clock, nor be prolonged after ten, neither should it exceed an hour in length.

RULES FOR FORMAL CALLS.

The lady of the house rises upon the entrance of her visitors, who at once advance to pay their respects to her before speaking to others. If too many callers are present to enable her to take the lead in conversation, she pays special attention to the latest arrivals, watching to see that no one is left alone, and talking to each of her guests in succession, or seeing that some one is doing so.

A lady who is not in her own house does not rise, either on the arrival or departure of ladies, unless there is some great difference of age. Attention to the aged is one of the marks of good breeding which is never neglected by the thoughtful and refined.

It is not customary to introduce residents of the same city, unless the hostess knows that an introduction will be agreeable to both parties. Strangers in the place are always introduced.

Ladies and gentlemen who meet in the drawing-room of a common friend are privileged to speak to each other without an introduction; though gentlemen generally prefer to ask for introductions. When introduced to any one, bow slightly, and enter at once into conversation. It shows a lack of good breeding not to do so.

When introductions are given, it is the gentleman who should be presented to the lady; when two ladies are introduced, it is the younger who is presented to the older.

A lady receiving gives her hand to a stranger as to a friend, when she wishes to bestow some mark of cordiality in welcoming a guest to her home, but a gentleman should not take the initiatory in handshaking. It is the lady's privilege to give or withhold, as she chooses.

A gentleman rises when those ladies with whom he is talking rise to take their leave. He also rises upon the entrance of ladies, but he does not offer seats to those entering, unless in his own house, or unless requested to do so by the hostess, and then he does not offer his own chair if others are available.

A call should not be less than fifteen minutes in duration, nor should it be so long as to become tedious. A bore is a person who does not know when you have had enough of his or her company, and gives more of it than is desirable. Choose a time to leave when there is a lull in the conversation, and the hostess is not occupied with fresh arrivals. Then take leave of your hostess, bowing to those you know as you leave the room, not to each in turn, but let one bow include all.

Calls ought to be made within three days after a dinner or tea party, if it is a first invitation; and if not, within a week. After a party or a ball, whether you have accepted the invitation or not, you call within a week.

A lady who has no regular reception day will endeavor to receive callers at any time. If she is occupied, she will instruct her servant to say that she is engaged; but a visitor once admitted into the house must be seen at any inconvenience.

A lady should never keep a caller waiting without sending to see whether a delay of a few minutes will inconvenience the caller. Servants should be instructed to return and announce to the person waiting that the lady will be down immediately. Any delay whatever should be apologized for.

If, on making a call, you are introduced into a room where you are unknown to those assembled, at once give your name and mention upon whom your call is made.

In meeting a lady or gentleman whose name you cannot recall, frankly say so, if you find it necessary. Sensible persons will prefer to recall themselves to your memory rather than to feel that you are talking to them without fully recognizing them. To affect not to remember a person is despicable, and reflects only on the pretender.

Gentlemen, as well as ladies, when making formal calls, send in but one card, no matter how many members of the family they may wish to see. If a guest is stopping at the house, the same rule is observed. If not at home, one card is left for the lady, and one for

the guest. The card for the lady may be folded so as
to include the family.

RULES FOR SUMMER RESORTS.

At places of summer resort, those who own their
cottages, call first upon those who rent them, and those
who rent, in turn, call upon each other, according to
priority of arrival. In all these cases there are exceptions; as, where there is any great difference in ages,
the younger then calling upon the older, if there has
been a previous acquaintance or exchange of calls. If
there has been no previous acquaintance or exchange of
calls, the older lady pays the first call, unless she takes
the initiative by inviting the younger to call upon her,
or by sending her an invitation to some entertainment,
which she is about to give. When the occupants of
two villas, who have arrived the same season, meet at
the house of a common friend, and the older of the two
uses her privilege of inviting the other to call, it would
be a positive rudeness not to call; and the sooner the
call is made, the more civil will it be considered. It is
equally rude, when one lady asks permission of another
to bring a friend to call, and then neglects to do it, after
permission has been given. If the acquaintance is not
desired, the first call can be the last.

CALLS MADE BY CARDS.

Only calls of pure ceremony—such as are made previous to an entertainment on those persons who are not
to be invited, and to whom you are indebted for any

attentions—are made by handing in cards; nor can a call in person be returned by cards. Exceptions to this rule comprise P. P. C. calls, cards left or sent by persons in mourning, and those which announce a lady's day for receiving calls, on her return to town, after an absence.

RECEPTION DAYS.

Some ladies receive only on certain days or evenings, which are once a week, once a fortnight, or once a month as the case may be, and the time is duly announced by cards. When a lady has made this rule it is considerate, on the part of her friends, to observe it, for it is sometimes regarded as an intrusion to call at any other time. The reason of her having made this rule may have been to prevent the loss of too much time from her duties, in the receiving of calls from her friends.

CALLS AFTER BETROTHAL.

When a betrothal takes place and it is formally announced to the relatives and friends on both sides, calls of congratulation follow. The bridegroom that is to be, is introduced by the family of the proposed bride to their connections and most intimate friends, and his family in return introduce her to relatives and acquaintances whom they desire her to know. The simplest way of bringing this about is by the parents leaving the cards of the betrothed, with their own, upon all families on their visiting list whom they wish to have the betrothed pair visit.

THE CARDS AND CALLS OF STRANGERS.

Strangers arriving are expected to send their cards to their acquaintances, bearing their direction, as an announcement that they are in the city. This rule is often neglected, but, unless it is observed, strangers may be a long time in town without their presence being known.

RETURNING A FIRST CALL.

A first call ought to be returned within three or four days. A longer delay than a week is considered an intimation that you are unwilling to accept the new acquaintance, unless some excuse for the remissness is made.

FORMING ACQUAINTANCE.

In an event of exchange of calls between two ladies, without meeting, who are known to each other only by sight, they should upon the first opportunity, make themselves acquainted with one another. The younger should seek the older, or the one who has been the recipient of the first attention should introduce herself, or seek an introduction, but it is not necessary to stand upon ceremony on such points. Ladies knowing each other by sight, bow, after an exchange of cards.

THE FIRST CALL.

When it becomes a question as to who shall call first, between old residents, the older should take the initiatory. Ladies, who have been in the habit of meeting for sometime without exchanging calls, sometimes say to each other: "I hope you will come and see me." and often the answer is made: "Oh, you must come and see me first!" That answer could only be given, with propriety, by a lady who is much the older of the two. The lady who extends the invitation makes the first advance, and the one who receives it should at least say: "I thank you—you are very kind," and then accept the invitation or not, as it pleases her. It is the custom for residents to make the first call upon strangers.

CALLS OF CONGRATULATION.

Calls of congratulation are made when any happy or auspicious event may have occurred in the family visited—such as a birth, marriage, or any piece of good fortune. Such visits may be made either similar to the morning or the evening call. Such visits may also be made upon the appointment of friends to any important office or honored position, or when a friend has distinguished himself by a notable public address or oration.

P. P. C. CALLS.

When persons are going abroad to be absent for a considerable period, if they have not time or inclination to take leave of all their friends by making formal calls, they will send to each of their friends a card with the letters P. P. C. written upon it. They are the initials of "Pour Prendre Conge"—to take leave—and may with propriety stand for "presents parting compliments." On returning home, it is customary that friends

should first call upon them. A neglect to do so, unless
for some good excuse, is sufficient cause to drop their
acquaintance. In taking leave of a family, you send as
many cards as you would if you were paying an ordinary visit.

VISITS OF CONDOLENCE.

Visits of condolence should be made within a week
after the event which occasioned them; but if the
acquaintance be slight, immediately after the family
appear at public worship. A card should be sent in,
and if your friends are able to receive you, your manners
and conversation should be in harmony with the character of your visit. It is deemed courteous to send in
a mourning card; and for ladies to make their calls in
black silk or plain-colored apparel. It denotes that they
sympathize with the afflictions of the family, and a
warm, heartfelt sympathy is always appreciated.

EVENING VISITS.

Evening visits are paid only to those with whom we
are well acquainted. They should not be frequent, even
where one is intimate, nor should they be protracted to
a great length. Frequent visits are apt to become tiresome to your friends or acquaintances, and long visits
may entitle you to the appellation of " bore."

If you should happen to pay an evening visit at a
house where a small party had assembled, unknown to
you, present yourself and converse for a few minutes
with an unembarrassed air, after which you may leave,

pleading as an excuse that you had only intended to make a short call. An invitation to stay and spend the evening, given for the sake of courtesy, should not be accepted. If urged very strongly to remain, and the company is an informal gathering, you may with propriety consent to do so.

KEEP AN ACCOUNT OF CALLS.

A person should keep a strict account of ceremonial calls, and take note of how soon calls are returned. By doing so, an opinion can be formed as to how frequently visits are desired. Instances may occur, when, in consequence of age or ill health, calls should be made without any reference to their being returned. It must be remembered that nothing must interrupt the discharge of this duty.

CALLS OF CEREMONY AMONG FRIENDS.

Among relatives and friends, calls of mere ceremony are unnecessary. It is, however, needful to make suitable calls, and to avoid staying too long, if your friend is engaged. The courtesies of society should be maintained among the nearest friends, and even the domestic circle.

"ENGAGED" OR "NOT AT HOME."

If a lady is so employed that she cannot receive callers she should charge the servant who goes to answer the bell to say that she is "engaged" or "not at home." This will prove sufficient with all well-bred people.

The servant should have her orders to say "engaged" or "not at home" before any one has called, so that the lady shall avoid all risk of being obliged to inconvenience herself in receiving company when she has intended to deny herself. If there are to be exceptions made in favor of any individual or individuals, mention their names specially to the servant, adding that you will see them if they call, but to all others you are "engaged."

A lady should always be dressed sufficiently well to receive company, and not keep them waiting while she is making her toilet.

A well-bred person always endeavors to receive visitors at whatever time they call, or whoever they may be, but there are times when it is impossible to do so, and then, of course, a servant is instructed beforehand to say "not at home" to the visitor. If, however, the servant admits the visitor and he is seated in the drawing room or parlor, it is the duty of the hostess to receive him or her at whatever inconvenience it may be to herself.

When you call upon persons, and are informed at the door that the parties whom you ask for are engaged, you should never insist in an attempt to be admitted, but should acquiesce at once in any arrangements which they have made for their convenience, and to protect themselves from interruption. However intimate you may be in any house you have no right, when an order has been given to exclude general visitors, and no exception has been made of you, to violate that exclusion, and declare that the party should be at home to you. There are times and seasons when a person desires to be left entirely alone, and at such times there is no friendship for which she would give up her occupation or her solitude.

GENERAL RULES REGARDING CALLS.

A gentleman in making a formal call should retain his hat and gloves in his hand on entering the room. The hat should not be laid upon a table or stand, but kept in the hand, unless it is found necessary from some cause to set it down. In that case, place it upon the floor. An umbrella should be left in the hall. In an informal evening call, the hat, gloves, overcoat and cane may be left in the hall.

A lady, in making a call, may bring a stranger, even a gentleman, with her, without previous permission. A gentleman, however, should never take the same liberty.

No one should prolong a call if the person upon whom the call is made is found dressed ready to go out.

A lady should be more richly dressed when calling on her friends than for an ordinary walk.

A lady should never call upon a gentleman except upon some business, officially or professionally.

Never allow young children, dogs or pets of any sort to accompany you in a call. They often prove disagreeable and troublesome.

Two persons out of one family, or at most three, are all that should call together.

It is not customary in cities to offer refreshments to

callers. In the country, where the caller has come from some distance, it is exceedingly hospitable to do so.

Calls in the country may be less ceremonious and of longer duration, than those made in the city.

A person making a call should not, while waiting for a hostess, touch an open piano, walk about the room examining pictures, nor handle any ornament in the room.

If there is a stranger visiting at the house of a friend, the acquaintances of the family should be punctilious to call at an early date.

Never offer to go to the room of an invalid upon whom you have called, but wait for an invitation to do so.

In receiving morning calls, it is unnecessary for a lady to lay aside any employment, not of an absorbing nature upon which she may happen to be engaged. Embroidery, crocheting or light needle-work are perfectly in harmony with the requirements of the hour, and the lady looks much better employed than in absolute idleness.

A lady should pay equal attention to all her guests. The display of unusual deference is alone allowable when distinguished rank or reputation or advanced age justifies it.

A guest should take the seat indicated by the hostess. A gentleman should never seat himself on a sofa beside her, nor in a chair in immediate proximity, unless she specially invites him to do so.

A lady need not lay aside her bonnet during a formal call, even though urged to do so. If the call be a friendly and unceremonious one, she may do so if she thinks proper, but not without an invitation.

A gentleman caller must not look at his watch during a call, unless, in doing so, he pleads some engagement and asks to be excused.

Formal calls are generally made twice a year; but only once a year is binding, when no invitations have been received that require calls in return.

In calling upon a person living at a hotel or boarding-house, it is customary to stop in the parlor and send your card to the room of the person called upon.

When a person has once risen to take leave, he should not be persuaded to prolong his stay.

Callers should take special pains to make their visits opportune. On the other hand, a lady should always receive her callers, at whatever hour or day they come, if it is possible to do so.

When a gentleman has called and not found the lady at home, it is civility on the part of the lady, upon the occasion of their next meeting, to express her regret at not seeing him. He should reciprocate the regret, and not reply unthinkingly or awkwardly: "Oh, it made no particular difference," "it was of no great consequence," or words to that effect.

After you have visited a friend at her country seat, or after receiving an invitation to visit her, a call is due her upon her return to her town residence. This is one of the occasions when a call should be made promptly and in person, unless you have a reason for wishing to discontinue the acquaintance; even then it would be

5

more civil to take another opportunity for dropping a
friend who wished to show a civility, unless her character
has been irretrievably lost in the meantime.

NEW-YEAR'S CALLS.

The custom of New-Year's calling is prevalent in all
cities, and most villages in the country, and so agreeable
a custom is it, that it is becoming more in favor every
year. This is the day when gentlemen keep up their
acquaintanceship with ladies and families, some of whom
they are unable to see, probably, during the whole year.
Of late it has been customary in many cities to publish
in one or more newspapers, a day or two before New
Years, a list of the ladies who will receive calls on that
day, and from this list gentlemen arrange their calls.
For convenience and to add to the pleasure of the day,
several ladies frequently unite in receiving calls at the
residence of one of their number, but this is usually done
when only one or two members of a family can receive.
Where there are several members of a family, who can
do so, they usually receive at their own home.

Gentlemen call either singly, in couples, by threes or
fours and sometimes even more, in carriages or on foot,
as they choose. Calls commence about ten o'clock in
the morning, and continue until about nine in the evening. When the gentlemen go in parties, they call upon
the lady friends of each, and if all are not acquainted,
those who are, introduce the others. The length of a
call is usually from five to fifteen minutes, but it is often

governed by circumstances, and may be prolonged to even an hour.

Refreshments are usually provided for the callers, and should always be offered, but it is not necessary that they should be accepted. If not accepted, an apology should be tendered, with thanks for the offer. The refreshments may consist of oysters, raw or scalloped, cold meats, salads, fruits, cakes, sandwiches, etc., and hot tea and coffee.

When callers are ushered into the reception-room, they are met by the ladies, when introductions are given, and the callers are invited to remove their overcoats, but it is optional with them whether they do so or not. It is also optional with them whether they remove their gloves. When gentlemen are introduced to ladies in making New-Year's calls, they are not thereby warranted in calling again upon any of these ladies, unless especially invited to do so. It is the lady's pleasure whether the acquaintance shall be maintained.

In making New-Year's calls, a gentleman leaves one card, whatever may be the number of ladies receiving with the hostess. If there is a basket at the door, he leaves a card for each of the ladies at the house, including lady guests of the family, provided there are any. The New-Year's card should not differ from an ordinary calling card. It should be plain, with the name engraved, or printed in neat script. It is not now considered in good taste to have "Happy New Year" or other words upon it, unless it may be the residence of the gentleman, which may be printed or written in the right hand corner, if deemed desirable. A gentleman does not make calls the first New-Year's after his marriage, but receives at home with his wife.

CHAPTER VI.

Etiquette of Visiting.

SOME of the social observances pertaining to visiting away from one's own home, and accepting the hospitalities of friends, are here given, and are applicable to ladies and gentlemen alike.

GENERAL INVITATIONS.

No one should accept a general invitation for a prolonged visit. "Do come and spend some time with me" may be said with all earnestness and cordiality, but to give the invitation real meaning the date should be definitely fixed and the length of time stated.

A person who pays a visit upon a general invitation need not be surprised if he finds himself as unwelcome as he is unexpected. His friends may be absent from home, or their house may be already full, or they may not have made arrangements for visitors. From these and other causes they may be greatly inconvenienced by an unexpected arrival.

It would be well if people would abstain altogether from this custom of giving general invitations, which really mean nothing, and be scrupulous to invite their desired guests at a stated time and for a given period.

LIMIT OF A PROLONGED VISIT.

If no exact length of time is specified, it is well for visitors to limit a visit to three days or a week, according to the degree of intimacy they may have with the family, or the distance they have come to pay the visit, announcing this limitation soon after arrival, so that the host and the hostess may invite a prolongation of the stay if they desire it, or so that they can make their arrangements in accordance. One never likes to ask of a guest, "How long do you intend to remain?" yet it is often most desirable to know.

TRUE HOSPITALITY.

Offer your guests the best that you have in the way of food and rooms, and express no regrets, and make no excuses that you have nothing better to give them.

Try to make your guests feel at home; and do this, not by urging them in empty words to do so, but by making their stay as pleasant as possible, at the same time being careful to put out of sight any trifling trouble or inconvenience they may cause you.

Devote as much time as is consistent with other engagements to the amusement and entertainment of your guests.

DUTIES OF THE VISITOR.

On the other hand, the visitor should try to conform as much as possible to the habits of the house which temporarily shelters him. He should never object to the hours at which meals are served, nor should he ever allow the family to be kept waiting on his account.

It is a good rule for a visitor to retire to his own apartment in the morning, or at least seek out some occupation or amusement of his own, without seeming to need the assistance or attention of host or hostess; for it is undeniable that these have certain duties which must be attended to at this portion of the day, in order to leave the balance of the time free for the entertainment of their guests.

If any family matters of a private or unpleasant nature come to the knowledge of the guest during his stay, he must seem both blind and deaf, and never refer to them unless the parties interested speak of them first.

The rule on which a host and hostess should act is to make their guests as much at ease as possible; that on which a visitor should act is to interfere as little as possible with the ordinary routine of the house.

It is not required that a hostess should spend her whole time in the entertainment of her guests. The latter may prefer to be left to their own devices for a portion of the day. On the other hand, it shows the worst of breeding for a visitor to seclude himself from the family and seek his own amusements and occupations regardless of their desire to join in them or entertain him.

You should try to hold yourself at the disposal of those whom you are visiting. If they propose to you to ride, to drive or walk, you should acquiesce as far as your strength will permit, and do your best to seem pleased at the efforts made to entertain you.

You should not accept invitations without consulting your host. You should not call upon the servants to do errands for you, or to wait upon you too much, nor keep the family up after hours of retiring.

If you have observed anything to the disadvantage of your friends, while partaking of their hospitality, it should never be mentioned, either while you are under their roof or afterwards. Speak only of what redounds to their praise and credit. This feeling ought to be mutual between host and guest. Whatever good is observed in either may be commented upon, but the curtain of silence must be drawn over their faults.

Give as little trouble as possible when a guest, but at the same time never think of apologizing for any little additional trouble which your visit may occasion. It would imply that you thought your friends incapable of entertaining you without some inconvenience to themselves.

Keep your room as neat as possible, and leave no articles of dress or toilet around to give trouble to servants.

A lady guest will not hesitate to make her own bed, if few or no servants are kept ; and in the latter case she will do whatever else she can to lighten the labors of her hostess as a return for the additional exertion her visit occasions.

INVITATIONS TO GUESTS.

Any invitation given to a lady guest should also
include the hostess, and the guest is justified in declining to accept any invitation unless the hostess is also
invited. Invitations received by the hostess should
include the guest. Thus, at all places of amusement and
entertainment, guest and host may be together.

FORBEARANCE WITH CHILDREN.

A guest should not notice nor find fault with the bad
behavior of the children in the household where visiting, and should put up with any of their faults, and
overlook any ill-bred or disagreeable actions on their
part.

GUESTS MAKING PRESENTS.

If a guest wishes to make a present to any member of
the family she is visiting, it should be to the hostess, or
if to any of the children, to the youngest in preference,
though it is usually better to give it to the mother.
Upon returning home, when the guest writes to the hostess, she expresses her thanks for the hospitality, and
requests to be remembered to the family.

TREATMENT OF A HOST'S FRIENDS.

If you are a guest, you must be very cautious as to the
treatment of the friends of your host or hostess. If you
do not care to be intimate with them, you must be careful not to show a dislike for them, or that you wish to
avoid them. You must be exceedingly polite and agree-

able to them, avoiding any special familiarity, and keep them at a distance without hurting their feelings. Do not say to your host or hostess that you do not like any of their friends.

LEAVE-TAKING.

Upon taking leave, express the pleasure you have experienced in your visit. Upon returning home it is an act of courtesy to write and inform your friends of your safe arrival, at the same time repeating your thanks.

A host and hostess should do all they can to make the visit of a friend agreeable ; they should urge him to stay as long as it is consistent with his own plans, and at the same time convenient to themselves. But when the time for departure has been fully fixed upon, no obstacle should be placed in the way of leave-taking. Help him in every possible way to depart, at the same time giving him a cordial invitation to renew the visit at some future period.

"Welcome the coming, speed the parting, guest,"

expresses the true spirit of hospitality.

CHAPTER VII.

Visiting and Calling Cards.

N authentic writer upon visiting cards says: "To the unrefined or under-bred, the visiting card is but a trifling and insignificant bit of paper; but to the cultured disciple of social law, it conveys a subtle and unmistakable intelligence. Its texture, style of engraving, and even the hour of leaving it combine to place the stranger, whose name it bears, in a pleasant or a disagreeable attitude, even before his manners, conversation and face have been able to explain his social position. The higher the civilization of a community, the more careful it is to preserve the elegance of its social forms. It is quite as easy to express a perfect breeding in the fashionable formalities of cards, as by any other method, and perhaps, indeed, it is the safest herald of an introduction for a stranger. Its texture should be fine, its engraving a plain script, its size neither too small, so that its recipients shall say to themselves, 'A whimsical person,' nor too large to suggest ostentation. Refinement seldom touches extremes in anything."

CALLING CARDS.

A card used in calling should have nothing upon it but the name of the caller. A lady's card should not bear her place of residence; such cards having, of late, been appropriated by the members of the demi-monde. The street and number always look better upon the card of the husband than upon that of the wife. When necessary, they can be added in pencil on the cards of the wife and daughter. A business card should never be used for a friendly call. A physician may put the prefix "Dr.," or the affix "M. D.," upon his card, and an army or navy officer his rank and branch of service.

WEDDING CARDS.

Wedding cards are only sent to those people whom the newly married couple desire to keep among their acquaintances, and it is then the duty of those receiving the cards to call first on the young couple.

An ancient custom, but one which has been recently revived, is for the friends of the bride and groom to send cards; these are of great variety in size and design, and resemble Christmas or Easter cards but are usually more artistic.

CHRISTMAS AND EASTER CARDS.

A very charming custom that is coming into vogue is the giving or sending of Easter and Christmas cards. These are of such elegant designs and variety of colors that the stationer takes great pride in decorating his shop windows with them; indeed some of them are so elegant as to resemble oil paintings. Books and other small offerings may accompany cards as a token of remembrance.

CARDS TO SERVE FOR CALLS.

A person may make a card serve the purpose of a call, and it may either be sent in an envelope, by messenger or left in person. If left in person, one corner should be turned down. To indicate that a call is made on all or several members of the family; the card for the lady of the house is folded in the middle. If guests are visiting at the house, a card is left for each guest.

ENCLOSING A CARD IN AN ENVELOPE.

To return a call made in person with a card inclosed in an envelope, is an intimation that visiting between the parties is ended. Those who leave or send their cards with no such intention, should not inclose them in an envelope. An exception to this rule is where they are sent in return to the newly married living in other cities, or in answering wedding cards forwarded when absent from home. P. P. C. cards are also sent in this way, and are the only cards that it is as yet universally considered admissible to send by post.

SIZE AND STYLE OF VISITING OR CALLING CARDS.

A medium sized is in better taste than a very large card for married persons. Cards bearing the name of the husband alone are smaller. The cards of unmarried men should also be small. The engraving in simple writing is preferred, and without flourishes. Nothing in cards can be more commonplace than large printed letters, be the type what it may. Young men should dispense with the "Mr." before their names.

CALLING CARDS.

CORNERS OF CARDS TURNED DOWN.

The signification of turning down the corners of cards are:

Visite—The right hand upper corner.

Felicitation—The left hand upper corner.

Condolence—The left hand lower corner.

P. P. C.
To Take Leave } The right hand lower corner.

Card, right hand end turned down—*Delivered in Person.*

CARD FOR MOTHER AND DAUGHTER.

The name of young ladies are sometimes printed or engraved on their mother's cards; both in script. It is, of course, allowable, for the daughter to have cards of her own.

Some ladies have adopted the fashion of having the daughter's name on the same card with their own and their husband's names.

GLAZED CARDS.

Glazed cards are quite out of fashion, as are cards and note paper with gilt edges. The fashion in cards, however, change so often, that what is in style one year, may not be the next.

P. P. C. CARDS.

A card left at a farewell visit, before a long protracted absence, has "P. P. C." (Pour Prendre Conge) written in one corner. It is not necessary to deliver such cards in person, for they may be sent by a messenger, or by post if necessary. P. P. C. cards are not left when the absence from home is only for a few months, nor by persons starting in mid-summer for a foreign country, as residents are then supposed to be out of town. They are sent to or left with friends by ladies just previous to their contemplated marriage to serve the purpose of a call.

CARDS OF CONGRATULATION.

Cards of congratulation must be left in person, or a congratulatory note, if desired, can be made to serve instead of a call; excepting upon the newly married. Calls in person are due to them, and to the parents who have invited you to the marriage. When there has been a reception after the ceremony, which you have been unable to attend, but have sent cards by some member of your family, your cards need not again represent you until they have been returned, with the new residence announced; but a call is due to the parents or relatives who have given the reception. When no wedding cards are sent you, nor the card of the bridegroom, you cannot call without being considered intrusive. One month after the birth of a child the call of congratulation is made by acquaintances.

LEAVE CARDS IN MAKING FIRST CALL.

In making the first calls of the season (in the autumn) both ladies and gentlemen should leave a card each, at every house called upon, even if the ladies are receiving. The reason of this is that where a lady is receiving morning calls, it would be too great a tax upon her memory to oblige her to keep in mind what calls she has to return or which of them have been returned, and in making out lists for inviting informally, it is often the card-stand which is first searched for bachelors' cards, to meet the emergency. Young men should be careful to write their street and number on their cards.

LEAVE CARDS AFTER AN INVITATION.

After an invitation, cards must be left upon those who have sent it, whether it is accepted or not. They must be left in person, and if it is desired to end the acquaintance the cards can be left without inquiring whether the ladies are at home.

Gentlemen should not expect to receive invitations from ladies with whom they are only on terms of formal visiting, until the yearly or autumnal call has been made, or until their cards have been left to represent themselves.

CARDS IN MEMORIAM.

These are a loving tribute to the memory of the departed; an English custom rapidly gaining favor with us; it announces to friends the death, of which they might remain in ignorance but for this mark of respect:

George A. Custer,
Lieutenant-Colonel Seventh Cavalry,
Brevet Major-General United States Army,
Born December 5th, 1839,
Harrison County, Ohio,
Killed, with his entire Command, in the
Battle of Little Big Horn,
June 25th, 1876.

Oh, Custer—Gallant Custer! man fore-doomed
To ride, like Rupert, spurred and waving-plumed,
Into the very jaws of death.

CARDS OF CONDOLENCE.

Cards of condolence left by mere acquaintances must be returned by "mourning cards" before such persons feel at liberty to make a call. When the bereaved are ready to receive calls (instead of the cards) of their acquaintances, "mourning cards" in envelopes, or otherwise, are returned to all those who have left their cards since the death, which was the occasion of the cards being left. Intimate friends, of course, do not wait for cards, but continue their calls, without regard to any ceremonious observances made for the protection of the bereaved. Acquaintances leaving cards should inquire after the health of the family, leaving the cards in person.

MOURNING CARDS.

On announcement of a death it is correct to call in person at the door; to make inquiries and leave your card, with lower left hand corner turned town. Unless close intimacy exists, it is not usage to ask to see the afflicted. Cards can be sent to express sympathy, but notes of condolence are permissible only from intimate friends.

A BRIDEGROOM'S CARD.

When only the family and the most intimate friends of a bride and bridegroom have been included in the invitation for the marriage, or where there has been no reception after the marriage at church, the bridegroom often sends his bachelor card (inclosed in an envelope) to those of his acquaintances with whom he wishes to continue on visiting terms. Those who receive a card should call on the bride, within ten days after she has taken possession of her home. Some persons have received such a card as an intimation that the card was to end the acquaintance. This mistake shows the necessity of a better understanding of social customs.

CHAPTER VIII.

Conversation.

THE character of a person is revealed by his conversation as much as by any one quality he possesses, for strive as he may he cannot always be acting.

IMPORTANCE OF CONVERSING WELL.

To be able to converse well is an attainment which should be cultivated by every intelligent man and woman. It is better to be a good talker than a good singer or musician, because the former is more widely appreciated, and the company of a person who is able to talk well on a great variety of subjects, is much sought after. The importance, therefore, of cultivating the art of conversation, cannot easily be over-estimated. It should be the aim of all intelligent persons to acquire the habit of talking sensibly and with facility upon all topics of general interest to society, so that they may both interest others and be themselves interested, in whatever company they may chance to be thrown.

TRAINING CHILDREN.

The training for this should be commenced in early childhood. Parents should not only encourage their children to express themselves freely upon everything that attracts their attention and interests them, but they should also incite their faculties of perception, memory and close observation, by requiring them to recount everything, even to its minutest details, that they may have observed in walking to and from school, or in taking a ride in a carriage or in the cars. By training a child to a close observation of everything he meets or passes, his mind becomes very active, and the habit having once been acquired, he becomes interested in a great variety of objects; sees more and enjoys more than one who has not been so trained.

CULTIVATING THE MEMORY.

A good memory is an invaluable aid in acquiring the art of conversation, and the cultivation and training of this faculty is a matter of importance. Early youth is the proper time to begin this training, and parents and teachers should give special attention to the cultivation of memory. When children are taken to church, or to hear a lecture, they should be required to relate or to write down from memory, such a digest of the sermon or lecture as they can remember. Adults may also adopt this plan for cultivating the memory, and they will be surprised to find how continued practice in this will improve this faculty. The practice of taking notes impairs rather than aids the memory, for then a person relies almost entirely in the notes taken, and does not tax the memory sufficiently. A person should also train himself to remember the names of persons whom he becomes acquainted with, so as to recall them whenever or wherever he may subsequently meet them. It is related of a large wholesale boot and shoe merchant of an eastern city, that he was called upon one day by one of his best customers, residing in a distant city, whom he had frequently met, but whose name, at the time, he could not recall, and received his order for a large bill of goods. As he was about to leave, the merchant asked his name, when the customer indignantly replied that he supposed he was known by a man from whom he had purchased goods for many years, and countermanding his order, he left the store, deaf to all attempts at explanation. Though this may be an extreme case, it illustrates the importance of remembering the names of people when circumstances require it.

HENRY CLAY'S MEMORY OF NAMES.

One secret of Henry Clay's popularity as a politician was his faculty of remembering the names of persons he had met. It is said of him that if he was once introduced to a person, he was ever afterwards able to call him by name, and recount the circumstances of their first meeting. This faculty he cultivated after he entered upon the practice of law in Kentucky, and soon after he began his political life. At that time his memory for names was very poor, and he resolved to improve it.

He adopted the practice, just before retiring at night, of recalling the names of all the persons he had met during the day, writing them in a note book, and repeating over the list the next morning. By this practice, he acquired in time, his wonderful faculty in remembering the names of persons he had become acquainted with.

WRITING AS AN AID TO CORRECT TALKING.

To converse correctly—to use correct language in conversation—is also a matter of importance, and while this can be acquired by a strict attention to grammatical rules, it can be greatly facilitated by the habit of writing down one's thoughts. In writing, strict regard is, or should be, paid to the correct use of language, and when a person, from constant writing, acquires the habit of using correct language, this habit will follow him in talking. A person who is accustomed to much writing, will always be found to use language correctly in speaking.

REQUISITES FOR A GOOD TALKER.

To be a good talker then, one should be possessed of much general information, acquired by keen observation, attentive listening, a good memory, extensive reading and study, logical habits of thought, and have a correct knowledge of the use of language. He should also aim at a clear intonation, well chosen phraseology and correct accent. These acquirements are within the reach of every person of ordinary ability, who has a determination to possess them, and the energy and perseverance to carry out that determination.

VULGARISMS.

In conversation, one must scrupulously guard against vulgarisms. Simplicity and terseness of language are the characteristics of a well educated and highly cultivated person. It is the uneducated or those who are but half educated, who use long words and high-sounding phrases. A hyperbolical way of speaking is mere flippancy, and should be avoided. Such phrases as "awfully pretty," "immensely jolly," "abominally stupid," "disgustingly mean," are of this nature, and should be avoided. Awkwardness of attitude is equally as bad as awkwardness of speech. Lolling, gesticulating, fidgeting, handling an eye-glass or watch chain and the like, give an air of *gaucherie*, and take off a certain percentage from the respect of others.

LISTENING.

The habit of listening with interest and attention is one which should be specially cultivated. Even if the talker is prosy and prolix, the well-bred person will appear interested, and at appropriate intervals make such remarks as shall show that he has heard and understood all that has been said. Some superficial people are apt to style this hypocrisy; but if it is, it is certainly a commendable hypocrisy, directly founded on that strict rule of good manners which commands us to show the same courtesy to others that we hope to receive ourselves. We are commanded to check our impulses, conceal our dislikes, and even modify our likings whenever or wherever these are liable to give offense or pain to others. The person who turns away with manifest displeasure, disgust or want of interest when another is addressing him, is guilty not only of an ill-bred, but a cruel act.

FLIPPANCY.

In conversation all provincialism, affectations of foreign accents, mannerisms, exaggerations and slang are detestable. Equally to be avoided are inaccuracies of expression, hesitation, an undue use of foreign words, and anything approaching to flippancy, coarseness, triviality or provocation. Gentlemen sometimes address ladies in a very flippant manner, which the latter are obliged to pass over without notice, for various reasons, while inwardly they rebel. Many a worthy man has done himself an irreparable injury by thus creating a lasting prejudice in the minds of those whom he might have made his friends, had he addressed them as though he considered them rational beings, capable of sustaining their part in a conversation upon sensible subjects. Flippancy is as much an evidence of ill-breeding as is the perpetual smile, the wandering eye, the vacant stare, and the half-opened mouth of the man who is preparing to break in upon the conversation.

BE SYMPATHETIC AND ANIMATED.

Do not go into society unless you make up your mind to be sympathetic, unselfish, animating, as well as animated. Society does not require mirth, but it does demand cheerfulness and unselfishness, and you must help to make and sustain cheerful conversation. The manner of conversation is as important as the matter.

COMPLIMENTS.

Compliments are said by some to be inadmissible. But between equals, or from those of superior position to those of inferior station, compliments should be not only acceptable but gratifying. It is pleasant to know that our friends think well of us, and it is always agreeable to know that we are thought well of by those who hold higher positions, such as men of superior talent, or women of superior culture. Compliments which are not sincere, are only flattery and should be avoided; but the saying of kind things, which is natural to the kind heart, and which confers pleasure, should be cultivated, at least not suppressed. Those parents who strive most for the best mode of training their children are said to have found that it is never wise to censure them for a fault, without preparing the way by some judicious mention of their good qualities.

SLANG.

All slang is vulgar. It lowers the tone of society and the standard of thought. It is a great mistake to suppose that slang is in any manner witty. Only the very young or the uncultivated so consider it.

FLATTERY.

Do not be guilty of flattery. The flattery of those richer than ourselves or better born is vulgar, and born of rudeness, and is sure to be received as emanating from unworthy motives. Testify your respect, your admiration, and your gratitude by deeds more than words. Words are easy but deeds are difficult. Few will believe the former, but the latter will carry confirmation with them.

SCANDAL AND GOSSIP.

Scandal is the least excusable of all conversational vulgarities. Envy prompts the tongue of the slanderer. Jealousy is the disturber of the harmony of all interests. A writer on this subject says: "Gossip is a troublesome sort of insect that only buzzes about your ears and never bites deep; slander is the beast of prey that leaps upon you from its den and tears you in pieces. Slander is the proper object of rage; gossip of contempt." Those who best understand the nature of gossip and slander, if the victims of both, will take no notice of the former, but will allow no slander of themselves to go unrefuted during their lifetime, to spring up in a hydra-headed attack upon their children. No woman can be too sensitive as to any charges affecting her moral character, whether in the influence of her companionship, or in the influence of her writings.

RELIGION AND POLITICS.

Religion and politics are topics that should never be introduced into general conversation, for they are subjects dangerous to harmony. Persons are most likely to differ, and least likely to preserve their tempers on

these topics. Long arguments in general company, however entertaining to the disputants, are very tiresome to
the hearers.

SATIRE AND RIDICULE.

Young persons appear ridiculous when satirizing or
ridiculing books, people or things. Opinions to be worth
the consideration of others should have the advantage
of coming from mature persons. Cultivated people are
not in the habit of resorting to such weapons as satire
and ridicule. They find too much to correct in themselves to indulge in coarse censure of the conduct of
others, who may not have had advantages equal to their
own.

TITLES.

In addressing persons with titles always add the name;
as "what do you think of it, Doctor Hayes?" not "what
do you think of it, Doctor?" In speaking of foreigners
the reverse of the English rule is observed. No matter
what the title of a Frenchman is, he is always addressed
as *Monsieur*, and you never omit the word *Madame*,
whether addressing a duchess or a dressmaker. The
former is "*Madame la Duchesse*," the latter plain
"*Madame*." Always give a foreigner his title. If General Sherman travels in Europe and is received by the
best classes with the dignity that his worth, culture and
position as an American general demand, he will never
be called Mr. Sherman, but his title will invariably precede his name. There are persons who fancy that the
omission of the title is annoying to the party who pos-

sesses it, but this is not the ground taken why the title should be given, but because it reveals either ignorance or ill-breeding on the part of those omitting it.

CHRISTIAN NAMES.

There is a class of persons, who from ignorance of the customs of good society, or from carelessness, speak of persons by their Christian names, who are neither relations nor intimate friends. This is a familiarity which, outside of the family circle, and beyond friends of the closest intimacy, is never indulged in by the well-bred.

INTERRUPTION.

Interruption of the speech of others is a great sin against good-breeding. It has been aptly said that if you interrupt a speaker in the middle of a sentence, you act almost as rudely as if, when walking with a companion, you were to thrust yourself before him and stop his progress.

ADAPTABILITY IN CONVERSATION.

The great secret of talking well is to adapt your conversation, as skillfully as may be, to your company. Some men make a point of talking common-place to all ladies alike, as if a woman could only be a trifler. Others, on the contrary, seem to forget in what respects the education of a lady differs from that of a gentleman, and commit the opposite error of conversing on topics with which ladies are seldom acquainted, and in which few, if any, are ever interested. A woman of sense has as much right to be annoyed by the one, as a woman of ordinary education by the other. If you really wish to be thought agreeable, sensible, amiable, unselfish and even well-informed, you should lead the way, in *tete-a-tete* conversations, for sportsmen to talk of their shooting, a mother to talk of her children, a traveler of his journeys and the countries he has visited, a young lady of her last ball and the prospective ones, an artist of his picture and an author of his book. To show any interest in the immediate concerns of people is very complimentary, and when not in general society one is privileged to do this. People take more interest in their own affairs than in anything else you can name, and if you manifest an interest to hear, there are but few who will not sustain conversation by a narration of their affairs in some form or another. Thackeray says: "Be interested by other people and by their affairs. It is because you yourself are selfish that that other person's self does not interest you."

CORRECT USE OF WORDS.

The correct use of words is indispensable to a good talker who would escape the unfavorable criticism of an educated listener. There are many words and phrases, used in some cases by persons who have known better, but who have become careless from association with others who make constant use of them. "Because that" and "but that" should never be used in connection, the word "that" being entirely superfluous. The word "vocation" is often used for "avocation." "Unhealthy" food is spoken of when it should be "unwholesome."

"Had not ought to" is sometimes heard for "ought not to;" "banister" for "baluster;" "handsful" and "spoonsful" for "handfuls" and "spoonfuls;" "it was him" for "it was he;" "it was me" for "it was I;" "whom do you think was there?" for "who do you think was there?"; "a mutual friend" for "a common friend;" "like I did" instead of "as I did;" "those sort of things" instead of "this sort of things;" "laying down" for "lying down;" "setting on a chair" for "sitting on a chair;" "try and make him" instead of "try to make him;" "she looked charmingly" for "she looked charming;" "loan" for "lend;" "to get along" instead of "to get on;" "cupalo" instead of "cupola;" "who" for "whom"—as, "who did you see" for "whom did you see;" double negatives, as, "he did not do neither of those things;" "lesser" for "least;" "move" instead of "remove;" "off-set" instead of "set-off," and many other words which are often carelessly used by those who have been better taught, as well as by those who are ignorant of their proper use.

SPEAKING ONE'S MIND.

Certain honest but unthinking people often commit the grievous mistake of "speaking their mind" on all occasions and under all circumstances, and oftentimes to the great mortification of their hearers. And especially do they take credit to themselves for their courage, if their freedom of speech happens to give offense to any of them. A little reflection ought to show how cruel and unjust this is. The law restrains us from inflicting bodily injury upon those with whom we disagree, yet there is no legal preventive against this wounding of the feeling of others.

UNWISE EXPRESSION OF OPINION.

Another class of people, actuated by the best of intentions, seem to consider it a duty to parade their opinions upon all occasions, and in all places without reflecting that the highest truth will suffer from an unwise and over-zealous advocacy. Civility requires that we give to the opinions of others the same toleration that we exact for our own, and good sense should cause us to remember that we are never likely to convert a person to our views when we begin by violating his notions of propriety and exciting his prejudices. A silent advocate of a cause is always better than an indiscreet one.

PROFANITY.

No gentleman uses profane language. It is unnecessary to add that no gentleman will use profane language in the presence of a lady. For profanity there is no excuse. It is a low and paltry habit, acquired from association with low and paltry spirits, who possess no sense of honor, no regard for decency and no reverence or respect for beings of a higher moral or religious nature than themselves. The man who habitually uses profane language, lowers his moral tone with every oath he utters. Moreover, the silliness of the practice, if no other reason, should prevent its use by every man of good sense.

PUBLIC MENTION OF PRIVATE MATTERS.

Do not parade merely private matters before a public or mixed assembly or to acquaintances. If strangers really wish to become informed about you or your affairs, they will find the means to gratify their curiosity without your advising them gratuitously. Besides, personal and family affairs, no matter how interesting they may be to the parties immediately concerned, are generally of little moment to outsiders. Still less will the well-bred person inquire into or narrate the private affairs of any other family or individual.

OSTENTATIOUS DISPLAY OF KNOWLEDGE.

In refined and intelligent society one should always display himself at his best, and make a proper and legitimate use of all such acquirements as he may happen to have. But there should be no ostentatious or pedantic show of erudition. Besides being vulgar, such a show subjects the person to ridicule.

PRUDERY.

Avoid an affectation of excessive modesty. Do not use the word "limb" for "leg." If legs are really improper, then let us, on no account, mention them. But having found it necessary to mention them, let us by all means give them their appropriate name.

DOUBLE ENTENDRES.

No person of decency, still less of delicacy, will be guilty of *double entendre*. A well-bred person always
7

refuses to understand a phrase of doubtful meaning. If the phrase may be interpreted decently, and with such interpretation would provoke a smile, then smile to just the degree called for by such interpretation, and no more. The prudery which sits in solemn and severe rebuke at a *double entendre* is only second in indelicacy to the indecency which grows hilarious over it, since both must recognize the evil intent. It is sufficient to let it pass unrecognized.

INDELICATE WORDS AND EXPRESSIONS.

Not so when one hears an indelicate word or expression, which allows of no possible harmless interpretation. Then not the shadow of a smile should flit across the lips. Either complete silence should be preserved in return, or the words, "I do not understand you," be spoken. A lady will always fail to hear that which she should not hear, or, having unmistakably heard, she will not understand.

VULGAR EXCLAMATIONS.

No lady should make use of any feminine substitute for profanity. The woman who exclaims "The Dickens!" or "Mercy!" or "Goodness!" when she is annoyed or astonished, is as vulgar in spirit, though perhaps not quite so regarded by society, as though she had used expressions which it would require but little stretch of the imagination to be regarded as profane.

WIT.

You may be witty and amusing if you like, or rather if you can; but never use your wit at the expense of others.

> " Wit's an unruly engine, wildly striking
> Sometimes a friend, sometimes the engineer;
> Hast thou the knack? pamper it not with liking;
> But if thou want it, buy it not too dear.
> Many affecting wit beyond their power
> Have got to be a dear fool for an hour."—HERBERT.

DISPLAY OF EMOTIONS.

Avoid all exhibitions of temper before others, if you find it impossible to suppress them entirely. All emotions, whether of grief or joy, should be subdued in public, and only allowed full play in the privacy of your own apartments.

IMPERTINENT QUESTIONS.

Never ask impertinent questions. Some authorities in etiquette even go so far as to say that *all* questions are strictly tabooed. Thus, if you wished to inquire after the health of the brother of your friend, you would say, "I hope your brother is well," not, "How is your brother's health ?"

THE CONFIDENCE OF OTHERS.

Never try to force yourself into the confidence of others ; but if they give you their confidence of their own free will, let nothing whatever induce you to betray it.   Never seek to pry into a secret, and never divulge one.

USE OF FOREIGN LANGUAGE.

Do not form the habit of introducing words and phrases of French or other foreign languages into common conversation.   This is only allowable in writing, and not then except when the foreign word or phrase expresses more clearly and directly than English can do the desired meaning.   In familiar conversation this is an affectation, only pardonable when all persons present are particularly familiar with the language.

PRETENSES.

Avoid all pretense at gentility.   Pass for what you are, and nothing more.   If you are obliged to make any little economies, do not be ashamed to acknowledge them as economies, if it becomes necessary to speak of them at all.   If you keep no carriage, do not be over-solicitous to impress upon your friends that the sole reason for this deficiency is because you prefer to walk. Do not be ashamed of poverty; but, on the other hand, do not flaunt its rags unmercifully in the faces of others. It is better to say nothing about it, either in excuse or defense.

DOGMATIC STYLE OF SPEAKING.

Never speak dogmatically or with an assumption of knowledge or information beyond that of those with whom you are conversing.   Even if you are conscious of this superiority, a proper and becoming modesty will lead you to conceal it as far as possible, that you may not put to shame or humiliation those less fortunate than yourself. If they discover your superiority of their own accord, they will have much more admiration for you than though you forced the recognition upon them. If they do not discover it, you cannot force it upon their perceptions, and they will only hold you in contempt for trying to do so. Besides, there is the possibility that you over-estimate yourself, and instead of being a wise man you are only a self-sufficient fool.

FAULT-FINDING.

Do not be censorious or fault-finding. Long and close friendship may sometimes excuse one friend in reproving or criticising another, but it must always be done in the kindest and gentlest manner, and in nine cases out of ten had best be left undone. When one is inclined to be censorious or critical, it is well to remember the scriptural injunction, "First cast the beam out of thine own eye, and then shalt thou see clearly to cast the mote out of thy brother's eye."

CONVERSING WITH LADIES.

A gentleman should never lower the intellectual standard of his conversation in addressing ladies. Pay them the compliment of seeming to consider them capable of an equal understanding with gentlemen. You will, no doubt, be somewhat surprised to find in how many cases the supposition will be grounded on fact, and in the few instances where it is not, the ladies will be pleased rather than offended at the delicate compliment you pay them. When you "come down" to commonplace or small-talk with an intelligent lady, one of two things is the consequence; she either recognizes the condescension and despises you, or else she accepts it as the highest intellectual effort of which you are capable, and rates you accordingly.

HOBBIES.

People with hobbies are at once the easiest and most difficult persons with whom to engage in conversation. On general subjects they are idealess and voiceless beyond monosyllables. But introduce their special hobby, and if you choose you need only to listen. There is much profit to be derived from the conversation of these persons. They will give you a clearer idea of the aspects of any subject or theory which they may have taken to heart, than you could perhaps gain in any other way.

The too constant riding of hobbies is not, however, to be specially recommended. An individual, though he may be pardoned in cultivating special tastes, should yet be possessed of sufficiently broad and general information to be able to converse intelligently on all subjects, and he should, as far as possible, reserve his hobby-riding for exhibition before those who ride hobbies similar to his own.

THINGS TO BE AVOIDED.

It must be remembered that a social gathering should never be made the arena of a dispute. Consequently every subject liable to provoke a discussion should be avoided. Even slight inaccuracy in a statement of facts or opinions should rarely be remarked on in conversation.

Do not permit yourself to lose your temper in society, nor show that you have taken offense at a supposed slight.

If anyone should assume a disagreeable tone of voice or offensive manner toward you, never return it in company, and, above all, do not adopt the same style of conversation with him. Appear not to notice it, and generally it will be discontinued, as it will be seen that it has failed in its object.

Avoid all coarseness and undue familiarity in addressing others. A person who makes himself offensively familiar will have few friends.

Never attack the character of others in their absence; and if you hear others attacked, say what you can consistently to defend them.

If you are talking on religious subjects, avoid all cant. Cant words and phrases may be used in good faith from the force of habit, but their use subjects the speaker to a suspicion of insincerity.

Do not ask the price of articles you observe, except from intimate friends, and then very quietly, and only for some good reason.

Do not appear to notice an error in language, either in pronunciation or grammar, made by the person with whom you are conversing, and do not repeat correctly the same word or phrase. This would be as ill-bred as to correct it when spoken.

Mimicry is ill-bred, and must be avoided.

Sneering at the private affairs of others has long ago been banished from the conversation of well-mannered people.

Never introduce unpleasant topics, nor describe revolting scenes in general company.

Never give officious advice. Even when sought for, give advice sparingly.

Never, directly or indirectly, refer to the affairs of others, which it may give them pain in any degree to recall.

Never hold your companion in conversation by the button-hole. If you are obliged to detain him forcibly in order to say what you wish, you are pressing upon him what is disagreeable or unwelcome, and you commit a gross breach of etiquette in so doing.

Especially avoid contradictions, interruptions and monopolizing all conversation yourself. These faults are all intolerable and very offensive.

To speak to one person in a company in ambiguous terms, understood by him alone, is as rude as if you had whispered in his ear.

Avoid stale and trite remarks on commonplace subjects; also all egotism and anecdotes of personal adventure and exploit, unless they should be called out by persons you are conversing with.

To make a classical quotation in a mixed company is considered pedantic and out of place, as is also an ostentatious display of your learning.

A gentleman should avoid talking about his business

or profession, unless such matters are drawn from him by the person with whom he is conversing. It is in bad taste, particularly, to employ technical or professional terms in general conversation.

Long arguments or heated discussions are apt to be tiresome to others, and should be avoided.

It is considered extremely ill-bred for two persons to whisper in society, or to converse in a language with which all persons are not familiar.

Avoid talking too much, and do not inflict upon your hearers interminably long stories, in which they can have but little interest.

CHAPTER IX.

Dinner Giving and Dining Out.

INING should be ranked among the fine arts. A knowledge of dinner-table etiquette is all important in many respects; but chiefly in this: that it is regarded as one of the strong tests of good breeding. Dinners are generally looked upon as entertainments for married people and the middle aged, but it is often desirable to have some young unmarried persons among the guests.

WHOM TO INVITE.

Those invited should be of the same standing in society. They need not necessarily be friends, nor even acquaintances, but, at dinner, as people come into closer contact than at a dance, or any other kind of a party, those only should be invited to meet one another who move in the same class of circles. Care must, of course, be taken that those whom you think agreeable to

each other are placed side by side around the festive
board. Good talkers are invaluable at a dinner party—
people who have fresh ideas and plenty of warm words
to clothe them in; but good listeners are equally invaluable.

INVITATIONS.

Invitations to dinner parties are not usually sent by
post, in cities, and are only answered by post where the
distance is such as to make it inconvenient to send the
note by hand. They are issued in the name of the gentleman and lady of the house, from two to ten days in
advance. They should be answered as soon as received,
without fail, as it is necessary that the host and hostess
should know who are to be their guests. If the invitation is accepted, the engagement should, on no account,
be lightly broken. This rule is a binding one, as the
non-arrival of an expected guest produces disarrangement of plans. Gentlemen cannot be invited without
their wives, where other ladies than those of the family
are present; nor ladies without their husbands, when
other ladies are invited with their husbands. This rule
has no exceptions. No more than three out of a family
should be invited, unless the dinner party is a very large
one.

MANNER OF WRITING INVITATIONS.

The invitations should be written on small note paper,
which may have the initial letter or monogram stamped
upon it, but good taste forbids anything more. The
envelope should match the sheet of paper. The invita-

tion should be issued in the name of the host and hostess.
The form of invitations should be as follows:

Mr. and Mrs. Potter request the pleasure of Mr. and Mrs. Barton's company at dinner on Thursday, the 18th of October, at 5 o'clock.

An answer should be returned at once, so that if the
invitation is declined the hostess may modify her
arrangements accordingly.

INVITATION ACCEPTED.

An acceptance may be given in the following form,
and may be sent either by post or messenger:

Mr. and Mrs. Barton have much pleasure in accepting Mr. and Mrs Potter's invitation for October 18th.

INVITATION DECLINED.

The invitation is declined in the following manner:

Mr. and Mrs. Barton regret that a previous engagement (or *whatever the cause may be*) *prevents their having the pleasure of accepting Mr. and Mrs. Potter's invitation at dinner for October 18th.*

Or,

Mr. and Mrs. Barton regret exceedingly that owing to (*whatever the preventing cause may be*), *they cannot have the pleasure of dining with Mr. and Mrs. Potter on Thursday, October 18th.*

Whatever the cause for declining may be, it should be stated briefly, yet plainly, that there may be no occasion for misunderstanding or hard feelings.

INVITATION TO TEA-PARTY.

The invitation to a tea-party may be less formal. It may take the form of a friendly note, something in this manner:

Dear Miss Summer :

We have some friends coming to drink tea with us to-morrow : will you give us the pleasure of your company also? We hope you will not disappoint us.

FAILING TO FILL AN ENGAGEMENT.

When it becomes absolutely necessary to break an engagement once made for dinner or tea, a note must be sent at once to the hostess and host, with full explanation of the cause, so that your place may be supplied, if possible.

PUNCTUALITY.

The hour generally selected in cities is after business hours, or from five to eight o'clock. In the country or villages it may be an hour or two earlier. To be punctual at the hour mentioned is obligatory. If you are too early you are in the way; if too late you annoy the hostess, cause impatience among the assembled guests, and perhaps spoil the dinner. Fifteen minutes is the longest time required to wait for a tardy guest.

THE SUCCESS OF A DINNER.

A host and hostess generally judge of the success of a dinner by the manner in which conversation has been sustained. If it has flagged often, it is considered proof that the guests have not been congenial; but if a steady stream of talk has been kept up, it shows that they have smoothly amalgamated, as a whole. No one should monopolize conversation, unless he wishes to win for himself the appellation of a bore, and be avoided as such.

THE TABLE APPOINTMENTS.

A snow-white cloth of the finest damask, beautiful china, glistening or finely engraved glass, and polished plate are considered essential to a grand dinner. Choice flowers, ferns and mosses tastefully arranged, add much to the beauty of the table. A salt-cellar should be within the reach of every guest. Napkins should be folded square and placed with a roll of bread upon each plate. The dessert is placed on the table amidst the flowers. An *epergne*, or a low dish of flowers, graces the centre; stands of bon-bons and confectionery are ranged on both sides of the table, which complete the decorations of the table. The name of each guest, written upon a card and placed one on each plate, marks the seat assigned.

ASSIGNING PARTNERS FOR DINNER.

The number at a dinner should not be less than six, nor more than twelve or fourteen. Then the host will be able to designate to each gentleman the lady whom he is to conduct to the table; but when the number exceeds this limit it is a good plan to have the name of each couple written upon a card and enclosed in an addressed envelope, ready to be handed to the gentleman by the servant, before entering the drawing-room, or left on a tray for the guests to select those which bear their names.

If a gentleman finds upon his card the name of a lady with whom he is unacquainted, he requests the host to present him immediately after he has spoken with the hostess, also to any members of the family with whom he is not acquainted.

INTRODUCTIONS.

All the guests should secure introductions to the one for whom the dinner is given. If two persons, unknown to each other, find themselves placed side by side at a table, they may enter into conversation without an introduction.

ARRANGEMENTS OF GUESTS AT THE TABLE.

When dinner is announced, the host offers his right arm to the lady he is to escort to the table. The others follow, arm in arm, the hostess being the last to leave the drawing-room. Age should take the precedence in proceed ing from the drawing-room to the dining-room, the younger falling back until the elder have advanced. The host escorts the eldest lady or the greatest stranger, or if there be a bride present, precedence is given to her, unless the dinner is given for another person, in which case he escorts the latter. The hostess is escorted either by the greatest stranger, or some gentleman whom she wishes to place in the seat of honor, which is at her right. The host places the lady whom he escorts at his right. The seats of the host and hostess may be in the middle and at opposite sides of the table, or at the opposite ends. Husbands should not escort their wives, or brothers their sisters, as this partakes of the nature of a family gathering.

DINNER A LA RUSSE.

The latest and most satisfactory plan for serving dinners is the dinner *a la Russe* (the Russian style)—all the food being placed upon a side table, and servants do the carving and waiting. This style gives an opportunity for more profuse ornamentation of the table, which, as the meal progresses, does not become encumbered with partially empty dishes and platters.

DUTIES OF SERVANTS.

The servants commence, in passing the dishes, one upon the right of the host and one upon the right of the hostess. A master or mistress should never censure the servants at dinner, however things may go wrong. Servants should wear thin-soled shoes that their steps may be noiseless, and if they should use napkins in serving (as is the English custom) instead of gloves, their hands and nails should be faultlessly clean. A good servant is never awkward. He avoids coughing, breathing hard or treading on a lady's dress; never lets any article drop, and deposits plates, glasses, knives, forks and spoons noiselessly. It is considered good form for a servant not to wear gloves in waiting at table, but to use a damask napkin, with one corner wrapped around the thumb, that he may not touch the plates and dishes with the naked hand.

SOUP.

Soup is the first course. All should accept it even if they let it remain untouched, because it is better to make a pretense of eating until the next course is served, than to sit waiting, or compel the servants to serve one before the rest. Soup should not be called for a second time. A soup-plate should never be tilted for the last spoonful.

FISH.

Fish follows soup and must be eaten with a fork, unless fish knives are provided. If fish knives are not provided, a piece of bread in the left hand answers the purpose as well, with the fork in the right hand. Fish may be declined, but must not be called for a second time.

THE SIDE DISHES.

After soup and fish come the side dishes, which must be eaten with the fork, though the knife is used in cutting meats and anything too hard for a fork.

GENERAL RULES REGARDING DINNER.

When the plate of each course is set before you, with the knife and fork upon it, remove the knife and fork at once. This matter should be carefully attended to, as the serving of an entire course is delayed by neglecting to remove them.

Greediness should not be indulged in. Indecision must be avoided. Do not take up one piece and lay it down in favor of another, or hesitate.

Never allow the servant, or the one who pours, to fill your glass with wine that you do not wish to drink. You can check him by touching the rim of your glass.

Cheese is eaten with a fork and not with a knife.

If you have occasion to speak to a servant, wait until you can catch his eye, and then ask in a low tone for what you want.

The mouth should always be kept closed in eating, and both eating and drinking should be noiseless.

Bread is broken at dinner. Vegetables are eaten with a fork.

Asparagus can be taken up with the fingers, if preferred. Olives and artichokes are always so eaten.

Fruit is eaten with silver knives and forks.

You are at liberty to refuse a dish that you do not wish to eat. If any course is set down before you that you do not wish, do not touch it. Never play with food, nor mince your bread, nor handle the glass and silver near you unnecessarily.

Never reprove a waiter for negligence or improper conduct; that is the business of the host.

When a dish is offered you, accept or refuse at once, and allow the waiter to pass on. A gentleman will see that the lady whom he has escorted to the table is helped to all she wishes, but it is officiousnsss to offer to help other ladies who have escorts.

If the guests pass the dishes to one another, instead of being helped by a servant, you should always help yourself from the dish, if you desire it at all, before passing it on to the next.

A knife should never, on any account, be put into the mouth. Many people, even well-bred in other respects, seem to regard this as an unnecessary regulation; but when we consider that it is a rule of etiquette, and that its violation causes surprise and disgust to many people, it is wisest to observe it.

Be careful to remove the bones from fish before eating. If a bone inadvertently should get into the mouth, the lips must be covered with the napkin in removing it. Cherry stones and grape skins should be removed from the mouth as unobtrusively as possible, and deposited on the side of the plate.

Never use a napkin in place of a handkerchief for wiping the forehead, face or nose.

Pastry should be eaten with a fork. Every thing that can be cut without a knife should be eaten with the fork alone. Pudding may be eaten with a fork or spoon.

Never lay your hand, or play with your fingers, upon the table. Do not toy with your knife, fork or spoon, make crumbs of your bread, or draw imaginary lines upon the table cloth.

Never bite fruit. An apple, peach or pear should be peeled with a knife, and all fruit should be broken or cut.

WAITING ON OTHERS.

If a gentleman is seated by the side of a lady or elderly person, politeness requires him to save them all trouble of procuring for themselves anything to eat or drink, and of obtaining whatever they are in want of at the table, and he should be eager to offer them what he thinks may be most to their taste.

PRAISING DISHES.

A hostess should not express pride regarding what is on her table, nor make apologies if everything she offers you is not to her satisfaction. It is much better that she should observe silence in this respect, and allow her guests to eulogize her dinner or not, as they deem proper. Neither is it in good taste to urge guests to eat, nor to load their plates against their inclination.

MONOPOLIZING CONVERSATION.

For one or two persons to monopolize a conversation which ought to be general, is exceedingly rude. If the dinner party is a large one, you may converse with those near you, raising the voice only loud enough to be distinctly heard by the persons you are talking with.

PICKING TEETH AT THE TABLE.

It is a mark of rudeness to pick your teeth at the table, and it should always be avoided. To hold your hand or napkin over your mouth does not avoid the rudeness of the act, but if it becomes a matter of necessity to remove some obstacle from between the teeth, then your open mouth should be concealed by your hand or napkin.

SELECTING A PARTICULAR DISH.

Never express a preference for any dish or any particular portion of a fowl or of meat, unless requested to do so, and then answer promptly, that no time may be wasted in serving you and others after you.

DUTIES OF HOSTESS AND HOST.

Tact and self-possession are demanded of the hostess, in order that she may perform her duties agreeably, which are not onerous. She should instruct her servants not to remove her plate until her guests have finished. If she speaks of any omission by which her servants have inconvenienced her guests, she must do it with dignity, not betraying any undue annoyance. She must put all her guests at their ease, and pay every possible attention to the requirements of each and all around her. No accident must disturb her; no disappointment embarrass her. If her precious china and her rare glass are broken before her eyes, she must seem to take but little or no notice of it.

The host must aid the hostess in her efforts. He should

have ease and frankness of manner, a calmness of temper that nothing can ruffle, and a kindness of disposition that can never be exhausted. He must encourage the timid, draw out the silent and direct conversation rather than sustain it himself.

No matter what may go wrong, a hostess should never seem to notice it to the annoyance of her guests. By passing it over herself, it will very frequently escape the attention of others. If her guests arrive late, she should welcome them as cordially as if they had come early, but she will commit a rudeness to those who have arrived punctually, if she awaits dinner for tardy guests for more than the fifteen minutes of grace prescribed by custom.

RETIRING FROM THE TABLE.

When the hostess sees that all have finished, she looks at the lady who is sitting at the right of the host, and the company rise, and withdraw in the order they are seated, without precedence. After retiring to the drawing-room, the guests should intermingle in a social manner. It is expected that the guests will remain from one to three hours after dinner.

ACCEPTING HOSPITALITY A SIGN OF GOOD WILL.

As eating with another under his own roof is in all conditions of society regarded as a sign of good-will, those who partake of proffered hospitalities, only to gossip about and abuse their host and hostess, should remember, that in the opinion of all honorable persons, they injure themselves by so doing.

CALLS AFTER A DINNER PARTY.

Calls should be made shortly after a dinner party by all who have been invited, whether the invitation be accepted or not.

RETURNING HOSPITALITY.

Those who are in the habit of giving dinner parties, should return the invitation before another is extended to them. Society is very severe upon those who do not return debts of hospitality, if they have the means to do so. If they never entertain anyone because of limited means, or for other good reasons, it is so understood, and it is not expected that they should make exceptions ; or if they are in the habit of giving other entertainments and not dinners, their debts of hospitality can be returned by invitations to whatever the entertainment might be. Some are deterred from accepting invitations by the feeling that they cannot return the hospitality in so magnificent a form. It is not the costly preparations, nor the expensive repast offered which are the most agreeable features of any entertainment, but it is the kind and friendly feeling shown. Those who are not deterred from accepting such invitations for this reason, and who enjoy the fruits of friendliness thus shown them, must possess narrow views of their duty, and very little self-respect, if, when an opportunity presents itself in any way to reciprocate the kind feeling manifested, they fail to avail themselves of it. True hospitality, however, neither expects nor desires any return.

EXPENSIVE DINNERS NOT THE MOST ENJOYABLE.

It is a mistake to think that in giving a dinner, it is indispensable to have certain dishes and a variety of wines, because others serve them. Those who entertain frequently often use their own discretion, and never feel obliged to do as others do, if they wish to do differently. Some of the most enjoyable dinners given are those which are least expensive. It is this mistaken feeling that people cannot entertain without committing all sorts of extravagances, which causes many persons, in every way well qualified to do incalculable good socially, to exclude themselves from all general society.

WINES AT DINNERS.

The *menu* of a dinner party is by some not regarded as complete, unless it includes one or more varieties of wine. When used it is first served after soup, but any guest may, with propriety, decline being served. This, however, must not be done ostentatiously. Simply say to the waiter, or whoever pours it, "not any; thank you." Wine, offered at a dinner party, should never be criticized, however poor it may be. A person who has partaken of wine, may also decline to have the glass filled again.

If the guests should include one or more people of well-known temperance principles, in deference to the scruples of these guests, wines or liquors should not be brought to the table. People who entertain should also be cautious as to serving wines at all. It is impossible to tell what harm you may do to some of your highly esteemed guests. It may be that your palatable wines may create an appetite for the habitual use of wines or stronger alcoholic liquors; or you may renew a passion long controlled and entombed; or you may turn a wavering will from a seemingly steadfast resolution to forever abstain. This is an age of reforms, the temperance reform being by no means the least powerful of these, and no ladies or gentlemen will be censured or misunderstood if they neglect to supply their dinner table with any kind of intoxicating liquor. Mrs. ex-President Hayes banished wines and liquors from her table, and an example set by the "first lady of the land" can be safely followed in every American household, whatever may have been former prevailing customs. It is safe to say that no "mistress of the White House" will ever set aside the temperance principles established by Mrs. Hayes.

CHAPTER X.

Table Manners and Etiquette.

T is of the highest importance that all persons should conduct themselves with the strictest regard to good breeding, even in the privacy of their own homes, when at table, a neglect of such observances will render one stiff and awkward in society. There are so many little points to be observed, that unless a person is habitually accustomed to observe them, he unconsciously commits some error, or will appear awkward and constrained upon occasions when it is important to be fully at ease. To be thoroughly at ease at such times is only acquired by the habitual practice of good manners at the table, and is the result of proper home training. It is the duty of parents to accustom their children, by example as well as by precept, to be attentive and polite to each other at every meal, as well as to observe proper rules of etiquette, and if they do so, they need never fear that they will be rude or awkward when they go abroad. Even when persons habitually eat alone, they should pay

due regard to the rules of etiquette, for by so doing they
form habits of ease and gracefulness which are requisite
in refined circles; otherwise they speedily acquire rude
and awkward habits which they cannot shake off without great difficulty, and which are at times embarrassing
to themselves and their friends. In private families it
should be observed as a rule to meet together at all
meals of the day around one common table, where the
same rules of etiquette should be rigidly enforced, as
though each member of the family were sitting at a
stranger's table. It is only by this constant practice of
the rules of good behaviour at home, that good manners
become easy when any of them go abroad.

THE BREAKFAST.

At the first meal of the day, even in the most orderly
households, an amount of freedom is allowed, which
would be unjustifiable at any other meal. The head of
the house may look over his morning paper, and the
various other members may glance over correspondence
or such books or studies as they are interested in. Each
may rise and leave the table when business or pleasure
dictates, without awaiting for the others or for a general signal.

The breakfast table should be simply decorated, yet
it may be made very attractive with its snowy cloth and
napkins, its array of glass, and its ornamentation of
fruits and flowers. Bread should be placed upon the
table, cut in slices. In eating, it must always be
broken, never cut, and certainly not bitten. Fruit should

be served in abundance at breakfast whenever practicable. There is an old adage which declares that "fruit is gold in the morning, silver at noon, and lead at night."

LUNCHEON.

In many of our large cities, where business prevents the head of the family from returning to dinner until a late hour, luncheon is served about midday and serves as an early dinner for children and servants. There is much less formality in the serving of lunch than of dinner. It is all placed upon the table at once, whether it consists of one or more courses. Where only one or two are at luncheon, the repast is ordinarily served on a tray.

DINNER.

The private family dinner should be the social hour of the day. Then parents and children should meet together, and the meal should be of such length as to admit of the greatest sociality. It is an old saying that chatted food is half digested. The utmost good feeling should prevail among all. Business and domestic cares and troubles should be, for the time, forgotten, and the pleasures of home most heartily enjoyed. In another chapter we have spoken at length upon fashionable dinner parties.

THE KNIFE AND FORK.

The knife and fork were not made for playthings, and should not be used as such when people are waiting at the table for the food to be served. Do not hold them erect in your hands at each side of your plate, nor cross

them on your plate when you have finished, nor make a
noise with them. The knife should only be used for
cutting meats and hard substances, while the fork, held
in the left hand, is used in carrying food into the mouth.
A knife must never, on any account, be put into the
mouth. When you send your plate to be refilled, do
not send your knife and fork, but put them upon a piece
of bread, or hold them in your hand.

GREEDINESS.

To put large pieces of food into your mouth appears
greedy, and if you are addressed when your mouth is
so filled, you are obliged to pause, before answering,
until the vast mouthful is masticated, or run the risk of
choking, by swallowing it too hastily. To eat very fast
is also a mark of greediness, and should be avoided.
The same may be said of soaking up gravy with bread,
scraping up sauce with a spoon, scraping your plate and
gormandizing upon one or two articles of food only.

GENERAL RULES ON TABLE ETIQUETTE.

Refrain from making a noise when eating, or supping
from a spoon, and from smacking the lips or breathing
heavily while masticating food, as they are marks of ill-
breeding. The lips should be kept closed in eating as
much as possible.

It is rude and awkward to elevate your elbows and
move your arms at the table, so as to incommode those
on either side of you.

Whenever one or both hands are unoccupied, they

should be kept below the table, and not pushed upon the table and into prominence.

Do not leave the table before the rest of the family or guests, without asking the head, or host, to excuse you, except at a hotel or boarding house.

Tea or coffee should never be poured into a saucer to cool, but sipped from the cup.

If a person wishes to be served with more tea or coffee, he should place his spoon in his saucer. If he has had sufficient, let it remain in the cup.

If by chance anything unpleasant is found in the food, such as a hair in the bread or a fly in the coffee, remove it without remark. Even though your own appetite be spoiled, it is well not to prejudice others.

Always make use of the butter-knife, sugar-spoon and salt-spoon, instead of using your knife, spoon or fingers.

Never, if possible, cough or sneeze at the table.

At home fold your napkin when you are done with it and place it in your ring. If you are visiting, leave your napkin unfolded beside your plate.

Eat neither too fast nor too slow.

Never lean back in your chair, nor sit too near or too far from the table.

Keep your elbows at your side, so that you may not inconvenience your neighbors.

Do not find fault with the food.

The old-fashioned habit of abstaining from taking the last piece upon the plate is no longer observed. It is to be supposed that the vacancy can be supplied, if necessary.

If a plate is handed you at the table, keep it yourself instead of passing it to a neighbor. If a dish is passed to you, serve yourself first, and then pass it on.

The host or hostess should not insist upon guests partaking of particular dishes; nor ask persons more than once, nor put anything on their plates which they have declined. It is ill-bred to urge a person to eat of anything after he has declined.

When sweet corn is served on the ear, the grain should be pared from it upon the plate, instead of being eaten from the cob.

Strive to keep the cloth as clean as possible, and use the edge of the plate or a side dish for potato skins and other refuse.

CHAPTER XI.

Receptions, Parties and Balls.

ORNING RECEPTIONS, as they are called, but more correctly speaking, afternoon parties, are generally held from four to seven o'clock in the afternoon. Sometimes a sufficient number for a quadrille arrange to remain after the assemblage has for the most part dispersed.

THE DRESS.

The dress for receptions is, for men, morning dress; for ladies, demi-toilet, with or without bonnet. No low-necked dress nor short sleeves should be seen at day receptions, nor white neck-ties and dress coats.

The material of a lady's costume may be of velvet, silk, muslin, gauze or grenadine, according to the season of the year, and taste of the wearer, but her more elegant jewelry and laces should be reserved for evening parties.

THE REFRESHMENTS.

The refreshments for "morning receptions" are generally light, consisting of tea, coffee, frozen punch,

9   (129)

claret punch, ices, fruit and cakes. Often a cold collation is spread after the lighter refreshments have been
served, and sometimes the table is set with all the varieties, and renewed from time to time.

INVITATIONS.

Invitations to a reception are simple, and are usually
very informal. Frequently the lady's card is sent with
the simple inscription, " At Home Thursday, from four
to seven." No answers are expected to these invitations,
unless "R. S. V. P." is on one corner. One visiting
card is left by each person who is present, to serve for
the after call. No calls are expected from those who
attend. Those who are not able to be present, call soon
after.

MUSICAL MATINEES.

A *matinee musicale* partakes of the nature of a reception, and is one of the most difficult entertainments
attempted. For this it is necessary to secure those persons possessing sufficient vocal and instrumental talent
to insure the success of the entertainment, and to arrange
with them a programme, assigning to each, in order, his
or her part. It is customary to commence with a piece
of instrumental music, followed by solos, duets, quar-
tettes, etc., with instrumental music interspersed, in not
too great proportions. Some competent person is needed
as accompanist. It is the duty of the hostess to maintain silence among her guests during the performance
of instrumental as well as vocal music. If any are un-
aware of the breach of good manners they commit in

talking or whispering at such times, she should by a gesture endeavor to acquaint them of the fact. It is the duty of the hostess to see that the ladies are accompanied to the piano; that the leaves of the music are turned for them, and that they are conducted to their seats again. When not intimately acquainted with them, the hostess should join in expressing gratification.

The dress at a musical matinee is the same as at a reception, only bonnets are more generally dispensed with. Those who have taken part, often remain for a hot supper.

PARTIES IN THE COUNTRY.

Morning and afternoon parties in the country, or at watering places, are of a less formal character than in cities. The hostess introduces such of her guests as she thinks most likely to be mutually agreeable. Music or some amusement is essential to the success of such parties.

SUNDAY HOSPITALITIES.

In this country it is not expected that persons will call after informal hospitalities extended on Sunday. All gatherings on that day ought to be informal. No dinner parties are given on Sunday, or, at least, they are not considered as good form in good society.

FIVE O'CLOCK TEA, COFFEE AND KETTLE-DRUMS.

Five o'clock tea, coffee and kettle-drums have recently been introduced into this country from England. For these invitations are usually issued on the lady's visiting card, with the words written in the left hand corner.

Five o'clock tea,

Wednesday, October 6.

Or, if for a kettle-drum:

Kettle-drum,

Wednesday, October 6.

No answers are expected to these invitations, unless there is an R. S. V. P. on the card. It is optional with those who attend, to leave cards. Those who do not attend, call afterwards. The hostess receives her guests standing, aided by other members of the family or intimate friends. For a kettle-drum there is usually a crowd, and yet but few remain over half an hour—the conventional time alloted—unless they are detained by music or some entertaining conversation. A table set in the dining-room is supplied with tea, coffee, chocolate, sandwiches, buns and cakes, which constitute all that is offered to the guests.

There is less formality at a kettle-drum than at a larger day reception. The time is spent in desultory conversation with friends, in listening to music, or such entertainment as has been provided.

Gentlemen wear the usual morning dress. Ladies wear the *demi-toilet*, with or without bonnets.

At five o'clock tea (or coffee), the equipage is on a side table, together with plates of thin sandwiches, and of cake. The pouring of the tea and passing of refreshments are usually done by some members of the family or friends, without the assistance of servants, where the number assembled is small; for, as a rule, the people who frequent these social gatherings, care more for social intercourse than for eating and drinking.

MORE FORMAL ENTERTAINMENTS.

Evening parties and balls are of a much more formal character than the entertainments that have been mentioned. They require evening dress. Of late years, however, evening dress is almost as much worn at grand dinners as at balls and evening parties, only the material is not of so diaphanous a character. Lace and muslin are out of place. Invitations to evening parties should be sent from a week to two weeks in advance, and in all cases they should be answered immediately.

BALLS.

The requisites for a successful ball are good music and plenty of people to dance. An English writer says, "The advantage of the ball is, that it brings young people together for a sensible and innocent recreation, and takes them away from silly, if not from bad ones; that it gives them exercise, and that the general effect of the beauty, elegance and brilliancy of a ball is to elevate rather than to deprave the mind." It may be that the round dance is monopolizing the ball room to a too great extent, and it is possible that these may be so frequent as to mar the pleasure of some persons who do not care to participate in them, to the exclusion of "square" and other dances. America should not be the only nation that confines ball room dancing to waltzes, as is done in some of our cities. There should be an equal number of waltzes and quadrilles, with one or two contra dances, which would give an opportunity to those who object (or whose parents object) to round dances to appear on the floor.

PREPARATIONS FOR A BALL.

There should be dressing-rooms for ladies and gentlemen, with a servant or servants to each. There should be cards with the names of the invited guests upon them, or checks with duplicates to be given to the guests ready to pin upon the wraps of each one. Each dressing-room should be supplied with a complete set of toilet articles. It is customary to decorate the house elaborately with flowers. Although this is an expensive luxury, it adds much to beautifying the rooms.

THE MUSIC.

Four musicians are enough for a "dance." When the dancing room is small, the flageolet is preferable to the horn, as it is less noisy and marks the time as well. The piano and violin form the mainstay of the band; but when the rooms are large enough, a larger band may be employed.

THE DANCES.

The dances should be arranged beforehand, and for large balls programmes are printed with a list of the dances. Usually a ball opens with a waltz, followed by a quadrille, and these are succeeded by galops, lancers, polkas, quadrilles and waltzes in turn.

INTRODUCTIONS AT A BALL.

Gentlemen who are introduced to ladies at a ball, solely for the purpose of dancing, wait to be recognized before speaking with ladies upon meeting afterwards, but they are at liberty to recall themselves by lifting their hats in passing. In England a ball-room acquaintance rarely goes any farther, until they have met at more balls than one; so, also, a gentleman cannot, after being introduced to a young lady, ask her for more than two dances during the same evening. In England an introduction given for dancing purposes does not constitute acquaintanceship. With us, as in Continental Europe, it does. It is for this reason that, in England, ladies are expected to bow first, while on the Continent it is the gentlemen who give the first marks of recognition, as it should be here, or better still, simultaneously, when the recognition is simultaneous. It is as much the gentleman's place to bow (with our mode of life) as it is the lady's. The one who recognizes first should be the first to show that recognition. Introductions take place in a ball room in order to provide ladies with partners, or between persons residing in different cities. In all other cases permission is asked before giving introductions. But where a hostess is sufficiently discriminating in the selection of her guests, those assembled under her roof should remember that they are, in a certain sense, made known to one another, and ought, therefore, to be able to converse freely without introductions.

RECEIVING GUESTS.

The custom of the host and hostess receiving together, is not now prevalent. The receiving devolves upon the hostess, but it is the duty of the host to remain within sight until after the arrivals are principally over, that he may be easily found by any one seeking him. The same duty devolves upon the sons, who, that evening, must share their attentions with all. The daughters, as well as the sons, will look after partners for the young ladies who desire to dance, and they will try to see that no one is neglected before they join the dancers themselves.

AN AFTER-CALL.

After a ball, an after-call is due the lady of the house at which you were entertained, and should be made as soon as convenient—within two weeks at the farthest. The call loses its significance entirely, and passes into remissness, when a longer time is permitted to elapse. If it is not possible to make a call, send your card or leave it at the door. It has become customary of late for a lady who has no weekly reception day, in sending invitations to a ball, to inclose her card in each invitation for one or more receptions, in order that the after-calls due her may be made on that day.

SUPPER.

The supper-room at a ball is thrown open generally at twelve o'clock. The table is made as elegant as beautiful china, cut-glass and an abundance of flowers can make it. The hot dishes are oysters, stewed, fried, broiled and scalloped, chicken, game, etc., and the cold dishes are such as boned turkey, *bœuf á la mode*, chicken salad, lobster salad and raw oysters. When supper is announced, the host leads the way with the lady to whom he wishes to show especial attention, who may be an elderly lady, or a stranger or a bride. The hostess remains until the last, with the gentleman who takes her to supper, unless some distinguished guest is present, with whom she leads the way. No gentleman should ever go into the supper-room alone, unless he has seen every lady enter before him. When ladies are left unattended, gentlemen, although strangers, are at liberty to offer their services in waiting upon them, for the host and hostess are sufficient guarantees for the respectability of their guests.

THE NUMBER TO INVITE.

Persons giving balls or dancing parties should be careful not to invite more than their rooms will accommodate, so as to avoid a crush. Invitations to crowded balls are not hospitalities, but inflictions. A hostess is usually safe, however, in inviting one-fourth more than her rooms will hold, as that proportion of regrets are apt to be received. People who do not dance will not, as a rule, expect to be invited to a ball or dancing party.

DUTIES OF GUESTS.

Some persons may be astonished to learn that any duties devolve upon the guests. In fact there are circles where all such duties are ignored.

It is the duty of every person who has at first accepted the invitation, and subsequently finds that it will be impossible to attend, to send a regret, even at the last moment, and as it is rude to send an acceptance with no intention of going, those who so accept will do well to remember this duty. It is the duty of every lady who attends a ball, to make her toilet as fresh as possible. It need not be expensive, but it should at least be clean; it may be simple, but it should be neither soiled nor tumbled. The gentlemen should wear evening dress.

It is the duty of every person to arrive as early as possible after the hour named, when it is mentioned in the invitation.

Another duty of guests is that each one should do all in his or her power to contribute to the enjoyment of the evening, and neither hesitate nor decline to be introduced to such guests as the hostess requests. It is not binding upon any gentleman to remain one moment longer than he desires with any lady. By constantly moving from one to another, when he feels so inclined, he gives an opportunity to others to circulate as freely; and this custom, generally introduced in our society, would go a long way toward contributing to the enjoyment of all. The false notion generally entertained that a gentleman is expected to remain standing by the side of a lady, like a sentinel on duty, until relieved by some other person, is absurd, and deters many who would gladly give a few passing moments to lady acquaintances, could they but know that they would be free to leave at any instant that conversation flagged, or that they desired to join another. In a society where it is not considered a rudeness to leave after a few sentences with one, to exchange some words with another, there is a constant interchange of civilities, and the men circulate through the room with that charming freedom which insures the enjoyment of all.

While the hostess is receiving, no person should remain beside her except members of her family who receive with her, or such friends as she has designated to assist her. All persons entering should pass on to make room for others.

SOME SUGGESTIONS FOR GENTLEMEN.

A gentleman should never attempt to step across a lady's train. He should walk around it. If by any accident he should tread upon any portion of her dress, he must instantly beg her pardon, and if by greater carelessness he should tear it, he must pause in his course and offer to escort her to the dressing-room so that she may have it repaired.

If a lady asks any favor of a gentleman, such as to send a servant to her with a glass of water, to take her into the ball-room when she is without an escort, to inquire whether her carriage is in waiting, or any of the numerous services which ladies often require, no gentleman will, under any circumstances, refuse her request.

A really well-bred man will remember to ask the daughters of a house to dance, as it is his imperative duty to do so; and if the ball has been given for a lady who dances, he should include her in his attentions. If he wishes to be considered a thorough-bred gentleman, he will sacrifice himself occasionally to those who are unsought and neglected in the dance. The consciousness of having performed a kind and courteous action will be his reward.

When gentlemen, invited to a house on the occasion of an entertainment, are not acquainted with all the members of the family, their first duty, after speaking to their host and hostess, is to ask some common friend to introduce them to those members whom they do not know. The host and hostess are often too much occupied in receiving to be able to do this.

DUTIES OF AN ESCORT.

A lady's escort should call for her and accompany her to the place of entertainment; go with her as far as the dressing-room, return to meet her there when she is prepared to go to the ball-room; enter the latter room with her and lead her to the hostess; dance the first dance with her; conduct her to the supper-room, and be ready to accompany her home whenever she wishes to go. He should watch during the evening to see that she is supplied with dancing partners. When he escorts her home she should not invite him to enter the house, and even if she does so, he should by all means decline the invitation. He should call upon her within the next two days.

GENERAL RULES FOR BALLS.

A young man who can dance, and will not dance, should stay away from a ball.

The lady with whom a gentleman dances last is the one he takes to supper. Therefore he can make no engagement to take out any other, unless his partner is already engaged.

Public balls are most enjoyable when you have your own party. The great charm of a ball is its perfect accord and harmony. All altercations, loud talking and noisy laughter are doubly ill-mannered in a ball-room. Very little suffices to disturb the whole party.

In leaving a ball, it is not deemed necessary to wish the lady of the house a good night. In leaving a small dance or party, it is civil to do so.

The difference between a ball and an evening party is, that at a ball there must be dancing, and at an evening party there may or may not be. A London authority defines a ball to be "an assemblage for dancing, of not less than seventy-five persons."

Common civility requires that those who have not been present, but who were among the guests invited, should, when meeting the hostess the first time after an entertainment, make it a point to express some acknowledgment of their appreciation of the invitation, by regretting their inability to be present.

When dancing a round dance, a gentleman should never hold a lady's hand behind him, or on his hip, or high in the air, moving her arm as though it were a pump handle, as seen in some of our western cities, but should hold it gracefully by his side.

Never forget ball-room engagements, nor confuse them, nor promise two dances to one person. If a lady has forgotten an engagement, the gentleman she has thus slighted must pleasantly accept her apology. Good-breeding and the appearance of good temper are inseparable.

It is not necessary for a gentleman to bow to his partner after a quadrille; it is enough that he offers his arm and walks at least half way round the room with her. He is not obliged to reman beside her unless he wishes to do so, but may leave her with any lady whom she knows.

Never be seen without gloves in a ball-room, or with those of any other color than white, unless they are of the most delicate hue.

Though not customary for a married couple to dance together in society, those men who wish to show their wives the compliment of such unusual attention, if they possess any independence, will not be deterred from doing so by their fear of any comments from Mrs. Grundy.

The sooner that we recover from the effects of the Puritanical idea that clergymen should never be seen at balls, the better for all who attend them. Where it is wrong for a clergyman to go, it is wrong for any member of his church to be seen.

In leaving a ball room before the music has ceased, if no members of the family are in sight, it is not necessary to find them before taking your departure. If, however, the invitation is a first one, endeavor not to make your exit until you have thanked your hostess for the entertainment. You can speak of the pleasure it has afforded you, but it is not necessary that you should say "it has been a grand success."

Young ladies must be careful how they refuse to dance, for unless a good reason is given, a gentleman is apt to take it as evidence of personal dislike. After a lady refuses, the gentleman should not urge her to dance, nor should the lady accept another invitation for the same dance. The members of the household should see that those guests who wish to dance are provided with partners.

Ladies leaving a ball or party should not allow gentlemen to see them to their carriages, unless overcoats and hats are on for departure.

When balls are given, if the weather is bad, an awning should be provided for the protection of those passing from their carriages to the house. In all cases, a broad piece of carpet should be spread from the door to the carriage steps.

Gentlemen should engage their partners for the approaching dance, before the music strikes up.

In a private dance, a lady cannot well refuse to dance

with any gentleman who invites her, unless she has a previous engagement. If she declines from weariness, the gentleman will show her a compliment by abstaining from dancing himself, and remaining with her while the dance progresses.

CHAPTER XII.

Etiquette of the Street.

THE manners of a person are clearly shown by his treatment of the people he meets in the public streets of a city or village, in public conveyances and in traveling generally. The true gentleman, at all times, in all places, and under all circumstances, is kind and courteous to all he meets, regards not only the rights, but the wishes and feelings of others, is deferential to women and to elderly men, and is ever ready to extend his aid to those who need it.

THE STREET MANNERS OF A LADY.

The true lady walks the street, wrapped in a mantle of proper reserve, so impenetrable that insult and coarse familiarity shrink from her, while she, at the same time, carries with her a congenial atmosphere which attracts all, and puts all at their ease.

A lady walks quietly through the streets, seeing and hearing nothing that she ought not to see and hear, recog-

nizing acquaintances with a courteous bow, and friends
with words of greeting. She is always unobtrusive,
never talks loudly, or laughs boisterously, or does anything to attract the attention of the passers-by. She
walks along in her own quiet, lady-like way, and by her
pre-occupation is secure from any annoyance to which a
person of less perfect breeding might be subjected.

A lady never demands attention and favors from a
gentleman, but, when voluntarily offered, accepts them
gratefully, graciously, and with an expression of hearty
thanks.

FORMING STREET ACQUAINTANCES.

A lady never forms an acquaintance upon the street,
or seeks to attract the attention or admiration of persons
of the other sex. To do so would render false her claims
to ladyhood, if it did not make her liable to far graver
charges.

RECOGNIZING FRIENDS IN THE STREET.

No one, while walking the streets, should fail, through
pre-occupation, or absent-mindedness, to recognize friends
or acquaintances, either by a bow or some form of salutation. If two gentlemen stop to talk, they should retire
to one side of the walk. If a stranger should be in company with one of the gentlemen, an introduction is not
necessary. If a gentleman meets another gentleman in
company with a lady whom he does not know, he lifts
his hat to salute them both. If he knows the lady, he
should salute her first. The gentleman who accompanies
a lady, always returns a salutation made to her.

A CROWDED STREET.

When a gentleman and lady are walking in the street, if at any place, by reason of the crowd, or from other cause, they are compelled to proceed singly, the gentleman should always precede his companion.

INTRUSIVE INQUIRIES.

If you meet or join or are visited by a person who has any article whatever, under his arm or in his hand, and he does not offer to show it to you, you should not, even if it be your most intimate friend, take it from him and look at it. That intrusive curiosity is very inconsistent with the delicacy of a well-bred man, and always offends in some degree.

THE FIRST TO BOW.

In England strict etiquette requires that a lady, meeting upon the street a gentleman with whom she has acquaintance, shall give the first bow of recognition. In this country, however, good sense does not insist upon an imperative following of this rule. A well-bred man bows and raises his hat to every lady of his acquaintance whom he meets, without waiting for her to take the initiative. If she is well-bred, she will certainly respond to his salutation. As politeness requires that each salute the other, their salutations will thus be simultaneous.

ALWAYS RECOGNIZE ACQUAINTANCES.

One should always recognize lady acquaintances in the street, either by bowing or words of greeting, a gen-

tleman lifting his hat. If they stop to speak, it is not
obligatory to shake hands. Shaking hands is not forbidden, but in most cases it is to be avoided in public.

GENTLEMAN MEETING A LADY.

BOWING TO STRANGERS WITH FRIENDS.

If a gentleman meets a friend, and the latter has a
stranger with him, all three should bow. If the gentleman stops his friend to speak to him, he should apologize to the stranger for detaining him. If the stranger
is a lady, the same deference should be shown as if she
were an acquaintance.

DO NOT LACK POLITENESS.

Never hesitate in acts of politeness for fear they will not be recognized or returned. One cannot be too polite so long as he conforms to rules, while it is easy to lack politeness by neglect of them. Besides, if courtesy is met by neglect or rebuff, it is not for the courteous person to feel mortification, but the boorish one; and so all lookers-on will regard the matter.

TALKING WITH A LADY IN THE STREET.

In meeting a lady it is optional with her whether she shall pause to speak. If the gentleman has anything to say to her, he should not stop her, but turn around and walk in her company until he has said what he has to say, when he may leave her with a bow and a lift of the hat.

LADY AND GENTLEMAN WALKING TOGETHER.

A gentleman walking with a lady should treat her with the most scrupulous politeness, and may take either side of the walk. It is customary for the gentleman to have the lady on his right hand side, and he offers her his right arm, when walking arm in arm. If, however, the street is crowded, the gentleman must keep the lady on that side of him where she will be the least exposed to crowding.

OFFERING THE ARM TO A LADY.

A gentleman should, in the evening, or whenever her safety, comfort or convenience seems to require it, offer a lady companion his arm. At other times it is not customary to do so unless the parties be husband and wife or engaged. In the latter case, it is not always advisable to do so, as they may be made the subject of unjust remarks.

KEEPING STEP.

In walking together, especially when arm in arm, it is desirable that the two keep step. Ladies should be particular to adapt their pace as far as practicable, to that of their escort. It is easily done.

OPENING THE DOOR FOR A LADY.

A gentleman should always hold open the door for a lady to enter first. This is obligatory, not only in the case of the lady who accompanies him, but also in that of any strange lady who chances to be about to enter at the same time.

ANSWERING QUESTIONS.

A gentleman will answer courteously any questions which a lady may address to him upon the street, at the same time lifting his hat, or at least touching it respectfully.

SMOKING UPON THE STREETS.

In England a well-bred man never smokes upon the streets. While this rule does not hold good in this country, yet no gentleman will ever insult a lady by smoking in the streets in her company, and in meeting and saluting a lady he will always remove his cigar from his mouth.

OFFENSIVE BEHAVIOR.

No gentleman is ever guilty of the offense of standing on street corners and the steps of hotels or other public places and boldly scrutinizing every lady who passes.

CARRYING PACKAGES.

A gentleman will never permit a lady with whom he is walking to carry a package of any kind, but will insist upon relieving her of it. He may even accost a lady when he sees her overburdened and offer his assistance, if their ways lie in the same direction.

SHOUTING.

Never speak to your acquaintances from one side of the street to the other. Shouting is a certain sign of vulgarity. First approach, and then make your communication to your acquaintance or friend in a moderately loud tone of voice.

TWO GENTLEMEN WALKING WITH A LADY.

When two gentlemen are walking with a lady in the street they should not be both upon the same side of her, but one of them should walk upon the outside and the other upon the inside.

CROSSING THE STREET WITH A LADY.

If a gentleman is walking with a lady who has his arm, and they cross the street, it is better not to disengage the arm, and go round upon the outside. Such effort evinces a palpable attention to form, and that is always to be avoided.

FULFILLING AN ENGAGEMENT.

When on your way to fill an engagement, if a friend stops you on the street you may, without committing a breach of etiquette, tell him of your appointment, and release yourself from any delay that may be occasioned by a long talk; but do so in a courteous manner, expressing regret for the necessity.

WALKING WITH A LADY ACQUAINTANCE.

A gentleman should not join a lady acquaintance on the street for the purpose of walking with her, unless he ascertains that his company would be perfectly agreeable to her. It might be otherwise, and she should frankly say so, if asked.

PASSING BEFORE A LADY.

When a lady wishes to enter a store, house or room, if a gentleman accompanies her, he should hold the door open and allow her to enter first, if practicable; for a gentleman must never pass before a lady anywhere if he can avoid it, or without an apology.

SHOPPING ETIQUETTE.

In inquiring for goods at a store or shop, do not say to the clerk or salesman, "I want" such an article, but, "Please show me" such an article, or some other polite form of address.

You should never take hold of a piece of goods or an article which another person is examining. Wait until it is replaced upon the counter, when you are at liberty to examine it.

It is rude to interrupt friends whom you meet in a store before they have finished making their purchases, or to ask their attention to your own purchases. It is rude to offer your opinion unasked, upon their judgment or taste, in the selection of goods.

It is rude to sneer at and depreciate goods, and exceedingly discourteous to the salesman. Use no deceit, but be honest with them, if you wish them to be honest with you.

Avoid **haggling down** the prices of articles in any way. If the price does not suit, you may say so quietly, and depart, but it is generally best to say nothing about it.

It is an insult for the salesman to offensively suggest that you can do better elsewhere, which should be resented by instant departure.

Ladies should not monopolize the time and attention of salesmen in small talk, while other customers are in the store to be waited upon.

Whispering in a store is rude. Loud and showy behaviour is exceedingly vulgar.

ETIQUETTE FOR PUBLIC CONVEYANCES.

In street cars, omnibuses and other public street conveyances, it should be the endeavor of each passenger to make room for all persons entering, and no gentleman will retain his seat when there are ladies standing. When a lady accepts a seat from a gentleman, she expresses her thanks in a kind and pleasant manner.

A lady may, with perfect propriety, accept the offer of services from a stranger in alighting from, or entering an omnibus or other public conveyance, and should always acknowledge the courtesy with a pleasant "Thank you, sir," or a bow.

Never talk politics or religion in a public conveyance.

Gentlemen should not cross their legs, nor stretch their feet out into the passage-way of a public conveyance.

AVOID CUTTING.

No gentleman will refuse to recognize a lady after she has recognized him, under any circumstances. A young lady should, under no provocation, "cut" a married lady. It is the privilege of age to first recognize those who are younger in years. No young man will fail to recognize an aged one after he has met with recognition. "Cutting" is to be avoided if possible. There are other ways of convincing a man that you do not know him, yet, to young ladies, it is sometimes the only means available to rid them of troublesome acquaintances. "Cutting" consists in returning a bow or recognition with a stare, and is publicly ignoring the acquaintance of the person so treated. It is sometimes done by words in saying, "Really I have not the pleasure of your acquaintance."

AVOIDING CARRIAGES.

For a lady to run across the street to avoid an approaching carriage is inelegant and also dangerous. To attempt to cross the street between the carriages of a funeral procession, is rude and disrespectful. The foreign custom of removing the hat and standing in a respectful attitude until the melancholy train has passed, is a commendable one to be followed in this country.

KEEP TO THE RIGHT.

On meeting and passing people in the street, keep to your right hand, except when a gentleman is walking alone; then he must always turn aside to give the preferred side of the walk to a lady, to anyone carrying a heavy load, to a clergyman or to an old gentleman.

SOME GENERAL SUGGESTIONS.

If a gentleman is walking with two ladies in a rain storm, and there is but one umbrella, he should give it to his companions and walk outside. Nothing can be more absurd than to see a gentleman walking between two ladies holding an umbrella which perfectly protects himself, but half deluges his companions with its dripping streams.

Never turn a corner at full speed or you may find yourself knocked down, or may knock down another, by the violent contact. Always look in the way you are going or you may chance to meet some awkward collision.

A young lady should, if possible, avoid walking alone in the street after dark. If she passes the evening with a friend, provision should be made beforehand for an escort. If this is not practicable, the person at whose house she is visiting should send a servant with her, or some proper person—a gentleman acquaintance present, or her own husband—to perform the duty. A married lady may, however, disregard this rule, if circumstances prevent her being able to conveniently find an escort.

A gentleman will always precede a lady up a flight of stairs, and allow her to precede him in going down.

Do not quarrel with a hack-driver about his fare, but pay him and dismiss him. If you have a complaint to make against him, take his name and make it to the proper authorities. It is rude to keep a lady waiting while you are disputing with a hack-man.

SUMMER AFTERNOON, CENTRAL PARK.

CHAPTER XIII.

Etiquette of Public Places.

ALL well-bred persons will conduct themselves at all times and in all places with perfect decorum. Wherever they meet people they will be found polite, considerate of the comfort, convenience and wishes of others, and unobtrusive in their behavior. They seem to know, as if by instinct, how to conduct themselves, wherever they may go, or in whatever society they may be thrown. They consider at all times the fitness of things, and their actions and speech are governed by feelings of gentleness and kindness towards everybody with whom they come into social relations, having a due consideration for the opinions and prejudices of others, and doing nothing to wound their feelings. Many people, however, either from ignorance, thoughtlessness or carelessness, are constantly violating some of the observances of etiquette pertaining to places of public assemblages. It is for this reason that rules are here given by which may be regulated the conduct of people in various public gatherings, where awkwardness and ostentatious display often call forth unfavorable criticism.

CONDUCT IN CHURCH.

A gentleman should remove his hat upon entering the auditorium.

When visiting a strange church, you should wait in the vestibule until an usher appears to show you to a seat.

A gentleman may walk up the aisle either a little ahead of, or by the side of a lady, allowing the lady to first enter the pew. There should be no haste in passing up the aisle.

People should preserve the utmost silence and decorum in church, and avoid whispering, laughing, staring, or making a noise of any kind with the feet or hands.

It is ill-mannered to be late at church. If one is unavoidably late, it is better to take a pew as near the door as possible.

Ladies always take the inside seats, and gentlemen the outside or head of the pew. When a gentleman accompanies a lady, however, it is customary for him to sit by her side during church services.

A person should never leave church until the services are over, except in some case of emergency.

Do not turn around in your seat to gaze at anyone, to watch the choir, to look over the congregation or to see the cause of any disturbing noise.

If books or fans are passed in church, let them be

offered and accepted or refused with a silent gesture of the head.

It is courteous to see that strangers are provided with books; and if the service is strange to them, the places for the day's reading should be indicated.

It is perfectly proper to offer to share the prayer-book or hymn-book with a stranger if there is no separate book for his use.

In visiting a church of a different belief from your own, pay the utmost respect to the services and conform in all things to the observances of the church—that is, kneel, sit and rise with the congregation. No matter how grotesquely some of the forms and observances may strike you, let no smile or contemptuous remark indicate the fact while in the church.

When the services are concluded, there should be no haste in crowding up the aisle, but the departure should be conducted quietly and decorously. When the vestibule is reached, it is allowable to exchange greetings with friends, but here there should be no loud talking nor boisterous laughter. Neither should gentlemen congregate in knots in the vestibule or upon the steps of the church and compel ladies to run the gauntlet of their eyes and tongues.

If a Protestant gentleman accompanies a lady who is a Roman Catholic to her own church, it is an act of courtesy to offer the holy water. This he must do with the ungloved right hand.

In visiting a church for the mere purpose of seeing the edifice, one should always go at a time when there

are no services being held. If people are even then
found at their devotions, as is apt to be the case in
Roman Catholic churches especially, the demeanor of
the visitor should be respectful and subdued and his
voice low, so that he may not disturb them.

INVITATION TO OPERA OR CONCERT.

A gentleman upon inviting a lady to accompany him
to opera, theatre, concert or other public place of amusement, must send his invitation the previous day. The
lady must reply immediately, so that if she declines,
there shall yet be time for the gentleman to secure
another companion.

It is the gentleman's duty to secure good seats for
the entertainment, or else he or his companion may be
obliged to take up with seats where they can neither see
nor hear.

CONDUCT IN OPERA, THEATER OR PUBLIC HALL.

On entering the hall, theater or opera house the gentleman should walk side by side with his companion
unless the aisle is too narrow, in which case he should
precede her. Upon reaching the seats, he should allow
her to take the inner one, assuming the outer one himself.

A gentleman should, on no account, leave the lady's
side from the beginning to the close of the performance.

If it is a promenade concert or opera, the lady may
be invited to promenade during the intermission. If she
declines, the gentleman must retain his position by her
side.

There is no obligation whatever upon a gentleman to give up his seat to a lady. On the contrary, his duty is solely to the lady whom he accompanies. He must remain beside her during the evening to converse with her between the acts, and to render the entertainment as agreeable to her as possible.

During the performance complete quiet should be preserved, that the audience may not be prevented from seeing or hearing. Between the acts it is perfectly proper to converse, but it should be done in a low tone, so as not to attract attention. Neither should one whisper. There should be no loud talking, boisterous laughter, violent gestures, lover-like demonstrations or anything in manners or speech to attract the attention of others.

It is proper and desirable that the actors be applauded when they deserve it. It is their only means of knowing whether they are giving satisfaction.

The gentleman should see that the lady is provided with a programme, and with libretto also if they are attending opera.

In passing out at the close of the performance the gentleman should precede the lady, and there should be no crowding or pushing.

If the means of the gentleman warrant him in so doing, he should call for his companion in a carriage. This is especially necessary if the evening is stormy. He should call sufficiently early to allow them to reach their destination before the performance commences.

It is unjust to the whole audience to come in late and make a disturbance in obtaining seats.

The gentleman should ask permission to call upon the lady the following day, which permission she should grant; and if she be a person of delicacy and tact, she will make him feel that he has conferred a real pleasure upon her by his invitation. Even if she finds occasion for criticism in the performance, she should be lenient in this respect, and seek for points to praise instead, that he may not feel regret at taking her to an entertainment which has proved unworthy.

REMAIN UNTIL THE PERFORMANCE CLOSES.

At a theatrical or operatic performance, you should remain seated until the performance is concluded and the curtain falls. It is exceedingly rude and ill-bred to rise and leave the hall while the play is drawing to a close, yet this severely exasperating practice has of late been followed by many well-meaning people, who, if they were aware of the extent to which they outraged the feelings of many of the audience, and unwittingly offered an insult to the actors on the stage, would shrink from repeating such flagrantly rude conduct.

CONDUCT IN PICTURE-GALLERIES.

In visiting picture-galleries one should always maintain the deportment of a gentleman or a lady. Make no loud comments and do not seek to show superior knowledge in art matters by gratuitous criticism. If you have not an art education you will probably only be giving publicity to your own ignorance. Do not stand in conversation before a picture, and thus obstruct the view of others who wish to see rather than talk. If you wish to converse with any anyone on general subjects, draw to one side, out of the way of those who want to look at the pictures.

CONDUCT AT CHARITY FAIRS.

In visiting a fancy fair make no comments on either the article or their price, unless you can praise. If you want them, pay the price demanded, or let them alone. If you can conscientiously praise an article, by all means do so, as you may be giving pleasure to the maker if she chances to be within hearing. If you have a table at a fair, use no unladylike means to obtain buyers. Not even the demands of charity can justify you in importuning others to purchase articles against their own judgment or beyond their means.

Never appear so beggarly as to retain the change, if a larger amount is presented than the price. Offer the change promptly, when the gentleman will be at liberty to donate it if he thinks best, and you may accept it with thanks. He is, however, under no obligation whatever to make such donation.

Be guilty of no loud talking or laughing, and by all means avoid conspicuous flirting in so public a place.

As a gentleman must always remove his hat in the presence of ladies, so he should remain with head uncovered, carrying his hat in his hand, in a public place of this character.

CONDUCT IN AN ARTIST'S STUDIO.

If you have occasion to visit an artist's studio, by no means meddle with anything in the room. Reverse no picture which stands or hangs with face to the wall; open no portfolio without permission, and do not alter by a single touch any lay-figure or its drapery, piece of furniture or article of *vertu* posed as a model. You do not know with what care the artist may have arranged these things, nor what trouble the disarrangement may cost him.

Use no strong expression either of delight or disapprobation at anything presented for your inspection. If a picture or a statue please you, show your approval and appreciation by close attention, and a few quiet, well chosen words, rather than by extravagant praise.

Do not ask the artist his prices unless you really intend to become a purchaser; and in this case it is best to attentively observe his works, make your choice, and trust the negotiation to a third person or to a written correspondence with the artist after the visit is concluded· You may express your desire for the work and obtain the refusal of it from the artist. If you desire to conclude the bargain at once you may ask his price, and if he names a higher one than you wish to give, you may say as much and mention the sum you are willing to pay, when it will be optional with the artist to maintain his first price or accept your offer.

It is not proper to visit the studio of an artist except by special invitation or permission, and at an appointed time, for you cannot estimate how much you may disturb him at his work. The hours of daylight are all golden to him; and steadiness of hand in manipulating a pencil is sometimes only acquired each day after hours of practice, and may be instantly lost on the irruption and consequent interruption of visitors.

Never take a young child to a studio, for it may do much mischief in spite of the most careful watching. At any rate, the juvenile visitor will try the artist's temper and nerves by keeping him in a constant state of apprehension.

If you have engaged to sit for your portrait never keep the artist waiting one moment beyond the appointed time. If you do so you should in justice pay for the time you make him lose.

A visitor should never stand behind an artist and watch him at his work; for if he be a man of nervous temperament it will be likely to disturb him greatly.

GENTLEMEN PASSING BEFORE LADIES.

Gentleman having occasion to pass before ladies who are already seated in lecture and concert rooms, theaters and other public places, should beg pardon for disturbing them; passing with their faces and never with their backs toward them.

WHERE GENTLEMEN MAY KEEP THEIR HATS ON.

At garden parties and at all assemblies held in the open air, gentlemen keep their hats on their heads. If draughts of cold air, or other causes, make it necessary for them to retain their hats on their heads, when in the presence of ladies within doors, they explain the necessity and ask permission of the ladies whom they accompany.

CHAPTER XIV.

Etiquette of Traveling.

HERE is nothing that tests the natural politeness of men and women so thoroughly as traveling. We all desire as much comfort as possible and as a rule are selfish. In these days of railroad travel, when every railway is equipped with elegant coaches for the comfort, convenience and sometimes luxury of its passengers, and provided with gentlemanly conductors and servants, the longest journeys by railroad can be made alone by self-possessed ladies with perfect safety and but little annoyance. Then, too, a lady who deports herself as such may travel from the Atlantic to the Pacific, from Maine to the Gulf of Mexico, and meet with no affront or insult, but on the contrary receive polite attentions at every point, from men who may chance to be her fellow-travelers. This may be accounted for from the fact that, as a rule in America, all men show a defferential regard for women, and are especially desirous of showing them such attentions as will render a long and lonesome journey as pleasant as possible.

DUTIES OF AN ESCORT.

However self-possessed and ladylike in all her deportment and general bearing a lady may be, and though
capable of undertaking any journey, howsoever long it
may be, an escort is at all times much more pleasant,
and generally acceptable. When a gentleman undertakes the escort of a lady, he should proceed with her
to the depot, or meet her there, a sufficient time before
the departure of the train to attend to the checking of
her baggage, procure her ticket, and obtain for her an
eligible seat in the cars, allowing her to choose such
seat as she desires. He will then dispose of her packages and hand-baggage in their proper receptacle, and
make her seat and surroundings as agreeable for her as
possible, taking a seat near her, or by the side of her if
she requests it, and do all he can to make her journey a
pleasant one.

Upon arriving at her destination, he should conduct
her to the ladies' waiting-room or to a carriage, until he
has attended to her baggage, which he arranges to have
delivered where the lady requests it. He should then
escort her to whatever part of the city she is going and
deliver her into the hands of her friends before relaxing
his care. On the following day he should call upon her
to inquire after her health. It is optional with the lady
whether the acquaintance shall be prolonged or not after
this call. If the lady does not wish to prolong the
acquaintance, she can have no right, nor can her friends,
to request a similar favor of him at another time.

THE DUTY OF A LADY TO HER ESCORT.

The lady may supply her escort with a sum of money ample to pay all the expenses of the journey before purchasing her ticket, or furnish him the exact amount required, or, at the suggestion of her escort, she may allow him to defray the expenses from his own pocket, and settle with him at the end of the journey. The latter course, however, should only be pursued when the gentleman suggests it, and a strict account of the expenses incurred must be insisted on.

A lady should give her attendant as little trouble and annoyance as possible, and she should make no unnecessary demands upon his good nature and gentlemanly services. Her hand-baggage should be as small as circumstances will permit, and when once disposed of, it should remain undisturbed until she is about to leave the car, unless she should absolutely require it. As the the train nears the end of her journey, she will deliberately gather together her effects preparatory to departure, so that when the train stops she will be ready to leave the car at once and not wait to hurriedly grab her various parcels, or cause her escort unnecessary delay.

A LADY TRAVELING ALONE.

A lady, in traveling alone, may accept services from her fellow-travelers, which she should always acknowledge graciously. Indeed, it is the business of a gentleman to see that the wants of an unescorted lady are attended to. He should offer to raise or lower her window if she seems to have any difficulty in doing it herself. He may offer his assistance in carrying her packages upon leaving the car, or in engaging a carriage or obtaining a trunk. Still, women should learn to be as self-reliant as possible; and young women particularly should accept proffered assistance from strangers, in all but the slightest offices, very rarely.

LADIES MAY ASSIST OTHER LADIES.

It is not only the right, but the duty of ladies to render any assistance or be of any service to younger ladies, or those less experienced in traveling than themselves. They may show many little courtesies which will make the journey less tedious to the inexperienced traveler, and may give her important advice or assistance which may be of benefit to her. An acquaintance formed in traveling, need never be retained afterwards. It is optional whether it is or not.

THE COMFORT OF OTHERS.

In seeking his own comfort, no passenger has a right to overlook or disregard that of others. If for his own comfort, he wishes to raise or lower a window he should consult the wishes of passengers immediately around him before doing so. The discomforts of traveling should be borne cheerfully, for what may enhance your own comfort may endanger the health of some fellow-traveler.

ATTENDING TO THE WANTS OF OTHERS.

See everywhere and at all times that ladies and elderly people have their wants supplied before you think of your own. Nor is there need for unmanly haste or pushing in entering or leaving cars or boats. There is always time enough allowed for each passenger to enter in a gentlemanly manner and with a due regard to the rights of others.

If, in riding in the street-cars or crossing a ferry, your friend insists on paying for you, permit him to do so without serious remonstrance. You can return the favor at some other time.

READING WHEN TRAVELLING.

If a gentleman in traveling, either on cars or steamboat, has provided himself with newspapers or other reading, he should offer them to his companions first. If they are refused, he may with propriety read himself, leaving the others free to do the same if they wish.

OCCUPYING TOO MANY SEATS.

No lady will retain possession of more than her rightful seat in a crowded car. When others are looking for accommodations she should at once and with all cheerfulness so dispose of her baggage that the seat beside her may be occupied by anyone who desires it, no matter how agreeable it may be to retain possession of it.

It shows a great lack of proper manners to see two

ladies, or a lady and gentleman turn over the sea't in front of them and fill it with their wraps and bundles, retaining it in spite of the entreating or remonstrating looks of fellow-passengers. In such a case any person who desires a seat is justified in reversing the back, removing the baggage and taking possession of the unused seat.

RETAINING POSSESSION OF A SEAT.

A gentleman in traveling may take possession of a seat and then go to purchase tickets or look after baggage or procure a lunch, leaving the seat in charge of a companion, or depositing traveling-bag or overcoat upon it to show that it is engaged. When a seat is thus occupied, the right of possession must be respected, and no one should presume to take a seat thus previously engaged, even though it may be wanted for a lady. A gentleman cannot, however, in justice, vacate his seat to take another in the smoking-car, and at the same time reserve his rights to the first seat. He pays for but one seat, and by taking another he forfeits the first.

It is not required of a gentleman in a railway car to relinquish his seat in favor of a lady, though a gentleman of genuine breeding will do so rather than allow the lady to stand or suffer inconvenience from poor accommodations.

In the street cars the case is different. No woman should be allowed to stand while there is a seat occupied by a man. The inconvenience to the man will be temporary and trifling at the most, and he can well afford to suffer it rather than to do an uncourteous act.

DISCRETION IN FORMING ACQUAINTANCES.

While an acquaintance formed in a railway car or on a steamboat, continues only during the trip, discretion should be used in making acquaintances. Ladies may, as has been stated, accept small courtesies and favors from strangers, but must check at once any attempt at familiarity. On the other hand, no man who pretends to be a gentleman will attempt any familiarity. The practice of some young girls just entering into womanhood, of flirting with any young man they may chance to meet, either in a railway car or on a steamboat, indicates low-breeding in the extreme. If, however, the journey is long, and especially if it be on a steamboat, a certain sociability may be allowed, and a married lady or a lady of middle age may use her privileges to make the journey an enjoyable one, for fellow-passengers should always be sociable to one another.

CHAPTER XV.

Riding and Driving.

ONE of the most exhilarating and enjoyable amusements that can be indulged in by either ladies or gentlemen is that of riding on horseback, and it is a matter of regret that it is not participated in to a greater extent than it is. The etiquette of riding, though meagre, is exact and important.

LEARNING TO RIDE.

The first thing to do is to learn to ride, and no one should attempt to appear in public until a few preliminary lessons in riding are taken. Until a person has learned to appear at ease on horseback, he or she should not appear in public. The advice given in the old rhyme should be kept in mind, viz:

> Keep up your head and your heart,
> Your hands and your heels keep down;
> Press your knees close to your horse's sides,
> And your elbows close to your own.

THE GENTLEMAN'S DUTY AS AN ESCORT.

When a gentleman contemplates riding with a lady, his first duty is to see that her horse is a proper one for her use, and one that she can readily manage. He must see that her saddle and bridle are perfectly secure,

and trust nothing of this kind to the stable men, without personal examination. He must be punctual at the appointed hour, and not keep the lady waiting for him clad in her riding costume. He should see the lady comfortably seated in her saddle before he mounts himself; take his position on the lady's right in riding, open all gates and pay all tolls on the road.

ASSISTING A LADY TO MOUNT.

The lady will place herself on the left side of the horse, standing as close to it as possible, with her skirts gathered in her left hand, her right hand upon the pommel, and her face toward the horse's head. The gentleman should stand at the horse's shoulder, facing the lady, and stooping, hold his hand so that she may place her foot in it. This she does, when the foot is lifted as she springs, so as to gently aid her in gaining the saddle. The gentleman must then put her foot in the stirrup, smooth the skirt of her riding habit, and give her the reins and her riding whip.

RIDING WITH LADIES.

In riding with one lady, a gentleman takes his position to the right of her. When riding with two or more, his position is still to the right unless one of them needs his assistance or requests his presence near her. He must offer all the courtesies of the road, and yield the best and shadiest side to the ladies. The lady must always decide upon the pace at which to ride. It is ungenerous to urge her or incite her horse to a faster gait than she feels competent to undertake.

If a gentleman, when riding alone, meets a lady who is walking and wishes to enter into conversation with her, he must alight and remain on foot while talking with her.

ASSISTING A LADY TO ALIGHT FROM HER HORSE.

After the ride, the gentleman must assist his companion to alight. She must first free her knee from the pommel, and be certain that her habit is entirely disengaged. He must then take her left hand in his right, and offer his left hand as a step for her foot. He then lowers his hand slowly and allows her to reach the ground gently without springing. A lady should not attempt to spring from the saddle.

DRIVING.

The choicest seat in a double carriage is the one facing the horses, and gentlemen should always yield this seat to the ladies. If only one gentleman and one lady are riding in a two-seated carriage, the gentleman must sit opposite the lady, unless she invites him to a seat by her side. The place of honor is on the right hand of the seat facing the horses. This is also the seat of the hostess, which she never resigns. If she is not driving, it must be offered to the most distinguished lady. A person should enter a carriage with the back to the seat, so as to prevent turning round in the carriage. A gentleman must be careful not to trample upon or crush a lady's dress. In driving, one should always remember that the rule of the road in meeting and passing another vehicle is to keep to the right.

ASSISTING LADIES TO ALIGHT.

A gentleman must first alight from a carriage, even if he has to pass before a lady in doing so. He must then assist the ladies to alight. If there is a servant with the carriage, the latter may hold open the door, but the gentleman must by all means furnish the ladies the required assistance. If a lady has occasion to leave the carriage before the gentleman accompanying her, he must alight to assist her out, and if she wishes to resume her seat, he must again alight to help her to do so.

In assisting a lady to enter a carriage, a gentleman will take care that the skirt of her dress is not allowed to hang outside. A carriage robe should be provided to protect her dress from the mud and dust of the road. The gentleman should provide the lady with her parasol, fan and shawl, and see that she is comfortable in every way, before he seats himself.

TRUSTING THE DRIVER.

While driving with another who holds the reins, you must not interfere with the driver, as anything of this kind implies a reproof, which is very offensive. If you think his conduct wrong, or are in fear of danger resulting, you may delicately suggest a change, apologizing therefor. You should resign yourself to the driver's control, and be perfectly calm and self-possessed during the course of a drive.

CHAPTER XVI.

Courtship and Marriage.

HE correct behavior of young men toward young ladies, and of young ladies toward young men, during that portion of their lives when they are respectively paying attention to, and receiving attention from, one another, is a matter which requires consideration in a work of this nature.

A GENTLEMAN'S CONDUCT TOWARD LADIES.

Young people of either sex, who have arrived at mature age, and who are not engaged, have the utmost freedom in their social intercourse in this country, and are at liberty to associate and mingle freely in the same circles with those of the opposite sex. Gentlemen are at liberty to invite their lady friends to concerts, operas, balls, etc., to call upon them at their homes, to ride and drive with them, and make themselves agreeable to all young ladies to whom their company is acceptable. In fact they are at liberty to accept invitations and give them *ad libitum*. As soon, however, as a young gentleman neglects all others, to devote himself to a single lady, he gives that lady reason to suppose that he is par ticularly attracted to her, and may give her cause to believe that she is to become engaged to him, without telling her so. A gentleman who does not contemplate matrimony should not pay too exclusive attention to any one lady.

A LADY'S CONDUCT TOWARD GENTLEMEN.

A young lady who is not engaged may receive calls and attentions from such unmarried gentlemen as she desires, and may accept invitations to ride, to concerts, theatres, etc. She should use due discretion, however, as to whom she favors by the acceptance of such invitations. A young lady should not allow special attention from anyone to whom she is not specially attracted, because, first, she may do injury to the gentleman in seeming to give his suit encouragement; and, secondly, she may keep away from her those whom she likes better, but who will not approach her under the mistaken idea that her feelings are already interested. A young lady should not encourage the addresses of a gentleman unless she feels that she can return his affections. It is the prerogative of a man to propose, and of a woman to accept or refuse, and a lady of tact and kind heart will exercise her prerogative before her suitor is brought to the humiliation of an offer which must result in a refusal.

No well-bred lady will too eagerly receive the atten- tions of a gentleman, no matter how much she admires him; nor, on the other hand, will she be so reserved as to altogether discourage him. A man may show considerable attention to a lady without becoming a lover; and so a lady may let it be seen that she is not disagreeable to him without discouraging him. She will be able to judge soon from his actions and deportment, as to his motive in paying her his attentions, and will treat him accordingly. A man does not like to be refused when he makes a proposal, and no man of tact will risk a refusal. Neither will a well-bred lady encourage a man to make a proposal, which she must refuse. She should endeavor, in discouraging him as a lover, to retain his friendship. A young man of sensibilities, who can take a hint when it is offered him, need not run the risk of a refusal.

PREMATURE DECLARATION.

It is very injudicious, not to say presumptuous, for a gentleman to make a proposal to a young lady on too brief an acquaintance. A lady who would accept a gentleman at first sight can hardly possess the discretion needed to make a good wife.

THOROUGH ACQUAINTANCE AS A BASIS FOR MARRIAGE.

Perhaps there is such a thing as love at first sight, but love alone is a very uncertain foundation upon which to base marriage. There should be thorough acquaintanceship and a certain knowledge of harmony of tastes and temperaments before matrimony is ventured upon.

PROPER MANNER OF COURTSHIP.

It is impossible to lay down any rule as to the proper mode of courtship and proposal. In France it is the business of the parents to settle all preliminaries. In England the young man asks the consent of the parents to pay addresses to their daughter. In this country the matter is left almost entirely to the young people.

It seems that circumstances must determine whether courtship may lead to engagement. Thus, a man may begin seriously to court a girl, but may discover before any promise binds them to each other, that they are entirely unsuited to one another, when he may, with perfect propriety and without serious injury to the lady, withdraw his attentions.

Certain authorities insist that the consent of parents must always be obtained before the daughter is asked to give herself in marriage. While there is nothing improper or wrong in such a course, still, in this country, with our social customs, it is deemed best in most cases not to be too strict in this regard. Each case has its own peculiar circumstances which must govern it, and it seems at least pardonable if the young man should prefer to know his fate directly from the lips of the most interested party, before he submits himself to the cooler judgment and the critical observation of the father and mother, who are not by any means in love with him, and who may possibly regard him with a somewhat jealous eye, as having already monopolized their daughter's affections, and now desires to take her away from them altogether.

PARENTS SHOULD EXERCISE AUTHORITY OVER DAUGHTERS.

Parents should always be perfectly familiar with the character of their daughter's associates, and they should exercise their authority so far as not to permit her to form any improper acquaintances. In regulating the social relations of their daughter, parents should bear in mind the possibility of her falling in love with any one with·whom she may come in frequent contact. Therefore, if any gentleman of her acquaintance is particularly ineligible as a husband, he should be excluded as far as practicable from her society.

A WATCHFUL CARE REQUIRED BY PARENTS.

Parents, especially mothers, should also watch with a jealous care the tendencies of their daughter's affections; and if they see them turning toward unworthy or undesirable objects, influence of some sort should be brought to bear to counteract this. Great delicacy and tact are required to manage matters rightly. A more suitable person may, if available, be brought forward, in the hope of attracting the young girl's attention. The objectionable traits of the undesirable suitor should be made apparent to her without the act seeming to be intentional; and if all this fails, let change of scene and surroundings by travel or visiting accomplish the desired result. The latter course will generally do it, if matters have not been allowed to progress too far and the young girl is not informed *why* she is temporarily banished from home.

AN ACCEPTABLE SUITOR.

Parents should always be able to tell from observation and instinct just how matters stand with their daughter; and if the suitor is an acceptable one and everything satisfactory, then the most scrupulous rules of etiquette will not prevent their letting the young couple alone. If the lover chooses to propose directly to the lady and consult her father afterward, consider that he has a perfect right to do so. If her parents have sanctioned his visits and attentions by a silent consent, he has a right to believe that his addresses will be favorably received by them.

REQUIREMENTS FOR A HAPPY MARRIAGE.

Respect for each other is as necessary to a happy marriage as that the husband and wife should have an affection for one another. Social equality, intellectual sympathy, and sufficient means are very important matters to be considered by those who contemplate matrimony.

It must be remembered that husband and wife, after marriage, have social relations to sustain, and perhaps it will be discovered, before many months of wedded life have passed, when there is a social inequality, that one of the two have made a sacrifice for which no adequate compensation has been or ever will be received. And so both lives become soured and spoiled, because neither receives nor can receive the sympathy which their efforts deserve, and because their cares are multiplied from a want of congeniality. One or the other may find that the noble qualities seen by the impulse of early love, were but the creation of an infatuated fancy, existing only in the mind where it originated.

Another condition of domestic happiness is intellectual sympathy. Man requires a woman who can make his home a place of rest for him, and woman requires a man of domestic tastes. While a woman who seeks to find happiness in a married life will never consent to be wedded to an idler or a pleasure-seeker, so a man of intelligence will wed none but a woman of intelligence and good sense. Neither beauty, physical characteristics nor other external qualifications will compensate for the absence of intellectual thought and clear and quick comprehensions. An absurd idea is held by some that intelligence and domestic virtues cannot go together; that an intellectual woman will never be content to stay at home to look after the interests of her household and children. A more unreasonable idea has never been suggested, for as the intellect is strengthened and cultured, it has a greater capacity of affection, of domesticity and of self-sacrifice for others.

Mutual trust and confidence are other requisites for happiness in married life. There can be no true love without trust. The responsibility of a man's life is in a woman's keeping from the moment he puts his heart into her hands. Without mutual trust there can be no real happiness.

Another requisite for conjugal happiness is moral and religious sympathy, that each may walk side by side in the same path of moral purpose and social usefulness, with joint hope of immortality.

PROPOSALS OF MARRIAGE.

Rules in regard to proposals of marriage cannot be laid down, for they are and should be as different as people. The best way is to apply to the lady in person, and receive the answer from her own lips. If courage should fail a man in this, he can resort to writing, by which he can clearly and boldly express his feelings. A spoken declaration should be bold, manly and earnest, and so plain in its meaning that there can be no misunderstanding. As to the exact words to be used, there can be no set formula; each proposer must be governed by his own ideas and sense of propriety in the matter.

DO NOT PRESS AN UNWELCOME SUIT.

A gentleman should evince a sincere and unselfish affection for his beloved, and he will show as well as feel that her happiness must be considered before his own. Consequently he should not press an unwelcome suit upon a young lady. If she has no affection for him, and does not conceive it possible even to entertain any, it is cruel to urge her to give her person without her love. The eager lover may believe, for the time being, that such possession would satisfy him, but the day will surely come when he will reproach his wife that she had no love for him, and he will possibly make that an excuse for all manner of unkindness.

A LADY'S FIRST REFUSAL.

It is not always necessary to take a lady's first refusal as absolute. Diffidence or uncertainty as to her own feelings may sometimes influence a lady to reply in the negative, and after-consideration cause her to regret that reply.

Though a gentleman may repeat his suit with propriety after having been once repulsed, still it should not be repeated too often nor too long, lest it should degenerate into importuning.

No lady worthy any gentleman's regard will say "no" twice to a suit which she intends ultimately to receive with favor. A lady should be allowed all the time she requires before making up her mind; and if the gentleman grows impatient at the delay, he is always at liberty to insist on an immediate answer and abide by the consequences of his impatience.

A LADY'S POSITIVE REFUSAL.

A lady who really means "no" should be able to so say it as to make her meaning unmistakable. For her own sake and that of her suitor, if she really desires the suit ended her denial should be positive, yet kind and dignified, and of a character to let no doubt remain of its being final.

TRIFLING WITH A LADY.

A man should never make a declaration in a jesting manner. It is most unfair to a lady. He has no right to trifle with her feelings for mere sport, nor has he a right to hide his own meaning under the guise of a jest.

A DOUBTFUL ANSWER.

Nothing can be more unfair or more unjustifiable than a doubtful answer given under the plea of sparing the suitor's feelings. It raises false hopes. It renders a man restless and unsettled. It may cause him to express himself or to shape his conduct in such a manner as he would not dream of doing were his suit utterly hopeless.

HOW TO TREAT A REFUSAL.

As a woman is not bound to accept the first offer that is made to her, so no sensible man will think the worse of her, nor feel himself personally injured by a refusal. That it will give him pain is most probable. A scornful "no" or a simpering promise to "think about it" is the reverse of generous.

In refusing, the lady ought to convey her full sense of the high honor intended her by the gentleman, and to add, seriously but not offensively, that it is not in accordance with her inclination, or that circumstances compel her to give an unfavorable answer.

UNLADYLIKE CONDUCT TOWARD A SUITOR.

It is only the contemptible flirt that keeps an honorable man in suspense for the purpose of glorifying herself by his attentions in the eyes of friends. Nor would any but a frivolous or vicious girl boast of the offer she had received and rejected. Such an offer is a privileged communication. The secret of it should be held sacred. No true lady will ever divulge to anyone, unless it may be to her mother, the fact of such an offer. It is the severest breach of honor to do so. A lady who has once been guilty of boasting of an offer should never have a second opportunity for thus boasting.

No true-hearted woman can entertain any other feeling than that of commiseration for the man over whose happiness she has been compelled to throw a cloud, while the idea of triumphing in his distress, or abusing his confidence, must be inexpressibly painful to her.

THE REJECTED SUITOR.

The duty of the rejected suitor is quite clear. Etiquette demands that he shall accept the lady's decision as final and retire from the field. He has no right to demand the reason of her refusal. If she assign it, he is bound to respect her secret, if it is one, and to hold it inviolable. To persist in urging his suit or to follow up the lady with marked attentions would be in the worst possible taste. The proper course is to withdraw as much as possible, from the circles in which she moves, so that she may be spared reminiscences which cannot be otherwise than painful.

PRESENTS AFTER ENGAGEMENT.

When a couple become engaged, the gentleman presents the lady with a ring, which is worn on the ring-finger of the right hand. He may also make her other small presents from time to time, until they are married, but if she has any scruples about accepting them, he can send her flowers, which are at all times acceptable.

CONDUCT OF THE FIANCEE.

The conduct of the *fiancee* should be tender, assiduous and unobtrusive. He will be kind and polite to the sisters of his betrothed and friendly with her brothers. Yet he must not be in any way unduly familiar or force himself into family confidences on the ground that he is to be regarded as a member of the family. Let the advance come rather from them to him, and let him show a due appreciation of any confidences which they may be pleased to bestow upon him. The family of the young man should make the first advances toward an acquaintance with his future wife. They should call upon her or write to her, and they may with perfect propriety invite her to visit them in order that they may become acquainted.

THE POSITION OF AN ENGAGED WOMAN.

An engaged woman should eschew all flirtations, though it does not follow that she is to cut herself off from all association with the other sex because she has chosen her future husband. She may still have friends and acquaintances, she may still receive visits and calls, but she must try to conduct herself in such a manner as to give no offense.

POSITION OF AN ENGAGED MAN.

The same rules may be laid down in regard to the other party to the contract, only that he pays visits instead of receiving them. Neither should assume a masterful or jealous attitude toward the other. They are neither of them to be shut up away from the rest of the world, but must mingle in society after marriage nearly the same as before, and take the same delight in friendship. The fact that they have confessed their love for each other ought to be deemed a sufficient guarantee of faithfulness; for the rest let there be trust and confidence.

THE RELATIONS OF AN ENGAGED COUPLE.

A young man has no right to put a slight upon his future bride by appearing in public with other ladies while she remains neglected at home. He is in future her legitimate escort. He should attend no other lady when she needs his services; she should accept no other escort when he is at liberty to attend her. A lady should not be too demonstrative of her affection during the days of her engagement. There is always the chance of "a slip 'twixt the cup and the lip;" and over-demonstrations of love are not pleasant to be remembered by a young lady, if the man to whom they are given by any chance fails to become her husband. An honorable man will never tempt his future bride to any such demonstration. He will always maintain a respectful and decorous demeanor toward her.

No young man who would shrink from being guilty of a great impropriety, should ever prolong his visits beyond ten o'clock, unless it be the common custom of the family to remain up and to entertain visitors to a later hour, and the visit paid is a family one and not a *tete-a-tete.* Two hours is quite long enough for a call; and the young man will give evidence of his affection no less than his consideration, by making his visits short, and, if need be, making them often, rather than by prolonging to unreasonable hours.

LOVERS' DISPUTES.

Neither party should try to make the other jealous for the purpose of testing his or her affection. Such a course is contemptible; and if the affections of the other are permanently lost by it, the offending party is only gaining his or her just deserts. Neither should there be provocation to little quarrels for the foolish delight of reconciliation. No lover will assume a domineering attitude over his future wife. If he does so, she will do well to escape from his thrall before she becomes his wife in reality. A domineering lover will be certain to be more domineering as a husband.

BREAKING AN ENGAGEMENT.

Sometimes it is necessary to break off an engagement. Many circumstances will justify this. Indeed anything which may occur or be discovered which shall promise to render the marriage an unsuitable or unhappy one is, and should be accepted as, justification for such rupture. Still, breaking an engagement is always a serious and distressing thing, and ought not to be contemplated without absolute and just reasons. It is generally best to break an engagement by letter. By this means one can express himself or herself more clearly, and give the true reason for his or her course much better than in a personal interview. The letter breaking the engagement should be accompanied by everything, in the way of portraits, letters or gifts, that has been received during the engagement. Such letters should be acknowledged in a dignified manner, and no efforts should be made or measures be taken to change the decision of the writer, unless it is manifest that he or she is greatly mistaken in his or her premises. A similar return of letters, portraits and gifts should be made.

Many men, in taking retrospective glances, remember how they were devoted to women, the memory of whom calls up only a vague sort of wonder how they ever could have fallen into the state of infatuation in which they once were. The same may be said of many women. Heart-breaking separations have taken place between young men and young women who have learned that the sting of parting does not last forever. The heart, lacerated by a hopeless or misplaced attachment, when severed from the cause of its woe, gradually heals and prepares itself to receive fresh wounds, for affection requires either a constant contemplation of, or intercourse, with its object, to keep it alive.

CHAPTER XVII.

Etiquette of Weddings.

THE circumstances under which weddings take place are so varied, and the religious forms observed in their solemnization so numerous, that to lay down rules applicable to all cases would be a matter of great difficulty, if not an impossibility. Consequently only those forms of marriage attended with the fullest ceremonies, and all the attendant ceremonials will here be given, and others may be modeled after them as the occasion may seem to require.

After the marriage invitations are issued, the *fiancee* does not appear in public. It is also *de rigueur* at morning weddings, that she does not see the bridegroom on the wedding-day, until they meet at the altar.

THE BRIDEMAIDS AND GROOMSMEN.

Only relatives and the most intimate friends are asked to be bridemaids—the sisters of the bride and of the bridegroom, where it is possible. The bridegroom chooses his best man and the groomsmen and ushers from his circle of relatives and friends of his own age, and from the relatives of his *fiancee* of a suitable age. The dresses of the bridemaids are not given unless their circumstances are such as to make it necessary.

THE BRIDAL COSTUME.

The most approved bridal costume for young brides is of white silk, high corsage, a long wide veil of white tulle, reaching to the feet, and a wreath of maiden-blush roses with orange blossoms. The roses she can continue to wear, but the orange blossoms are only suitable for the ceremony.

COSTUMES OF THE BRIDEGROOM AND USHERS.

The bridegroom and ushers, at a morning wedding, wear full morning dress, dark blue or black frock coats, or cut-aways, light neckties, and light trousers. The bridegroom wears white gloves. The ushers wear gloves of some delicate color.

PRESENTS OF THE BRIDE AND BRIDEGROOM.

Where the bride makes presents to the bridemaids on her wedding-day, they generally consist of some articles of jewelry, not costly, and given more as a memento of the occasion than for their own intrinsic worth. The bridegroom sometimes gives the groomsmen a scarf pin of some quaint device, or some other slight memento of the day, as a slight acknowledgment of their services.

CEREMONIALS WHEN THERE ARE NO USHERS OR BRIDE-MAIDS.

When there are no bridemaids or ushers the marriage ceremonials at the church are as follows: The members of the bride's family proceed to the church before the bride, who follows with her mother. The bridegroom awaits them at the church and gives his arm to the bride's mother. They walk up the aisle to the altar, the mother falling back to her position on the left. The father, or relative representing him, conducts the bride to the bridegroom, who stands at the altar with his face turned toward her as she approaches, and the father falls back to the left. The relatives follow, taking their places standing; those of the bride to the left, those of the groom to the right. After kneeling at the altar for a moment, the bride, standing on the left of the bridegroom, takes the glove off from her left hand, while he takes the glove off from his right hand. The service then begins. The father of the bride gives her away by bowing when the question is asked, which is a much simpler form than stepping forward and placing his daughter's hand in that of the clergyman. Perfect self-control should be exhibited by all parties during the ceremony.

The bride leaves the altar, taking the bridegroom's right arm, and they pass down the aisle without looking to the right or left. It is considered very bad form to recognize acquaintances by bows and smiles while in the church.

The bride and bridegroom drive away in their own carriage, the rest following in their carriages.

When the circle of friends on both sides is very extensive, it has become customary of late to send invitations to such as are not called to the wedding breakfast, to attend the ceremony at church. This stands in the place of issuing cards. No one must think of calling on the newly married couple who has not received an invitation to the ceremony at church, or cards after their establishment in their new home.

The latest New York form for conducting the marriage ceremony is substantially as follows:

When the bridal party has arranged itself for entrance, the ushers, in pairs march slowly up to the altar and turn to the right. Behind them follows the groom alone. When he reaches the altar he turns, faces the aisle, and watches intently for the coming of his bride. After a slight interval the bridemaids follow, in pairs, and at the altar turn to the left. After another brief interval, the bride, alone and entirely veiled, with her eyes cast down, follows her companions. The groom comes forward a few steps to meet her, takes her hand, and places her at the altar. Both kneel for a moment's silent devotion. The parents of the bride, having followed her, stand just behind her and partly to the left. The services by the clergyman now proceed as usual.

While the bride and bridegroom are passing out of the church, the bridemaids follow slowly, each upon the arm of an usher, and they afterward hasten on as speedily as possible to welcome the bride at her own door, and to arrange themselves about the bride and groom in the reception room, half of the ladies upon her side and half upon his—the first bridemaid retaining the place of honor.

THE USHERS' DUTIES.

The ushers at the door of the reception room offer themselves as escorts to parties, who arrive slowly from the church, conducting them to the bridal party, and there presenting them by name. This announcement becomes necessary when two families and two sets of friends are brought together for the first time. If ladies are present without gentlemen, the ushers accompany them to the breakfast or refreshment room, or provide them with attendants.

At the church the ushers are the first to arrive. They stand by the inner entrance and offer their arms to escort the ladies, as they enter, to their proper seats in the church. If a lady be accompanied by a gentleman, the latter follows the usher and the lady to the seat shown her. The ushers, knowing the two families, understand where to place the nearer, and where the remoter relatives and friends of the bridal party, the groom's friends being arranged upon the right of the entrance, and the bride's upon the left. The distribution of guests places the father (or guardian) of the bride at the proper place during the ceremony.

ANOTHER FORM OF CHURCH CEREMONIALS.

The ceremonials for the entry to the church by the bridal party may be varied to suit the taste. Precedents for the style already described are found among the highest social circles in New York and other large cities, but there are brides who prefer the fashion of their grandmothers, which is almost strictly an American fashion. In this style, the bridemaids, each leaning upon the arm of a groomsman, first pass up the aisle to the altar, the ladies going to their left, and the gentlemen to their right. The groom follows with the bride's mother, or some one to represent her, leaning on his arm, whom he seats in a front pew at the left. The bride follows, clinging to the arm of her father (or near relative), who leads her to the groom. The father waits at her left and a step or two back of her, until asked to give her away, which he does by taking her right hand and placing it in that of the clergyman. After this he joins the mother of the bride in the front pew, and becomes her escort while they pass out of the church.

In case there are no bridemaids, the ushers walk into church in pairs, just in advance of the groom, and parting at the altar, half of them stand at one side and half at the other. While the clergyman is congratulating the bride, they pass out in pairs, a little in advance of the wedded couple.

WEDDINGS AT HOME.

Weddings at home vary but little from those at church. The music, the assembling of friends, the *entree* of the bridal party to the position selected, are the same. An altar of flowers, and a place of kneeling can be easily arranged at home. The space behind the altar need be no wider than is allowed for the clergyman to stand. The altar is generally only a fender or railing entirely wound and concealed by greenery or blossoms. Other floral accessories, such as the marriage-bell, horseshoe, or white dove, etc., can be arranged with ease by a skillful florist, if desired.

When the marriage ceremony is concluded, the party turn in their places and face their friends, who proceed to congratulate them. If space be required, the kneeling stool and floral altar may be removed, a little later, without observation.

THE EVENING WEDDING.

If the wedding occur in the evening, the only difference in the ceremonials from those in the morning is that the ushers or groomsmen wear full evening dress, and the bridal pair retire quietly to dress for their journey before the dancing party disperses, and thus leave unobserved. At the morning wedding only bridemaids, ushers and relatives remain to witness the departure of the pair.

"AT HOME" RECEPTIONS.

When the newly married couple commence life in a home of their own, it is customary to issue "at home" cards for a few evenings, at an early date after the wedding, for informal receptions. Only such persons are invited as the young couple choose to keep as friends, or perhaps only those whom they can afford to retain. This is a suitable opportunity to carefully re-arrange one's social list, and their list of old acquaintances may be sifted at the time of the beginning of housekeeping This custom of arranging a fresh list is admitted as a social necessity, and nobody is offended.

CALLS.

All guests and friends who receive "at home" invitations, or who are invited to the church, are required by etiquette to call upon the family of the bride, or to leave their cards, within ten days after the wedding.

THE WEDDING RING.

All churches at present use the ring, and vary the sentiment of its adoption to suit the customs and ideas of their own rites. A jeweled ring has been for many years the sign and symbol of betrothal, but at present a plain gold circlet, with the date of the engagement inscribed within, is generally preferred. The ring is removed by the groom at the altar, passed to the clergyman and used in the ceremony. A jeweled ring is placed upon her hand by the groom on the way home from the church, or as soon after the service as is convenient. It stands guard over its precious fellow, and is a confirmation of the first promise.

THE MARRIAGE CEREMONIALS OF A WIDOW.

The marriage ceremonials of à widow differ from that of a young lady in not wearing the veil and orange blossoms. She may be costumed in white and have her maids at the altar if she pleases. This liberty, however, has only been given her within a few years. On her wedding cards of invitation, her maiden name is used as a part of her proper name; which is done in respect to her parents. Having dropped the initials of her dead husband's name when she laid aside her mourning, she uses her Christian name. If she has sons or unmarried daughters at the time she becomes again a wife, she may prefix the last name of her children to her new one on all ceremonious occasions in which they are interested in common with herself. This respect is really due them, and etiquette permits it, although our social usages do not command its adoption. The formalities which follow the marriage of a widow can seldom be regulated in the same manner as those of a younger bride. No fixed forms can be arranged for entertainments, which must be controlled by circumstances.

INVITATIONS.

Wedding invitations should be handsomely engraved in script. Neither Old English nor German text are admissible in invitations. The following is given as the latest form for invitations:

Mr. & Mrs. Theodore Grosser

request your presence at the marriage
of their daughter,

Miss Felicia Grosser
to
Mr. Julius C. Forsyth,

on Wednesday, September 5th, at
12 o'clock.

St. Luke's Church,
Cass Avenue.

This invitation requires no answer. Friends living in
other towns and cities receiving it, inclose their cards,
and send by mail. Residents call on the family within
the prescribed time, or as soon after as possible.

The invitation to the wedding breakfast is enclosed
in the same envelope, generally conveyed on a square
card, the same size as the sheet of note paper which
bears the invitation for the ceremony after it has been

once folded across the middle.   The following is one of
the adopted forms:

At Home,

Wednesday, September 5th,

from 12 until 3 o'clock.

20 Main Avenue.

The separate cards of the bride and groom are no
longer necessary.

The card of admission to the church is narrower, and
is plainly engraved in large-script, as follows:

St. Luke's Church,

Ceremony at 12 o'clock.

Generally only half an hour intervenes between the
ceremony and the reception.

DUTIES OF THOSE INVITED.

People who receive "At Home" wedding invitations,
are expected to acknowledge them as soon as received,
and never fail to accept, unless for some very good reason.   Guests invited to the house, or to a marriage feast
following the ceremony, should not feel at liberty to
decline from any whim or caprice.

REQUIREMENTS OF THE BRIDEMAIDS AND USHERS.

Bridesmaids and ushers should allow nothing but illness or some unavoidable accident to prevent them from officiating, thus showing their appreciation of the friendship which has caused their selection to this honored position. If by reason of sudden affliction, some one of the bridemaids or ushers is prevented from attending, a substitute should, if possible, be provided immediately. The reasons for this, however, should be well understood, that no opportunity may be given for uncharitable comments.

BRIDAL PRESENTS.

When bridal presents are given, they are sent to the bride previous to the day of the marriage ceremony. As the universal bridal present has fallen into disuse, this custom is not now considered obligatory, and if immediate friends and relatives desire to make presents, it should be spontaneous, and in no sense considered obligatory. These presents are not put on exhibition as formerly, but are acknowledged by the bride in a private note to the donor. It is not now considered in good form to talk about these contributions.

ARRANGEMENTS FOR THE CEREMONIES.

In weddings at churches a master of ceremonies is often provided, who is expected to be at the church as soon as the doors are opened. He arranges beforehand for the spreading of a carpet from the church door to the pavement, and if the weather be inclement, he sees that an awning is also spread. He also sees that a white ribbon is stretched across the main aisle of the church, far enough back from the altar to afford sufficient room for all invited guests to occupy the front pews of the main aisle. Sometimes an arch of flowers extends over the aisle, so as to divide those who come in wedding garments, from those who do not. The organist should be early at his post, and is expected to play during the arrival of guests. The order of the religious part of the marriage ceremony is fixed by the church in which it occurs.

THE WEDDING FEES.

There is no prescribed fee for performing the marriage ceremony. It is regulated according to the means and liberality of the bridegroom, but no less amount than five dollars should be given under any circumstances.

THE CONGRATULATIONS.

At wedding receptions, friends who congratulate the newly married couple should address the bride first, if they have any previous acquaintance with her, then the bridegroom, then the bridemaids, and after that the parents and family of the bride and groom. They should give their good wishes to the bride and congratulate the bridegroom. If they are acquainted with the bridegroom and not with the bride, let them address him first and he will introduce them to his bride.

THE BRIDAL TOUR.

The honeymoon of repose, exempt from all claims of society, is now prescribed by the dictates of common sense and fashion, and the same arbiters unite in condemning the harrassing bridal tour. It is no longer *de rigueur* to maintain any secrecy as to their plans for traveling, when a newly married couple depart upon a tour

CHAPTER XVIII.

Home Life and Etiquette.

OME is the woman's kingdom, and there she reigns supreme. To embellish that home, to make happy the lives of her husband and the dear ones committed to her trust, is the honored task which it is the wife's province to perform. All praise be to her who so rules and governs in that kingdom, that those reared beneath her roof "shall rise up and call her blessed."

A HOME.

After marriage one of the first requirements for happiness is a home. This can seldom be found in a boarding house or at a hotel, and not always beneath the parental roof of either husband or wife. It will oftenest be found in a house or even a cottage apart from the immediate association of relatives or friends, acquaintances or strangers, and here husband and wife may begin in reality, that new life of which they have had fond dreams; and upon their own actions must depend their future welfare.

HOME COMPANIONSHIP.

Husband and wife should remember, when starting out upon their newly wedded life, that they are to be life companions, that the affection they have possessed and expressed as lovers must ripen into a life-long devotion to one another's welfare and happiness, that the closest friendship must be begotten from their early love, and that each must live and work for the other.

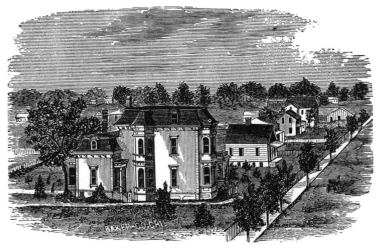

They must seek to be congenial companions to each other, so that every hour they pass together will be mutually enjoyable. They should aim to have the same tastes, so that what one enjoys will be alike enjoyable to the other, and what is distasteful to one shall be no less so to the other. Each should yield in matters where it is right to yield, and be firm only where duty is concerned. With a firm trust in one another they should

14

ever abide, that each may say to the world, "I possess one on whose character and heart I can lean as upon a rock."

CONDUCT OF HUSBAND AND WIFE.

Let neither ever deceive the other, or do anything to shake the other's confidence, for once deceived, the heart can never wholly trust again. Fault-finding should only be done by gentle and mild criticism, and then with loving words and pleasant looks. Make allowances for one another's weaknesses, and at the same time endeavor to mutually repress them. For the sake of mutual improvement the husband and wife should receive and give corrections to one another in a spirit of kindness, and in doing so they will prepare themselves for the work God gives the parents of training lives for usefulness here and hereafter. Their motto should be "faithful unto death in all things," and they must exercise forbearance with each other's peculiarities.

Let both preserve a strict guard over their tongues, that neither may utter anything rude, contemptuous or severe, and guard their tempers, that neither may ever grow passionate or become sullen or morose in one another's presence. They should not expect too much from each other; if either offends, it is the part of the other to forgive, remembering that no one is free from faults, and that we are all constantly erring.

If, perchance, after they have entered upon the stern realities of life, they find that they have made a mistake, that they are not well mated, then they must accept the inevitable and endure to the end, "for better or for

worse;" for only in this way can they find consolation
for having found out, when too late, that they were
unfitted for a life-long companionship. A journalist has
said: "No lessons learned by experience, however
sharply taught and sadly earned, can enlighten the
numbed senses which love has sent to sleep by its magic
fascination; and things as plain as the sun in heaven to
others are dark as night, unfathomable as the sea, to
those who let themselves love before they prove."

DUTIES OF THE WIFE TO HER HUSBAND.

The wife should remember that upon her, to the
greatest extent, devolves the duty of making home
happy. She should do nothing to make her husband
feel uncomfortable, either mentally or physically, but
on the other hand she should strive to the utmost of
her ability to do whatever is best calculated to please
him, continually showing him that her love, plighted
upon the altar, remains steadfast, and that no vicissitudes of fortune can change or diminish it.

She should never indulge in fits of temper, hysterics,
or other habits of ill-breeding, which, though easy to
conquer at first, grow and strengthen with indulgence,
if she would retain her husband as her lover and her
dearest and nearest friend. She should be equally as
neat and tidy respecting her dress and personal appearance at home as when she appears in society, and
her manners towards her husband should be as kind
and pleasing when alone with him as when in company.
She should bear in mind that to retain the good opinion

of her husband is worth far more than to gain the good opinion of hundreds of the devotees of society, and that as she possesses the love and confidence of her husband, so will she receive the respect and esteem of all his friends.

She should be careful not to confide to another any small misunderstandings or petty quarrels between herself and husband, should any occur. This is the surest method of widening any breach of harmony that may occur between husband and wife, for the more such misunderstandings are talked about, and the more advice she receives from her confidants, there is less probability that harmonious relations will be speedily resumed.

THE WIFE A HELPMATE.

A wife should act openly and honorably in regard to money matters, keeping an exact account of her expenditures, and carefully guarding against any extravagances; and while her husband is industriously at work, she should seek to encourage him, by her own frugality, to be economical, thrifty, enterprising and prosperous in his business, that he may be better enabled, as years go by and family cares press more heavily on each, to afford all the comforts and perhaps some of the luxuries of a happy home. No condition is hopeless when the wife possesses firmness, decision and economy, and no outward prosperity can counteract indolence, folly and extravagance at home. She should consult the disposition and tastes of her husband, and endeavor to lead him to high and noble thoughts, lofty aims, and temporal comfort; be ever ready to welcome him home, and in his companionship draw his thoughts from business and lead him to the enjoyment of home comforts and happiness. The influence of a good wife over her husband may be very great, if she exerts it in the right direction. She should, above all things, study to learn the disposition of her husband, and if, perchance, she finds herself united to a man of quick and violent temper, the utmost discretion, as well as perfect equanimity on her own part is required, for she should have such perfect control over herself as to calm his perturbed spirits.

A HUSBAND'S DUTIES.

It must not be supposed that it devolves upon the wife alone to make married life and home happy. She must be seconded in her noble efforts by him who took her from her own parental fireside and kind friends, to be his companion through life's pilgrimage. He has placed her in a new home, provided with such comforts as his means permit, and the whole current of both their lives have been changed. His constant duty to his wife is to be ever kind and attentive, to love her as he loves himself, even sacrificing his own personal comfort for her happiness. From his affection for her, there should grow out a friendship and fellowship, such as is possessed for no other person. His evenings and spare moments should be devoted to her, and these should be used for their intellectual, moral and social advancement.

The cares and anxieties of business should not exclude

the attentions due to wife and family, while he should carefully keep her informed of the condition of his business affairs. Many a wife is capable of giving her husband important advice about various details of his business, and if she knows the condition of his pecuniary affairs, she will be able to govern her expenditures accordingly.

It is the husband's duty to join with his wife in all her endeavors to instruct her children, to defer all matters pertaining to their discipline to her, aiding her in this respect as she requires it. In household matters the wife rules predominant, and he should never interfere with her authority and government in this sphere. It is his duty and should be his pleasure to accompany her to church, to social gatherings, to lectures and such places of entertainment as they both mutually enjoy and appreciate. In fact he ought not to attend a social gathering unless accompanied by his wife, nor go to an evening entertainment without her. If it is not a fit place for his wife to attend, neither is it fit for him.

While he should give his wife his perfect confidence in her faithfulness, trusting implicitly to her honor at all times and in all places, he should, on his part, remain faithful and constant to her, and give her no cause of complaint. He should pass by unnoticed any disagreeable peculiarities and mistakes, taking care at the proper time, and without giving offense, to remind her of them, with the idea of having her correct them. He should never seek to break her of any disagreeable habits or peculiarities she may possess, by ridiculing them. He should encourage her in all her schemes for promoting the welfare of her household, or in laudable endeavors to promote the happiness of others, by engaging in such works of benevolence and charity as the duties of her home will allow her to perform.

The husband, in fact, should act toward his wife as becomes a perfect gentleman, regarding her as the "best lady in the land," to whom, above all other earthly beings, he owes paramount allegiance. If he so endeavors to act, his good sense and judgment will dictate to him the many little courtesies which are due her, and which every good wife cannot fail to appreciate. The observance of the rules of politeness are nowhere more desirable than in the domestic circle, between husband and wife, parents and children.

CHAPTER XIX.

Home Training.

OUR earliest and best recollections are associated with home. There the first lessons of infancy are learned. The mother's heart is the child's first school-room. The parents' examples are first imitated by the child, whose earliest impressions are gained from them. In no way are evil habits more effectually propagated than by example, and therefore parents should be what they wish their children to be.

THE MOTHER'S INFLUENCE.

To the mother belongs the privilege of planting in the hearts of her children those seeds of love, which, nurtured and fostered, will bear the fruit of earnest and useful lives. It is she who must fit them to meet the duties and emergencies of life, and in this work of training she keeps her heart fresh and young, and thereby insures the growth of those powers with which nature has endowed her.

As the faculties of man, woman or child are brought into active exercise, so do they become strengthened, and the mother, in doing her work in the training of her children, grows in wisdom, in knowledge and in power, thus enabling her the better to perform her duties.

PARENTS SHOULD SET GOOD EXAMPLES.

As children first acquire knowledge and habits from the examples of their parents, the latter should be circumspect in all their actions, manners and modes of speech. If you wish your children's faces illumined with good humor, contentment and satisfaction, so that they will be cheerful, joyous and happy, day by day, then must your own countenance appear illumined by the sunshine of love. Kind words, kind deeds and loving looks are true works of charity, and they are needed in our home circle.

> Never a tear bedims the eye,
> That time and patience can not dry;
> Never a lip is curved with pain,
> That can not be kissed into smiles again.

Your children will form habits of evil speaking if they hear you deal lightly with the reputation of another—if they hear you slander or revile your neighbor. If you wish your child to show charity toward the erring, you must set the example by the habitual exercise of that virtue yourself. Without this your teaching will be of but little avail. If you take pleasure in dwelling upon the faults of others, if you refuse to cover over their infirmities with the mantle of charity, your example will nullify your teaching, and your admonitions will be lost.

COURTESIES IN THE HOME CIRCLE.

Mothers should early train their children to regard all the courtesies of life as scrupulously toward each other as to mere acquaintances and strangers. This is the only way in which you can secure to them the daily enjoyment of a happy home. When the external forms of courtesy are disregarded in the family circle, we are sure to find contention and bickering perpetually recurring. Rudeness is a constant source of bickering. Each will have his own way of being rude, and each will be angry at some portion of the ill-breeding of all the rest, thus provoking accusations and retorts. Where the rule of life is to do good and to make others happy, there will be found the art of securing a happy home. It is said that there is something higher in politeness than Christian moralists have recognized. In its best forms, none but the truly religious man can show it, for it is the sacrifice of self in the habitual matters of life— always the best test of our principles—together with a respect for man as our brother, under the same great destiny.

EARLY MORAL TRAINING.

The true test of the success of any education is its efficiency in giving full use of the moral and intellectual faculties wherewith to meet the duties and the struggles of life, and not by the variety of knowledge acquired. The development of the powers of the mind and its cu tivation are the work of a teacher; moral training is the work of the mother, and commences long before one word of precept can be understood. Children should be early taught to regard the rights of others, that they may early learn the rights which property confers and not entertain confused ideas upon this subject.

FORMATION OF HABITS.

Virtue is the child of good habits, and the formation of habits may be said to almost constitute the whole work of education. The mother can create habits which shall mold character and enable the mind to maintain that habitual sense of duty which gives command over the passions, and power to fight temptation, and which makes obedience to principle comparatively easy, under most circumstances. The social and domestic life are marred by habits which have grown into a second nature. It is not in an occasional act of civility that the charm of either home or society consists, but in continued practice of courtesy and respect for the rights and feelings of those around us. Whatever may be the precepts for a home, the practices of the fireside will give form to the habits. Parents who indulge in gossip, scandal, slander and tale-telling, will rear children possessing the same tastes and deteriorating habits. A parent's example outlines the child's character. It sinks down deep into his heart and influences his whole life for good or for evil. A parent should carefully avoid speaking evil of others, and should never exhibit faults requiring the mantle of charity to cover. A parent's example should be such as to excite an abhorrence of evil speaking, of tattling and of uncharitable construction of the motives of others. Let the mother begin the proper training of her children in early life and she will be able to so mold their characters that not only will they acquire the habit of bridling the tongue, but they will learn to avoid the presence of the slanderer as they do a deadly viper.

POLITENESS AT HOME.

Genuine politeness is a great fosterer of domestic love, and those who are habitually polished at home are those who exhibit good manners when abroad. When parents receive any little attention from their children, they should thank them for it. They should ask a favor only in a courteous way; never reply to questions in monosyllables, or indulge in the rudeness of paying no attention to a question, for such an example will be surely followed by the children. Parents sometimes thoughtlessly allow their children to form habits of disrespect in the home circle, which crop out in the bad manners that are found in society.

HOW TO REPROVE.

Parents should never check expressions of tenderness in their children, nor humiliate them before others. This will not only cause suffering to little sensitive hearts, but will tend to harden them. Reproof, if needed, should be administered to each child singly and alone.

CHEERFULNESS AT THE TABLE.

Children should not be prohibited from laughing and talking at the table. Joyousness promotes the circulation of the blood, enlivens and invigorates it, and sends it to all parts of the system, carrying with it animation, vigor and life. Controversy should not be permitted at the table, nor should any subjects which call forth political or religious difference. Every topic introduced should be calculated to instruct, interest or amuse. Business matters, past disappointments and mishaps should not be alluded to, nor should bad news be spoken of at the table, nor for half an hour before. All conversation should be of joyous and gladsome character, such as will bring out pleasant remarks and agreeable associations. Reproof should never be administered at the table, either to a child or to a servant; no fault found with anything, and no unkind word should be spoken. If remarks are to be made of absent ones, they should be of a kind and charitable nature. Thus will the family table be the center of pleasant memories in future years, when the family shall have been scattered far and near, and some, perhaps, have been laid in their final resting-place.

TRAIN CHILDREN FOR SOME OCCUPATION.

Chancellor Kent says: "Without some preparation made in youth for the sequel of life, children of all conditions would probably become idle and vicious when they grow up, from want of good instruction and habits, and the means of subsistence, or from want of rational and useful occupations. A parent who sends his son into the world without educating him in some art, science, profession or business, does great injury to mankind, as well as to his son and his own family, for he defrauds the community of a useful citizen, and bequeaths to it a nuisance. That parent who trains his child for some special occupation, who inspires him with a feeling of genuine self-respect, has contributed a useful citizen to society."

BAD TEMPER.

Dread an insubordinate temper, and deal with it as one of the greatest evils. Let the child feel by your manner that he is not a safe companion for the rest of the family when he is in anger. Allow no one to speak to him at such times, not even to answer a question. Take from him books, and whatever he may have, and place him where he shall feel that the indulgence of a bad temper shall deprive him of all enjoyment, and he will soon learn to control himself.

SELFISHNESS.

Selfishness that binds the miser in his chains, that chills the heart, must never be allowed a place in the family circle. Teach the child to share his gifts and pleasures with others, to be obliging, kind and benevolent, and the influence of such instruction may come back into your own bosom, to bless your latest hours.

HOME MAXIMS FOR TRAINING CHILDREN.

Remember that children are men and women in miniature, and though they should be allowed to act as children, still our dealings with them should be manly and not morose. Remember also that every word, tone and gesture, nay, even your dress, makes an impression.

Never correct a child on suspicion, or without understanding the whole matter, nor trifle with a child's feelings when under discipline.

Be always mild and cheerful in their presence, communicative, but never extravagant, trifling or vulgar in language or gesture. Never trifle with a child nor speak beseechingly when it is doing wrong.

Always follow commands with a close and careful watch, until the thing is done, allowing no evasion and no modification, unless the child ask for it, and it be expressly granted.

Never reprove children severely in company, nor hold them up to ridicule, nor make light of their failings.

Never speak in an impatient, pitiful manner, if you have occasion to find fault.

Never say to a child, "I don't believe what you say," nor even imply your doubts. If you have such feelings, keep them to yourself and wait; the truth will eventually be made plain.

Never disappoint the confidence a child places in you, whether it be a thing placed in your care or a promise.

Always give prompt attention to a child when he

speaks, so as to prevent repeated calls, and that he may learn to give prompt attention when you call him.

Never try to impress a child with religious truth when in anger, or talk to him of God, as it will not have the desired effect. Do it under more favorable circum-stances.

At the table a child should be taught to sit up and behave in a becoming manner, not to tease when denied, nor to leave his chair without asking. A parent's wish at such time should be a law from which no appeal should be made.

Even in sickness gentle restraint is better for a child than indulgence.

There should never be two sets of manners, the one for home and the other for company, but a gentle behavior should be always required.

MUSIC.
"A protection against vice,
An incentive to virtue."

CHAPTER XX.

Home Culture.

HE work of home culture should be made a matter of great importance to every one, for upon it depends the happiness of earthly homes, as well as our fitness for the enjoyment of the eternal home in heaven. The sufferings endured here, friend for friend, parents for children, unrequited sacrifices, cares and tears, all tend to discipline us, and prepare us for the recompense which eternity brings.

CULTIVATE MORAL COURAGE.

Moral courage will be cultivated in your children as they observe that you say and do whatever you conscientiously believe to be right and true, without being influenced by the views of others; thus showing them that you fear nothing so much as failing to do your duty. Perhaps this may be difficult to do, but every mother can at least show her appreciation of moral courage when she sees it exhibited by others, and in this way incite its growth in the souls of her children. Moral courage is a rare endowment, and those who possess it are able to act with perfect independence of the opinions of others, and govern themselves only by the laws of propriety, uprightness and charity.

THE PERNICIOUS INFLUENCE OF INDOLENCE.

If you would preserve your children from the pernicious influence of indolence and all its corrupting tendencies, you must be earnest in purpose, active, energetic and fervent in spirit. Earnestness sharpens the faculties; indolence corrodes and dulls them. By the former we rise higher and higher, by the latter we sink lower and lower. Indolence begets discontent, envy and jealousy, while labor elevates the mind and character. Cultivate in your children habits of thought which will keep their minds occupied upon something that will be of use or advantage, and prevent them from acquiring habits of idleness, if you would secure their future well-being.

It has been said that he who performs no useful act in society, who makes no human being happier, is leading a life of utter selfishness—a life of sin—for a life of selfishness is a life of sin. There is nowhere room for idleness. Work is both a duty and a necessity of our nature, and a befitting reward will ever follow it. To foster and encourage labor in some useful form, is a duty which parents should urge upon their children, if they should seek their best good.

SELF-RESPECT.

It is the mother's duty to see that her children protect themselves from the many pit-falls which surround them, such as malice, envy, conceit, avariciousness, and other evils, by being clad in the armor of self-respect; and then they will be able to encounter temptation and corruption, unstained and unpolluted. This feeling of self-respect is something stronger than self-reliance, higher than pride. It is an energy of the soul which masters the whole being for its good, watching with a never-ceasing vigilance. It is the sense of duty and the sense of honor combined. It is an armor, which, though powerless to shield from sorrows that purify and invigorate, yet will avert all hostile influences that assail, from whatever source they come. The mother having once made her children conscious that always and everywhere they carry with them such an angel to shield, warn and rescue them, may let them go out into the world, and fear nothing from the wiles and temptations which may beset them.

RESULTS OF GOOD-BREEDING IN THE HOME CIRCLE.

The laws of good-breeding in no place bear more gratifying results than in the home circle. Here, tempered with love, and nurtured by all kindly impulses, they bear the choicest fruit. A true lady will show as much courtesy, and observe the duties of politeness as unfailingly, toward every member of her family as toward her most distinguished guest. A true gentleman will feel bound to exercise courtesy and kindness in his intercourse with those who depend upon him for protection and example. Children influenced by such examples at home, will never fail to show to their elders the respect due them, to their young companions the same consideration for their feelings which they expect to meet with in return, nor to servants that patience which even the best too often require. In such a home peace and good will are the household gods.

FAULT-FINDING AND GRUMBLING.

The oil of civility is required to make the wheels of domestic life run smoothly. The habit of fault-finding and grumbling indulged in by some, is an exceedingly vexatious one, and will, in time, ruffle the calmest spirit and the sweetest temper. It is the little annoyances, perplexities and misfortunes which often render life a burden; the little omission of minor duties and the committing of little faults that perpetually scourge us and keep the heart sore. Constant fault-finding, persistent misrepresentations of motives, suspicions of evil where no evil was intended, will complete the work in all but the finest and most heroic natures. They alone can stand the fiery test, coming out purer and stronger for the ordeal. Children who habitually obey the commandment, "Be kind to one another," will find in mature life, how strong the bonds of affection may be that bind the members of the household together.

FAMILY JARS NOT TO BE MADE PUBLIC.

Whatever may be the family disagreements, they should never be made known outside of the home circle, if it can be avoided. Those who expose the faults of the members of their family are severely judged by the world, and no provocation can be a good excuse for it. It is exceedingly vulgar, not to say unchristianlike, for the members of the same family to be at enmity with one another.

YIELDING TO ONE ANOTHER.

One of the greatest disciplines of human life, is that which teaches us to yield our wills to those who have a claim upon us to do so, even in trifling, every-day affairs; the wife to the husband, children to parents, to teachers and to one another. In cases where principle is concerned, it is, of course, necessary to be firm, which requires an exercise of moral courage.

CONFLICTING INTERESTS.

Conflicting interests are a fruitful source of family difficulties. The command of Christ to the two brothers who came to Him with their disputes, "Beware of covetousness," is as applicable among members of the same family now, as it was when those words were spoken. It is better that you have few or no business transactions with any one who is near and dear to you, and connected by family ties. In business relations men are apt to be very exact, because of their habits of business, and this exactness is too often construed by near friends and relatives as actuated by purely selfish motives. Upon this rock many a bark of family love has been wrecked.

RELIGIOUS EDUCATION.

It is well to remember that every blessing of our lives, every joy of our hearts and every ray of hope shed upon our pathway, have had their origin in religion, and may be traced in all their hallowed, healthful influences to the Bible. With the dawn of childhood, then, in the earliest days of intelligence, should the mind be impressed and stored with religious truth, and nothing should be allowed to exclude or efface it. It should be taught so early that the mind will never remember when it began to learn; it will then have the character of innate, inbred principles, incorporated with their very being.

OBEDIENCE.

If you would not have all your instructions and counsels ineffectual, teach your children to obey. Government in a family is the great safeguard of religion and morals, the support of order and the source of prosperity. Nothing has a greater tendency to bring a curse upon a family than the insubordination and disobedience of children, and there is no more painful and disgusting sight than an ungoverned child.

INFLUENCE OF EXAMPLE.

Never forget that the first book children read is their parents' example—their daily deportment. If this is forgotten you may find, in the loss of your domestic peace, that while your children well know the right path, they follow the wrong.

Childhood is like a mirror, catching and reflecting images all around it. Remember that an impious, profane or vulgar thought may operate upon the heart of a young child like a careless spray of water upon polished steel, staining it with rust that no efforts can thoroughly efface.

Improve the first ten years of life as the golden opportunity, which may never return. It is the seed time, and your harvest depends upon the seed then sown.

THE INFLUENCE OF BOOKS.

Few mothers can over-estimate the influence which the companionship of books exerts in youth upon the habits and tastes of their children, and no mother who has the welfare of her children at heart will neglect the important work of choosing the proper books for them to read, while they are under her care. She should select for them such as will both interest and instruct, and this should be done during the early years, before their minds shall have imbibed the pernicious teachings of bad books and sensational novels. The poison imbibed from bad books works so secretly that their influence for evil is even greater than the influence of bad

associates. The mother has it in her power to make
such books the companions and friends of her children
as her good judgment may select, and to impress upon
them their truths, by conversing with them about the
moral lessons or the intellectual instructions they contain. A taste may be easily cultivated for books on
natural science and for history, as well as for those that
teach important and wholesome lessons for the young,
such as are contained in the works of Mrs. Edgeworth,
Mrs Child, Mrs. Yonge, and many other books written
for the young.

CHAPTER XXI.

Woman's Higher Education.

IT has been seen that in the rearing and training of her children, woman has a great work to perform; that in this work she exerts an incalculable influence upon untold numbers, and that she molds the minds and characters of her sons and daughters. How important, then, that she should cultivate her mental faculties to the highest extent, if for no other reason than to fit herself the better for the performance of this great duty of educating her children. How important it is, also, that she should look to the higher education of her daughters, who, in turn, will become mothers of future generations, or may, perhaps, by some vicissitude of fortune, become dependent upon their own resources for support. With the highest culture of the mental faculties, woman will be best enabled to faithfully perform whatever she may undertake.

TRAIN YOUNG WOMEN TO SOME OCCUPATION.

Owing to the changes in social and industrial life
which have crowded many women from their homes into
business and public life, women must train for their
branch of labor as men train for their work, if they wish
to attain any degree of success. Even where women
have independent fortunes, their lives will be all the
happier if they have been trained to some occupation,
that, in case of reverses, may be made a self-sustaining
one. A young woman who is able to support herself,
increases her chances for a happy marriage, for, not
being obliged to rely upon a husband for support or for
a home, she is able to judge calmly of an offer when it
comes, and is free to accept or decline, because of her
independence. Women are capable of and adapted to
a large number of employments, which have hitherto
been kept from them, and some of these they are slowly
wrenching from the hands of the sterner sex. In order
that women may enter the ranks of labor which she
is forcing open to herself, she needs a special education
and training to fit her for such employment.

EDUCATION OF GIRLS TOO SUPERFICIAL.

The school instruction of our girls is too superficial.
There is a smattering of too many branches, where two
or three systematically studied and thoroughly mastered,
would accomplish much more for them in the way of a
sound mental training, which is the real object of education. The present method of educating young girls is

to give them from five to ten studies, in which they prepare lessons, and this, too, at an age when their physical
development suffers and is checked by excess of mental
labor. Such a course of instruction, bestowing only a
smattering of many branches, wastes the powers of the
mind, and deters, rather than aids, self-improvement.
It is only a concentration of the mind upon the thorough
acquisition of all it undertakes that strengthens the
reflective, and forms the reasoning, faculties, and thus
helps to lay a solid foundation for future usefulness.
The word education means to educe, to draw out the
powers of the mind; not the cramming into it of facts,
dates and whole pages to be repeated *verbatim.*

AN EDUCATION APPROPRIATE TO EACH SEX.

The fact is becoming more palpable every year that
there is an education appropriate to each sex; that identical education for the two sexes is so unnatural, that
physiology protests against it and experience weeps over
it. The physiological motto in education is, " Educate
a man for manhood, a woman for womanhood, and both
for humanity." Herbert Spencer, in speaking of the
want of a proper course of education for girls, says:
" It is an astonishing fact that, though on the treatment
of offspring depend their lives or deaths, and their
moral welfare or ruin, yet not one word of instruction
on treatment of offspring is ever given to those who
will, by and by, be parents." It will thus be seen, that
as women have the care, the training and the education
of children, they need an education in a special direc-

tion, and should have a very thorough one, to prepare them for the task.

WOMEN SHOULD HAVE A KNOWLEDGE OF THE LAWS OF HEALTH.

Physiology is one of the branches of that higher education, which should be thoroughly pursued by women to enable them to fulfill the various duties of their allotted stations. Yet it is also desirable that they should have a thorough knowledge of all branches that they undertake, and a mastery of the studies pursued by them; for the want of thoroughness in woman's education is an obstacle to success in all branches of labor. But woman should especially have a thorough knowledge of the laws of physiology and hygiene. If she becomes a mother, such knowledge will enable her to guard better the lives and health of her children. She will understand that when she sends out her child insufficiently clad, and he comes home chilled through, that his vitality, his power of resisting disease, is wasted. She will know that by taking the necessary precautions, she may save the child's life; that she must not take him thus chilled, to the fire or into a room highly heated, but that by gentle exercise or friction, she must restore the circulation of the blood, and in using such precautions, she may ward off the attacks of disease that would surely follow if they were neglected. This is but a single case, for there are instances of almost daily occurrence when a proper knowledge of the laws of health will ward off disease, in her own case, as well as in those of various members of her household. The diseases which carry off children, are for the most part, such as ought to be under the control of the women who love them, pet them, educate them, and who would, in many cases, lay down their lives for them.

RESULT OF IGNORANCE OF SANITARY LAWS.

Ignorance of the laws of ventilation in sleeping-rooms and school-rooms is the cause of a vast amount of disease. From ignorance of the signs of approaching disease, children are often punished for idleness, listlessness, sulkiness and wilfulness, and this punishment is too often by confinement in a closed room, and by an increase of tasks; when what is really needed is more oxygen, more open-air exercise, and less study. These forms of ignorance have too often resulted in malignant typhus and brain fevers. Knowledge of the laws of hygiene will often spare the waste of health and strength in the young, and will also spare anxiety and misery to those who love and tend them. If the time devoted to the many trashy so-called "accomplishments" in a young lady's education, were given to a study of the laws of preserving health, how many precious lives might be spared to loving parents, and how many frail and delicate forms, resulting from inattention to physical training, might have become strong and beautiful temples of exalted souls. We are all in duty bound to know and to obey the laws of nature, on which the welfare of our bodies depends, for the full enjoyment of our faculties can only be attained when the body is in perfect health.

IDLENESS A SOURCE OF MISERY.

Perhaps the greatest cause of misery and wretchedness in social life is idleness. The want of something to do is what makes people wicked and miserable. It breeds selfishness, mischief-making, envy, jealousy and vice, in all its most dreadful forms. It is the duty of mothers to see that their daughters are trained to habits of industry, that their minds are at all times occupied, that they are well informed as to household duties, and to the duties of married life, for upon a knowledge of household details may depend their life-long happiness or misery. It is frequently the case, that a girl's education ends just as her mind is beginning to mature and her faculties are beginning to develop. Her education ends when it ought properly to begin. She enters upon marriage entirely unprepared, and, perchance, by some misfortune, she is thrown penniless upon the world with no means of obtaining a livelihood, for her education has never fitted her for any vocation. Not having been properly taught herself, she is not able to teach, and she finds no avenue of employment open to her. An English clergyman, writing upon this subject, says: "Let girls take a serious interest in art; let them take up some congenial study, let it be a branch of science or history. Let them write. They can do almost anything they try to do, but let their mothers never rest until they have implanted in their daughters' lives one growing interest beyond flirtation and gossip, whether it be work at the easel, music, literature, the structure of the human body and the laws of health, any solid interest that will occupy their thoughts and their hearts. Idleness, frivolity and ignorance can only be put down by education and employment. In the last resort, the spirit of evil becomes teacher and task-master."

WOMEN SHOULD CULTIVATE A SPIRIT OF INDEPENDENCE.

In this country more than any other, women should, to some extent, cultivate a spirit of independence. They should acquire a knowledge of how business is transacted, of the relation between capital and labor, and of the value of labor, skilled and unskilled. As housekeepers, they would then be saved from many annoyances and mistakes. If they chance to be left alone, widows, or orphans possessing means, they would be saved from many losses and vexatious experiences by knowing how to transact their own business. And those women who are obliged to take care of themselves, who have no means, how necessary is it that they should have a thorough knowledge of some occupation or business by which they can maintain themselves and others dependent upon them. In this country, the daughter brought up in affluence, may, by some rapid change of fortune, be obliged, upon arriving at maturity, to be among the applicants for whatever employment she may be fitted. If she has been trained to some useful occupation, or if her faculties have been developed by a thoroughness of study of any subject she has undertaken, she will be better qualified to prepare herself to fill any position which may be open to her. With a mind drilled by constant study she will the more quickly acquire a knowledge aud grasp the details of any subject or business to which she may devote herself.

HEALTH AND LIFE DEPENDENT UPON A HIGHER CULTURE.

Not only wealth and comfort, but health and life are dependent upon a higher form of culture, a more thorough course of education than is now the standard. Not more, but fewer branches of study and a more thorough comprehension of those pursued. Not only are the health and life of each woman dependent upon the kind and degree of the education she receives, but the health and lives of great numbers may depend upon it. In proportion as she has a knowledge of the laws and nature of a subject will she be able to work at it easily, rapidly and successfully. Knowledge of physical laws saves health and life, knowledge of the laws of intellect saves wear and tear of the brain, knowledge of the laws of political economy and business affairs saves anxiety and worrying.

CULTIVATION OF THE MORAL SENSE.

A well educated moral sense prevents idleness and develops a well regulated character, which will preserve from excess those tenderer emotions and deeper passions of woman, which are potent in her for evil or for good, in proportion as they are undisciplined and allowed to run wild, or are trained and developed into a noble and harmonious self-restraint.

The girl who has so educated and regulated her intellect, her tastes, her emotions and her moral sense, as to be able to discern the true from the false, will be ready for the faithful performance of whatever work in life is allotted to her; while she who is allowed to grow up ignorant, idle, vain, frivolous, will find herself fitted for no state of existence, and, in after years, with feelings of remorse and despair over a wasted life, may cast reproach upon those in whose trust was reposed her early education.

It is not for women alone that they should seek a higher education of their faculties and powers but for the sake of the communities in which they live, for the sake of the homes in which they rule and govern, and govern immortal souls, and for the sake of those other homes in the humbler walks of life, where they owe duties as ministering spirits as well as in their own, for in proportion as they minister to the comfort and health of others, so do they exalt their own souls. Women should seek a higher education in order that they may elevate themselves, and that they may prepare themselves for whatever duty they may be called upon to perform. In social life we find that the truest wives, the most patient and careful mothers, the most exemplary house-keepers, the model sisters, the wisest philanthropists and the women of the greatest social influence are women of cultivated minds.

16

CHAPTER XXII.

The Art of Letter Writing.

FRENCH writer says, that the writing a note or letter, the wording of a regret, the prompt or the delayed answering of an invitation, the manner of a salutation, the neglect of a required attention, all betray to the well-bred the degree or the absence of good-breeding.

A person who has self-respect as well as respect for others, should never carelessly write a letter or note.

REQUIREMENTS FOR CORRECT WRITING.

The letter or note should be free from all flourishes. The rules of punctuation should be followed as nearly as possible, and no capital letters used where they are not required. Ink-blots, erasures and stains on the paper are inadmissible. Any abbreviations of name, rank or title are considered rude, beyond those sanctioned by custom. No abbreviations of words should be indulged in, nor underlining of words intended to be made emphatic. All amounts of money or other numbers should be written, reserving the use of numerical figures for dates only. It is a good form to have the address of the writer printed at the top of the sheet, especially for all business letters. For letters of friendship and notes, pure white paper and envelopes are in better taste than tinted or colored, and the paper should be of a superior quality. When a page is once written from left to right side, it should not be written over again from top to bottom.

ANONYMOUS LETTERS.

No attention should ever be paid to anonymous letters. The writers of such stamp themselves as cowardly, and cowards do not hesitate to say or write what is not true when it suits their purpose. All statements made in such letters should be regarded as false, and the writers as actuated by some bad motives. Anonymous letters should be burned at once, for they are not to be noticed.

LETTERS AND NOTES.

The writing of notes in the third person is generally confined to notes of invitation, and such notes are never signed.

When a letter is upon business, commencing "Sir" or "Dear Sir," the name of the person addressed may be written either at the beginning or at the close of the letter, in the left hand corner. In letters commencing with the name of the person to whom you are writing, as, "My Dear Mrs. Brown," the name should not be repeated in the left hand corner.

No notes should be commenced very high or very low on the page, but nearer the top than the middle of the sheet.

MANNER OF ADDRESS.

In addressing a clergyman, it is customary to commence "Reverend Sir," or "Dear Sir." It is not now customary to write "B. A." or "M. A." after his name.

Doctors of divinity and medicine are thus distinguished: "To the Rev. John Blair, D. D.," or "Rev. Dr. Blair;" "To G. T. Roscoe, M. D.," "Doctor Roscoe" or "Dr. Roscoe."

The President of the United States and Governors of States, are addressed "His Excllency." U. S. Senators, members of Congress and men distinguished by holding various political offices of an honorable nature, are addressed as "Honorable."

The superscription or address should be written upon the envelope as legibly as possible, beginning a little to the left of the center of the envelope. The number of the house and name of the street may be written immediately under this line, or in the lower left hand corner, as the writer sees fit. The postage stamp should be securely fixed in the upper right hand corner of the envelope. The following forms will show the appearance of a properly addressed envelope:

STAMP.

Thos. Y. Stevens, Esq.

Chicago,

796 Ashland Ave.   Ills.

STAMP.

Mr. Thos. Y. Stevens,

796 Ashland Avenue,

Chicago,

Ills.

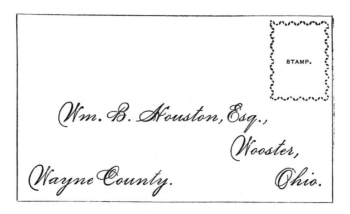

In sending a letter in care of another person the following form is the manner in which the envelope should be addressed:

In sending a letter by a friend or acquaintance, and not through the mail, acknowledge the courtesy of your friend on the envelope. The letter should not be sealed. The following is the proper form:

Mrs. Julia C. Wheeler,

734 Simson Street,

Kindness (or Politeness) of

James Steinfield.

Dayton,

Ohio.

A note or letter sent to a friend residing in the same place, by a messenger, may be addressed as follows, or bear the full address:

Miss Mary Wyman,

Presented.

FORM OF A LETTER.

Denver, May 13, 1881.

My Esteemed Friend:

I received your very good letter, and hasten to reply. I am overjoyed at the prospects of a speedy return to the ancient, but delightful "City of the Straits," and anticipate spending a pleasant summer with you and my many friends. We are making preparations to leave June 5th.

Your old friend,

Joe J. Wilson.

Geo. W. Smyth,
Detroit, Mich.

DEGREES OF FORMALITY OBSERVED.

In commencing and signing notes and letters there is a difference of opinion in the degrees of formality to be observed, but generally this scale is used according to the degree of acquaintance or friendship. "Madam" or "Sir," "Dear Madam" or "Dear Sir," "My Dear Madam" or "My Dear Sir," "Dear Mrs. Brown" or "Dear Mr. Brown," "My Dear Mrs Brown" or "My Dear Mr. Brown," "My Dear Friend." In closing a note, the degrees are implied as follows: "Truly Yours" or "Yours Truly," "Very Truly Yours," "Sincerely Yours," "Cordially Yours," "Faithfully Yours," "Affectionately Yours." The proper words should be carefully selected, as the conclusion of a note or letter makes an impression on the person reading it. To aged persons the form, "With great respect, sincerely yours," recommends itself as a proper form. "Yours, etc.," is considered a rude ending. If you are sufficiently well acquainted with a person to address her "My Dear Mrs. ———," do not sign "Yours Truly," or "Truly Yours," as this is the form to be used in writing to strangers or in business letters

SIGNATURE OF LADIES.

A married lady should not sign herself with the "Mrs." before her baptismal name, or a single lady with the "Miss." In writing to strangers who do not know whether to address you as Mrs. or Miss, the address should be given in full, after signing your letter; as "Mrs. John Smith," followed by the direction; or if unmarried, the "Miss" should be placed in brackets a short distance preceding the signature.

Only the letters of unmarried ladies and widows are addressed with their baptismal names. The letters of married ladies are addressed with their husbands' names, as "Mrs John Smith."

LETTERS OF INTRODUCTION.

Letters of introduction should be brief and carefully worded. Give in full the name of the person introduced, the city or town he is from, intimating the mutual pleasure that you believe the acquaintance will confer, adding a few remarks concerning the one introduced, as circumstances seem to require. Modest persons sometimes shrink from delivering letters of introduction which appear to them to be undeservedly complimentary. Letters of introduction are left unsealed, to be sealed before delivery by the one introduced. They should receive immediate attention by the parties who receive them. When a gentleman delivers such a letter to a lady, he is at liberty to call upon her, sending her his card to ascertain whether she will receive him then, or appoint another hour that will be more convenient. The same rule is to be observed by those whose stay in the city is short. He may also send it to her with his card bearing his address.

A letter of introduction should not be given, unless

the person writing it is very well acquainted with the one whom he introduces, and the one to whom he writes. If the person who receives such a letter is really well-bred, you will hear from him or her within twenty-four hours, for a letter of introduction is said to be like a draft, it must be cashed at sight. The one receiving it either invites you to dine, or to meet others, or to a drive, or to visit some place of amusement. Too great caution cannot be exercised in giving a letter which makes such demands upon an acquantance.

When the letter of introduction is left with a card, if there is a gentleman in the family, he may call upon the stranger the next day, unless some engagement prevents, when he should send his card with an invitation. If the letter introduces a gentleman to a lady, she may write a note of invitation in answer, appointing a time for him to call.

The following is an appropriate form for a letter of introduction.

New York, Dec. 20, 1880.

Dear Sir:

I take great pleasure in introducing to you my esteemed friend, Miss Ida A. Thornton, a young lady of culture and refinement, who will spend a few months in your city. I am sure that an acquaintance with her will be a pleasure to you, as it will also be to Miss Thornton. Any favor you may show her during her stay in your city, I will consider a personal favor.

Yours Sincerely,

Mrs. J. Q. A. Jones.

To Geo. Morris,

Chicago.

The envelope containing a letter of introduction, should be addressed as follows:

Geo. Morris, Esq.
1671 Jackson Street,
Chicago,
Introducing   Ill.
Miss Ida A. Thornton.

NOTES OF CONGRATULATION OR CONDOLENCE.

Notes of congratulation and condolence should be brief, and the letter should only be sent by near and intimate friends. Do not allude to any subject except the one for which you are offering your congratulations or sympathy. Such notes should be made expressive of real feeling, and not be mere matters of form.

INVITATION TO A RECEPTION.

For a general reception, invitations are printed on cards. Their style is like the following, and do not require an answer unless "R. S. V. P." is upon one corner.

Mrs. J. L. Ashton,
At home,
Wednesday Evening, Jan. 6,
8 to 11 P. M.   No. 248 James St

INVITATION TO A BALL.

The "At Home" form of invitation for a reception is often adopted for a ball with the word "Dancing" in one corner, though many people use the "At Home" form only for receptions. For balls the hours are not limited as at receptions. When the above form is not used for a ball, the invitation may read as follows:

"Mrs. Blair requests the pleasure of Miss Milton's company at a ball, on Tuesday, February 7, at 9 o'clock."

Invitations to a ball are always given in the name of the lady of the house, and require an answer, which should not be delayed. If the invitation is accepted, the answer should be as follows:

"Miss Milton accepts with pleasure Mrs. Blair's kind invitation for Tuesday, February 7."

If it is found impossible to attend, a note of regrets, something like the following, should be sent:

"Miss Milton regrets that intended absence from home (or whatever may be the preventing cause) prevents her accepting Mrs. Blair's kind invitation for February 7."

INVITATION TO A LARGE PARTY.

The invitation to a large party is similar to that for a ball, only the words "at a ball" are omitted, and the hour may be earlier. The notes of acceptance and regret are the same as for a ball. If the party is a small one, it should be indicated by inserting the words, "to a small evening party," so that there may be no misunderstanding. A large party calls for full evening dress, and it would be embarrassing for a lady or gentleman to go to a house in full evening dress, expecting to find a large party there in similar costumes, and meet only a few friends and acquaintances plainly dressed. If there is any special feature which is to give character to the evening, it is best to mention this fact in the note of invitation. Thus the words "musical party," "to take part in dramatic readings," "amateur theatricals," will denote the character of the evening's entertainment. If you have programmes, enclose one in the invitation.

INVITATION TO A PUBLIC ENTERTAINMENT.

An invitation from a gentleman to a lady to attend a concert, lecture, theatre, opera or other amusement, may read as follows:

"Mr. Hayden would be pleased to have Miss Morton's company to the Academy of Music, on Monday evening, November 8, when 'Richelieu' will be played by Edwin Booth's Company."

An invitation of this kind demands an immediate answer of acceptance or regrets. A previous engagement may be a reason for rejection.

DINNER INVITATIONS.

These are written in the name of the husband and wife, and demand an immediate reply. This form may be used:

"Mr. and Mrs. Eugene Snow request the pleasure of Mr. and Mrs. Horace Allen's company at dinner, on Tuesday, the 13th of January, at 7 o'clock."

A note of acceptance may read as follows:

"Mr. and Mrs. Horace Allen accept with pleasure Mr. and Mrs. Eugene Snow's kind invitation to dine with them on Tuesday, the 13th inst., at 7 o'clock."

A note of regret may read:

"Mr. and Mrs. Horace Allen regret exceedingly that sickness in the family (or whatever the cause may be) prevents the acceptance of Mr. and Mrs. Eugene Snow's kind invitation to dine with them on Tuesday, January 13th."

INVITATIONS TO TEA.

An invitation to a tea-drinking may be less formal and should partake more of the nature of a private note; thus:

"Dear Miss Brock: Some friends are coming to drink tea with me on Thursday, and I should be glad of the pleasure of your company also. Please do not disappoint me."

An invitation of this informal nature needs no reply, unless "R. S. V. P." is appended, in which case the answer must be returned, if possible, by the messenger who brought it, or sent at once, as your friend may depend upon having a certain number of people at her tea-drinking, and if you cannot go, she will want to supply your place.

LESS FORMAL INVITATIONS.

Invitations of a less formal character are sent for charades, private theatricals, and for archery, croquet, sailing and garden parties; but, however informal the invitation (except only when a visiting card is used) on no account neglect to give immediate attention to it, by sending an acceptance or a regret, for any want of courtesy in this respect is unpardonable.

PROMPTNESS IN ANSWERING.

All invitations requiring answers should be answered as soon as possible after receiving them. The French have a saying, applicable to all notes of invitation, to the effect that it is as important to reply as promptly to a note requiring an answer, as it is to a question in speaking. All refined people who are accustomed to the best social forms, consider that it would be an unpardonable negligence to omit for a single day replying to an invitation or a note requiring a reply.

In accepting dinner invitations, repeat the hour and day named in your letter of acceptance, in order that if any mistake has been made it may be corrected.

Promptly acknowledge all attentions you receive, such as receiving presents of books, flowers, etc.

17

EXPRESSIONS TO BE USED.

The expression "presents compliments" has become obsolete in the writing of invitations. The expression "kind" or "very kind" invitation has taken the place of "polite," in notes of acceptance or regret. Be particular to distinguish between "go" and "come," you go to a friend's house and your friend comes to your house.

TIME TO SEND INVITATIONS.

Invitations for parties and entertainments of a formal nature, can be sent out for a week or two weeks before the entertainment is to take place. A notice of not less than one week is expected for such invitations. They should be printed or engraved on small note paper or large cards, with the envelopes to match, with no colors in the monogram, if one is used.

INVITATIONS FOR SEVERAL MEMBERS OF A FAMILY.

It is not considered good form to have one card of invitation answer for several persons belonging to the same family, or to address an invitation " Mrs. Blank and family," as it indicates a scarcity of cards. One card or invitation may be sent to Mr. and Mrs. Blank, and one each to the several members of the family who are to be invited.

THE LEAST FORMAL INVITATIONS.

The least formal, of formal invitations, is when a lady sends or leaves her own visiting card with the invitation upon it. An invitation of this kind need not be answered unless an " R. S. V. P." (*Respondez s'il vous plait*), is on the card. You go or not, as you please, but if you do not go, you call, or leave a card as soon after as is convenient.

UNCIVIL ANSWERS.

Uncivil and curt, not to say rude, answers are sometimes returned to invitations, more frequently the result of carelessness in their writers than of premeditated rudeness.

" Mr. and Mrs. Adam Brown regret that they cannot accept Mrs. Smith's invitation for Wednesday evening," is a rude form of regret.

" Mr. and Mrs. Adam Brown decline Mrs. Moses Smith's invitation for Friday evening,"

is a still ruder form.

A curt and thoughtless reply is:

" Mr. and Mrs. Adam Brown's compliments and regrets for Friday evening."

REASONS FOR REGRETS.

" All regrets from persons who are not able to accept invitations, should contain a reason for regretting," is a rule strictly observed in our best society, and is considered especially binding in answering a first invitation. If persons are in mourning, they regret that a recent bereavement prevents them from accepting. Those contemplating being absent from home, regret that contemplated absence from home prevents them from accept-

ing. "A previous engagement " is made the excuse
when there is an engagement either at home or away
from it, and also when one has no inclination to accept;
which makes it quite necessary for those who really
regret their inability to accept, to mention what that
engagement is.

THE FAMILY LETTER.

It seems hardly necessary to give the form of a letter
from one member of a family to another. It is often
the case that letters sent from home to an absent member are decidedly unsatisfactory, if not to a great extent
of little interest outside of one or two facts mentioned.
Consequently some hint as to what those letters should
be, are here given. They should be written as though
the writer were talking, using familiar expressions, and
such peculiarities as the writer possesses in ordinary
speech should find a place in the letter. The writer
may speak of many trivial things at and about home,
and gossipy matters in the neighborhood, and should
keep the absent one posted upon all minor facts and
occurrences, as well as the more important ones. The
writer may make inquiries as to how the absent one is
enjoying himself, whether he finds any place better than
home, and ask such other questions as he may desire,
concluding with sincere expressions of affection from
various members of the family. The absent one may,
in like manner, express himself freely on all subjects,
describe his journey minutely, and speak of whatever
he may feel deep interest in. In short, a family letter
may be as gossipy as the writer can make it, without

much regard to an attempt at showy or dignified composition.

THE LETTER OF FRIENDSHIP.

This should be of a more dignified tone, contain less trivialties than the family letter, and should embrace matters that will be of interest to both. A letter of friendship should be answered in due time, according to the intimacy of the parties, but should not be delayed long enough to allow the friendship to cool, if there is a desire to keep it warm.

THE LOVE LETTER.

Of this it may be only said, that while it may be expressive of sincere esteem and affection, it should be of a dignified tone, and written in such a style, that if it should ever come under the eyes of others than the party to whom it was written, there may be found in it nothing of which the writer may be ashamed, either of silliness or of extravagant expression.

BUSINESS LETTERS.

These should be brief and to the point, should be of plain chirography, and relate to the business in hand, in as few words and as clearly as possible. Begin at once without apology or explanation, and finish up the matter pertaining to the business. If an apology or explanation is due, it may be made briefly at the close of the letter, after the business has been attended to. A letter on business should be answered at once, or as soon as possible after receiving it.

It is allowable, in some cases, upon receiving a brief business letter, to write the reply on the same page, beneath the original letter, and return both letter and answer together.

Among business letters may be classed all correspondence relating to business, applications for situations, testimonials regarding the character of a servant or employe; letters requesting the loan of money or an article, and letters granting or denying the favor; while all forms of drawing up notes, drafts and receipts may properly be included. The forms of some of these are here given.

LETTERS REQUESTING EMPLOYMENT.

A letter of this kind should be short, and written with care and neatness, that the writer may both show his penmanship and his business-like qualities, which are often judged of by the form of his letter. It may be after this fashion:

NEW YORK, March 1, 1880.

MESSRS. LORD & NOBLE,

DEAR SIRS:

Having heard that you are in need of more assistance in your establishment (or store, office) I venture to ask you for employment. I can refer you to Messrs. Jones & Smith, my late employers, as to my qualifications, should you decide to consider my application.

Yours truly,

JAMES ROBERTS.

LETTERS REGARDING THE CHARACTER OF A SERVANT.

DEAR MADAM: Sarah Riley, having applied to me for the position of cook, refers me to you for a character. I feel particularly anxious to obtain a good servant for the coming winter, and shall therefore feel obliged by your making me acquainted with any particulars referring to her character, and remain, madam,

Your very obedient servant,
MRS. GEORGE STONE.

To MRS. ALFRED STARK.

MRS. GEORGE STONE,

DEAR MADAM: It gives me pleasure to say that Sarah Riley lived with me for two years, and during that time I found her active, diligent and efficient. She is a superior cook, and I have full confidence in her honesty. I feel that I can recommend her with full confidence of her being likely to give you satisfaction. I am, madam,

Your very obedient servant,
MRS. ALFRED STARK.

MRS. GEORGE STONE,

DEAR MADAM: In replying to your note of inquiry, I beg to inform you that Sarah Riley, who lived with me in the capacity of cook, left my services because I did not find her temper and habits in all respects satisfactory. She was thoroughly competent as a cook, but in other respects I cannot conscientiously recommend her. I remain,

Yours, very truly,
MRS. ALFRED STARK.

NOTES, DRAFTS, BILLS AND RECEIPTS.

The following are forms of notes, drafts, receipts, etc.:

Promissory Note Without Interest.

$500.   CINCINNATI, O., June 6, 1880.

Sixty days after date, I promise to pay Samuel Arch-
over, or order, at my office in Cincinnati, five hundred
dollars, value received.

TIMOTHY MORTGRAVE.

Promissory Note With Interest but not Negotiable.

$125.30.   CHICAGO, Sept. 2, 1880.

For value received, I promise to pay Daniel Cartright
one hundred and twenty-five dollars and thirty cents, on
August 12th next, with interest at seven per cent. after
January 1, 1881.

JOHN S. ALLBRIGHT.

A Negotiable Note Payable to Bearer.

$75.   DETROIT, MICH., Oct. 8, 1881.

Thirty days after date, for value received, I promise
to pay Silas G. Smithers, or bearer, at my office in
Detroit, seventy-five dollars with interest from date.

SAMUEL Q. PETTIBONE.

Form of a Receipt.

$25.   NEW YORK, Nov. 3, 1880.

Received from James O. Mitchell, twenty-five dollars
to apply on account.   SMITH, JONES & Co.

Form of a Draft, Time from Sight.

$1,000.   DETROIT, MICH., July 7, 1880.

At ten days sight, pay to the order of J. Smith & Co.,
one thousand dollars, and charge the same to the account of   SHEPARD & NILES.

To SAMUEL STOKER & Co.,
       Indianapolis, Ind.

A Draft or Order " Without Grace."

$175.   CINCINNATI, OHIO, Aug. 12, 1880.

At sight, without grace, pay to F. B. Dickerson & Co., one hundred and seventy-five dollars, and charge to the account of   H. S. MOREHOUSE.

To TRADERS' NATIONAL BANK,
       Cincinnati, Ohio.

Form of a Bill.

                     BUFFALO, N. Y., Dec. 6, 1880.
MARTIN HUGHES, Dr.
            To JOHN J. HART.

Four volumes History of France, at $2.50 per volume, $10.00.

                     Received payment.

CHAPTER XXIII.

General Rules of Conduct.

IN society, everybody should receive equal attention, the young as well as the old. A high authority says, "If we wish our young people to grow up self-possessed and at ease, we must early train them in those graces by giving them the same attention and consideration we do those of maturer years. If we snub them, and systematically neglect them, they will acquire an awkwardness and a deprecatory manner, which will be very difficult for them to overcome."

GRACEFULNESS OF CARRIAGE.

Physical education is indispensable to every well-bred man and woman. A gentleman should not only know how to fence, to box, to ride, to shoot and to swim, but he should also know how to carry himself gracefully, and how to dance, if he would enjoy life to the utmost. A graceful carriage can best be attained by the aid of a drilling master, as dancing and boxing are taught. A man should be able to defend himself from ruffians, if attacked, and also to defend women from their insults. Dancing and calisthenics are also essential for a lady, for the better the physical training, the more graceful and self-possessed she will be. Every lady should know how to dance, whether she intends to dance in society or not. Swimming, skating, archery, games of lawn-tennis, and croquet, riding and driving, all aid in strengthening the muscles and giving open air exercise, and are therefore desirable recreations for the young of both sexes.

ATTITUDE.

Awkwardness of attitude is a mark of vulgarity. Lolling, gesticulating, fidgeting, handling an eye-glass, a watch-chain or the like, gives an air of *gaucherie*. A lady who sits cross-legged or sidewise on her chair, who stretches out her feet, who has a habit of holding her chin, or twirling her ribbons or fingering her buttons; a man who lounges in his chair, nurses his leg, bites his nails, or caresses his foot crossed over on his knee, shows clearly a want of good home training. Each should be quiet and graceful, either in their sitting or standing position, the gentleman being allowed more freedom than the lady. He may sit cross-legged if he wish, but should not sit with his knees far apart, nor with his foot on his knee. If an object is to be indicated, you must move the whole hand, or the head, but never point the finger.

COUGHING, SNEEZING, ETC.

Coughing, sneezing, clearing the throat, etc., if done at all, must be done as quickly as possible. Snuffing, hawking and expectorating must never be done in society. A sneeze can be checked by pressing the thumb or fingers firmly across the bridge of the nose. If not checked, the face should be buried in the handkerchief, during the act of sneezing, for obvious reasons.

ANECDOTES, PUNS AND REPARTEES.

Anecdotes should be seldom brought into a conversation. Puns are always regarded as vulgar. Repartee should be indulged in with moderation, and never kept up, as it degenerates into the vulgarity of an altercation.

A SWEET AND PURE BREATH.

The breath should be kept sweet and pure. Onions are the forbidden fruit, because of their offensiveness to the breath. No gentleman should go into the presence of ladies smelling of tobacco.

SMOKING.

It is neither respectful nor polite to smoke in the presence of ladies, even though they have given permission, nor should a gentleman smoke in a room which ladies are in the habit of frequenting. In those homes when the husband is permitted to smoke in any room of the house, the sons will follow the father's example, and the air of the rooms becomes like that of a public house.

SUPPRESSION OF EMOTION.

Suppression of undue emotion, whether of laughter, of anger, or of mortification, of disappointment, or of selfishness in any form, is a mark of good breeding.

A GOOD LISTENER.

To be a good listener is almost as great an art as to be a good talker; but it is not enough only to listen, you must endeavor to seem interested in the conversation of those who are talking. Only the low-bred allow their impatience to be manifest.

GIVE PRECEDENCE TO OTHERS.

Give precedence to those older or of higher social position than yourself, unless they required you to take the precedence, when it is better to obey than to refuse. Be more careful to give others their rank of precedence than to take your own.

BE MODERATE.

Always express your own opinions with modesty, and, if called upon, defend them, but without that warmth which may lead to hard feelings. Do not enter into argument. Having spoken your mind, and thus shown you are not cowardly in your beliefs and opinions, drop the subject and lead to some other topic. There is seldom any profit in idle discussion.

SINGING AND PLAYING IN SOCIETY.

A lady in company should never exhibit any anxiety to sing or play: but being requested to do so, if she intends to comply, she should do so at once, without waiting to be urged. If she refuses, she should do so in a manner that shall make her decision final. Having complied, she should not monopolize the evening with her performances, but make room for others.

RECEIVING AND MAKING PRESENTS.

Emerson says: "Our tokens of love are for the most part barbarous, cold and lifeless, because they do not represent our life. The only gift is a portion of thyself. Therefore let the farmer give his corn; the miner his gem; the sailor coral or shells; the painter his picture, and the poet his poem." To persons of refined nature, whatever the friend creates takes added value as part of themselves—part of their lives, as it were, having gone into it. People of the highest rank, abroad, will often accept, with gratitude, a bit of embroidery done by a friend, a poem inscribed to them by an author; a painting executed by some artist; who would not care for the most expensive bauble that was offered them. Mere costliness does not constitute the soul of a present; it is the kind feeling that it manifests which gives it its value. People who possess noble natures do not make gifts where they feel neither affection nor respect, but their gifts are bestowed out of the fullness of kind hearts

A present should be acknowledged without delay, but you must not follow it quickly by a return. It is to be taken for granted that a gift is intended to afford pleasure to the recipient, not to be regarded as a question of investment or exchange. Never allude to a present you have given, unless you have reason to believe that it has not been received by the person to whom it was sent

Unmarried ladies should not accept presents from gentlemen who are neither related nor engaged to them, nor indebted to them for some marked favors. A married lady may accept presents from a gentleman who is indebted to her for hospitality.

In presenting a book to a friend, do not write in it the name of the person to whom it is given. But this is a rule better honored in its breach than in its observance, when the giver of the book is its author.

Presents made by a married lady to a gentleman, should be in the name of both herself and her husband.

Never refuse a present if offered in kindness, unless the circumstances are such that you cannot, with propriety, receive it. Nor, in receiving a present, make such comments as would seem to indicate that your friend cannot afford to make the present. On the other hand, never make a present which you cannot afford to make. In that case the recipient, if he or she knows anything of your circumstances, will think that you had better kept it yourself.

GOVERNING OUR MOODS.

We should subdue our gloomy moods before we enter society. To look pleasantly and to speak kindly is a duty we owe to others. Neither should we afflict them with any dismal account of our health, state of mind or outward circumstances. Nevertheless, if another makes us the confidant of his woes, we should strive to appear sympathetic, and if possible help him to be stronger under them. A lady who shows by act, or expresses in plain, curt words, that the visit of another is unwelcome, may perhaps pride herself upon being no hypocrite. But she is, in reality, worse. She is grossly selfish. Courtesy requires her, for the time being, to forget her own feelings, and remember those of her visitor, and thus it is her duty to make that visitor happy while she remains.

A LADY DRIVING WITH A GENTLEMAN.

When a lady offers to drive a gentleman in her phaeton, he should walk to her house, if he accepts the invitation, unless, the distance being great, she should propose to call for him. In that case he will be on the watch, so as not to keep her waiting, and, if possible, meet her on the way.

AN INVITATION CANNOT BE RECALLED.

An invitation, once given, cannot be recalled, even from the best motives, without subjecting the one who recalls it to the charge of being either ignorant or regardless of all conventional rules of politeness. There is but one exception to this rule, and that is when the invitation has been delivered to the wrong person.

AVOID TALKING OF PERSONALITIES.

Avoid speaking of your birth, your travels and of all personal matters, to those who may misunderstand you, and consider it boasting. When induced to speak of them, do not dwell too long upon them, and do not speak boastfully.

ABOUT PERSONS' NAMES.

Do not speak of absent persons, who are not relatives or intimate friends, by their Christian names or sur-names, but always as Mr. ——, or Mrs. ——, or Miss ——. Never name anyone by the first letter of his name, as "Mr. C." Give a foreigner his name in full when speaking of him.

SHUN GOSSIP AND TALE-BEARING.

Gossip and tale-bearing are always a personal confes-sion either of malice or imbecility. The young of both sexes should not only shun these things, but, by the most thorough culture, relieve themselves from all temp-tation in that direction.

REMOVING THE HAT.

A gentleman never sits in the house with his hat on in the presence of ladies. Indeed, a gentleman instinc-tively removes his hat as soon as he enters a room, the habitual resort of ladies. A gentleman never retains

his hat in a theatre or other place of public entertain·
ment

TREATMENT OF INFERIORS.

Never affect superiority. In the company of an inferior never let him feel his inferiority. If you invite
an inferior as your guest, treat him with all the politeness and consideration you would show an equal.

INTRUDING ON PRIVACY.

Never enter a private room anywhere without knock-
ing. Sacredly respect the private property of others,
and let no curiosity tempt you to pry into letters, desks,
packets, trunks, or other belongings of another. It is
ill-mannered to read a written paper lying upon a table
or desk; whatever it may be, it is certainly no business
of yours. No person should ever look over the shoulder
of another who is reading or writing. You must not
question a servant or child upon family affairs. Never
betray an implied confidence, even if you have not been
bound to secrecy.

KEEPING ENGAGEMENTS.

Nothing is more rude than to make an engagement,
be it of business or pleasure, and break it. If your
memory is not sufficiently retentive to keep all the engagements you make, carry a little memorandum book,
and enter them there.

VALUE OF POLITENESS.

Chesterfield says: " As learning, honor and virtue
are absolutely necessary to gain you the esteem and

admiration of mankind, politeness and good-breeding are equally necessary to make you welcome and agreeable in conversation and common life. Great talents, such as honor, virtue, learning and arts, are above the generality of the world, who neither possess them themselves, nor judge of them rightly in others; but all people are judges of the lesser talents, such as civility, affability, and an obliging, agreeable address and manner; because they feel the good effects of them, as making society easy and pleasing."

ADAPTING YOURSELF TO OTHERS.

Conform your conduct as far as possible to the company you chance to be with, only do not throw yourself into improper company. It is better even to laugh at and join in with vulgarity, so that it do not degenerate into indecency, than to set yourself up as better, and better-mannered than those with whom you may chance to be associated. True politeness and genuine good manners often not only permit but absolutely demand a temporary violation of the ordinary obligations of etiquette.

A WOMAN'S GOOD NAME.

Let no man speak a word against a woman at any time, or mention a woman's name in any company where it should not be spoken. "Civility," says Lord Chesterfield, "is particularly due to all women; and remember that no provocation whatsoever can justify any man in not being civil to every woman; and the greatest man

would justly be reckoned a brute if he were not civil to
the meanest woman.   It is due to their sex, and is the
only protection they have against the superior strength
of ours."

DO NOT CONTRADICT.

Never directly contradict anyone.   Say, "I beg your
pardon, but I think you are mistaken or misinformed,"
or some such similar phrase which shall break the weight
of direct contradiction.   Where the matter is unimport-
ant it is better to let it pass without correction.

EXPRESSING UNFAVORABLE OPINIONS.

You should be exceedingly cautious about expressing
an unfavorable opinion relative to a young lady to a
young man who appears to be attracted by, and attentive to her.   If they should marry, the remembrance of
your observations will not be pleasurable to yourself nor
the married parties.

A CONVERSATION CHECKED.

If a person checks himself in a conversation, you
should not insist on hearing what he intended to say.
There is some good reason for checking himself, and it
might cause him unpleasant feelings to urge him to carry
out his first intentions.

VULGARITIES.

Some of the acts which may be classed as vulgarities
when committed in the presence of others are given:

To sit with your back to a person, without asking to
be excused

To stand or sit with the feet wide apart.

To hum, whistle or sing in suppressed tones.

To stand with the arms akimbo; to lounge or yawn, or to do anything which shows disrespect, selfishness or indifference.

To correct inaccuracies in the statements of others, or their modes of speech.

To use profane language, or stronger expression than the occasion justifies.

To chew tobacco and its unnecessary accompaniment, spitting, are vulgar in the extreme.

MISCELLANEOUS RULES.

A gentleman precedes a lady passing through a crowd; ladies precede gentlemen under ordinary circumstances.

Give your children, unless married, their Christian names only, or say "my daughter" or "my son," in speaking of them to any one except servants.

Ladies in escorting each other, never offer to take the arm.

Acknowledge an invitation to stop with a friend, or any unusual attention without delay.

Never boast of birth, money or friends, or of any superior advantages you may possess.

Never ridicule others, be the object of your ridicule present or absent.

Always show respect for the religious opinions and observances of others, no matter how much they may differ from your own.

You should never scratch your head, pick your teeth, clean your nails or pick your nose in company.

Never lean your head against the wall, as you may disgust your wife or hostess by soiling the paper of her room.

Never slam a door or stamp noisily on entering a room.

Always be punctual. You have no right to waste the time of others by making them wait for you.

Always hand a chair for a lady, pick up her glove and perform any little service she may seem to require.

Never attract attention to yourself by talking or laughing loudly in public gatherings.

Keep yourself quiet and composed under all circumstances. Do not get fidgety. If you feel that time drags heavily, do not let this be apparent to others by any visible sign of uneasiness.

Refrain from absent-mindedness in the presence of others. You pay them a poor compliment if you thus forget them.

Never refuse to accept an apology for an offense, and never hesitate to make one, if one is due from you.

Never answer another rudely or impatiently. Reply courteously, at whatever inconvenience to yourself.

Never intrude upon a business man or woman in business hours unless you wish to see them on business.

Never engage a person in private conversation in presence of others, nor make any mysterious allusions which no one else understands.

On entering a room, bow slightly as a general salutation, before speaking to each of the persons assembled.

Do not seem to notice by word or glance, the deformity of another.

To administer reproof to anyone in the presence of others is very impolite. To scold at any time is unwise.

Never undertake a commission for a friend and neglect to perform it.

Never play a practical joke upon anyone, or answer a serious remark by a flippant one.

Never lend a borrowed book, and never keep such a book a single day after you are done with it.

Never pass between two persons who are talking together; and never pass before persons when it is possible to pass behind them. When such an act is absolutely necessary, always apologize for so doing.

"Never speak of a man's virtues before his face, or his faults behind his back," is a maxim to be remembered.

Another maxim is, "In private watch your thoughts; in your family watch your temper; in society watch your tongue."

Never address a mere acquaintance by his or her Christian name. It is a presumption at which the acquaintance may take offense.

Haughtiness and contempt are among the habits to be avoided. The best way is to deal courteously with the rude as well as with the courteous.

In the presence of others, talk as little of yourself as possible, or of the business or profession in which you are engaged.

It shows a want of courtesy to consult your watch, either at home or abroad. If at home, it appears as though you were tired of your company, and wished them to be gone. If abroad, it appears as though the hours dragged heavily, and you were calculating how soon you would be released.

Do not touch or handle any of the ornaments in the house where you visit. They are intended to be admired, not handled by visitors.

Do not read in company. A gentleman or lady may, however, look over a book of engravings or a collection of photographs with propriety.

Every species of affectation should be avoided, as it is always detected, and exceedingly disagreeable.

WASHINGTON'S MAXIMS.

Mr. Sparks, in his biography of Washington, has given to the public a collection of Washington's directions as to personal conduct, which he called his "Rules of Civility and Decent Behavior in Company." We give these rules entire, as the reader may be interested in learning the principles which governed the conduct of the "Father of his Country."

Every action in company ought to be with some sign of respect to those present.

In the presence of others sing not to yourself with a humming voice, nor drum with your fingers or feet.

Speak not when others speak, sit not when others stand, and walk not when others stop.

Turn not your back to others, especially in speaking;

jog not the table or desk on which another reads or writes; lean not on anyone.

Be no flatterer, neither play with anyone that delights not to be played with.

Read no letters, books or papers in company; but when there is a necessity for doing it, you must not leave. Come not near the books or writings of anyone so as to read them unasked; also look not nigh when another is writing a letter.

Let your countenance be pleasant, but in serious matters somewhat grave.

Show not yourself glad at the misfortune of another, though he were your enemy.

They that are in dignity or office have in all places precedency, but whilst they are young, they ought to respect those that are their equals in birth or other qualities, though they have no public charge.

It is good manners to prefer them to whom we speak before ourselves, especially if they be above us.

Let your discourse with men of business be short and comprehensive.

In visiting the sick do not presently play the physician if you be not knowing therein.

In writing or speaking, give to every person his due title according to his degree and the custom of the place.

Strive not with your superiors in argument, but always submit your judgment to others with modesty.

Undertake not to teach your equal in the art he himself professes; it savors arrogancy.

When a man does all he can though it succeeds not well, blame not him that did it.

Being to advise or reprehend anyone, consider whether it ought to be in public or in private, presently or at some other time, also in what terms to do it; and in reproving show no signs of choler, but do it with sweetness and mildness.

Mock not nor jest at anything of importance; break no jests that are sharp or biting, and if you deliver anything witty or pleasant, abstain from laughing thereat yourself.

Wherein you reprove another be unblamable yourself, for example is more prevalent than precept.

Use no reproachful language against any one, neither curses or revilings.

Be not hasty to believe flying reports to the disparagement of anyone.

In your apparel be modest, and endeavor to accommodate nature rather than procure admiration. Keep to the fashion of your equals, such as are civil and orderly with respect to time and place.

Play not the peacock, looking everywhere about you to see if you be well decked, if your shoes fit well, if your stockings set neatly and clothes handsomely.

Associate yourself with men of good quality if you esteem your reputation, for it is better to be alone than in bad company.

Let your conversation be without malice or envy, for it is a sign of a tractable and commendable nature; and in all cases of passion admit reason to govern.

Be not immodest in urging your friend to discover a secret.

Utter not base and frivolous things amongst grown and learned men, nor very difficult questions or subjects amongst the ignorant, nor things hard to be believed.

Speak not of doleful things in time of mirth nor at the table; speak not of melancholy things, as death and wounds; and if others mention them, change, if you can, the discourse. Tell not your dreams but to your intimate friends.

Break not a jest when none take pleasure in mirth. Laugh not aloud, nor at all without occasion. Deride no man's misfortunes, though there seem to be some cause.

Speak not injurious words, neither in jest nor earnest. Scoff at none, although they give occasion.

Be not forward, but friendly and courteous, the first to salute, hear and answer, and be not pensive when it is time to converse.

Detract not from others, but neither be excessive in commending.

Go not thither where you know not whether you shall be welcome or not. Give not advice without being asked; and when desired, do it briefly.

If two contend together, take not the part of either unconstrained, and be not obstinate in your opinions; in things indifferent be of the major side.

Reprehend not the imperfection of others, for that belongs to parents, masters and superiors.

Gaze not on the marks or blemishes of others, and ask not how they came. What you may speak in secret to your friend deliver not before others.

Speak not in an unknown tongue in company, but in your own language; and that as those of quality do, and not as the vulgar. Sublime matters treat seriously.

Think before you speak; pronounce not imperfectly, nor bring out your words too heartily, but orderly and distinctly.

When another speaks, be attentive yourself, and disturb not the audience. If any hesitate in his words, help him not, nor prompt him without being desired; interrupt him not, nor answer him till his speech be ended.

Treat with men at fit times about business, and whisper not in the company of others.

Make no comparisons; and if any of the company be commended for any brave act of virtue, commend not another for the same.

Be not apt to relate news if you know not the truth thereof. In discoursing of things that you have heard, name not your author always. A secret discover not.

Be not curious to know the affairs of others, neither approach to those who speak in private.

Undertake not what you cannot perform; but be careful to keep your promise.

When you deliver a matter, do it without passion and indiscretion, however mean the person may be you do it to.

When your superiors talk to anybody, hear them; neither speak nor laugh.

In disputes be not so desirous to overcome as not to give liberty to each one to deliver his opinion, and submit to the judgment of the major part, especially if they are judges of the dispute.

Be not tedious in discourse, make not many digressions, nor repeat often the same matter of discourse.

Speak no evil of the absent, for it is unjust.

Be not angry at table, whatever happens; and if you have reason to be so show it not; put on a cheerful countenance, especially if there be strangers, for good humor makes one dish a feast.

Set not yourself at the upper end of the table; but if it be your due, or the master of the house will have it so, contend not, lest you should trouble the company.

When you speak of God or his attributes, let it be seriously, in reverence and honor, and obey your natural parents.

Let your recreations be manful, not sinful.

Labor to keep alive in your breast that little spark of celestial fire called conscience.

CHAPTER XXIV.

Anniversary Weddings.

HE custom of celebrating anniversary weddings has, of late years, been largely practiced, and they have become a very pleasant means of social reunion among the relatives and friends of both husband and wife. Often this is the only reason for celebrating them, and the occasion is sometimes taken advantage of to give a large party, of a more informal nature than could be given under other circumstances. The occasion becomes one of the memorable events in the life of the couple whose wedding anniversary is celebrated. It is an occasion for recalling the happy event which brought to each a new existence, and changed the current of their lives. It is an occasion for them to receive congratulations upon their past married life, and wishes for many additional years of wedded bliss.

Upon these occasions the married couple sometimes appear in the costumes worn by them on their wedding day, which they have preserved with punctilious care, and when many years have intervened the quaintness and oddity of the style of dress from the prevailing style is a matter of interest, and the occasion of pleasant comments. The couple receive their guests together, who upon entering the drawing-room, where they are receiving, extend to them their congratulations and wishes for continued prosperity and happiness. The various anniversaries are designated by special names, indicative of the presents suitable on each occasion, should guests deem it advisable to send presents. It may be here stated that it is entirely optional with parties invited as to whether any presents are sent or taken. At the earlier anniversaries, much pleasantry and amusement is occasioned by presenting unique and fantastic articles, gotten up for the occasion. When this is contemplated, care should be taken that they should not be such as are liable to give offense to a person of sensitive nature.

THE PAPER, COTTON AND LEATHER WEDDING.

The first anniversay of the wedding-day is called the Paper Wedding, the second the Cotton Wedding, and the third the Leather Wedding. The invitations to the first should be issued on a grey paper, representing thin cardboard. Presents, if given should be solely articles made of paper.

The invitations for the cotton wedding should be neatly printed on fine white cloth, and presents should be of articles of cotton cloth.

For the leather wedding invitations should be issued upon leather, tastily gotten up, and presents, of course, should be articles made of leather.

THE WOODEN WEDDING.

The wooden wedding is the fifth anniversay of the marriage. The invitations should be upon thin cards of wood, or they may be written on a sheet of wedding note paper, and a card of wood enclosed in the envelope. The presents suitable to this occasion are most numerous, and may range from a wooden paper knife or trifling article for kitchen use up to a complete set of parlor or kitchen furniture.

THE TIN WEDDING.

The tenth anniversary of the marriage is called the tin wedding. The invitations for this anniversary may be made upon cards covered with a tin card inclosed. The guests, if they desire to accompany their congratulations with appropriate presents, have the whole list of articles manufactured by the tinner's art from which to select.

THE CRYSTAL WEDDING.

The crystal wedding is the fifteenth anniversary. Invitations may be on thin, transparent paper, or colored sheets of prepared gelatine, or on ordinary wedding note-paper, enclosing a sheet of mica. The guests make their offerings to their host and hostess of trifles of glass, which may be more or less valuable, as the donor feels inclined.

THE CHINA WEDDING.

The china wedding occurs on the twentieth anniversary of the wedding-day. Invitations should be issued on exceedingly fine, semi-transparent note-paper or cards. Various articles for the dining or tea-table or for the toilet-stand, vases or mantel ornaments, all are appropriate on this occasion.

THE SILVER WEDDING.

The silver wedding occurs on the twenty-fifth marriage anniversary. The invitations issued for this wedding should be upon the finest note-paper, printed in bright silver, with monogram or crest upon both paper and envelope, in silver also. If presents are offered by any of the guests, they should be of silver, and may be the merest trifles, or more expensive, as the means and inclinations of the donors incline.

THE GOLDEN WEDDING.

The close of the fiftieth year of married life brings round the appropriate time for the golden wedding. Fifty years of married happiness may indeed be crowned with gold. The invitations for this anniversary celebration should be printed on the finest note-paper in gold, with crest or monogram on both paper and envelopes in highly-burnished gold. The presents, if any are offered, are also in gold.

THE DIAMOND WEDDING.

Rarely, indeed, is a diamond wedding celebrated. This should be held on the seventy-fifth anniversary of the marriage-day. So seldom are these occurrences that custom has sanctioned no particular style or form to be observed in the invitations. They might be issued upon diamond-shaped cards, enclosed in envel. opes of a corresponding shape. There can be no general offering of presents at such a wedding, since diamonds in any number are beyond the means of most persons.

PRESENTS AT ANNIVERSARY WEDDINGS.

It is not, as before stated, required that an invitation to an anniversary wedding be acknowledged by a valuable gift, or indeed by any. The donors on such occasions are usually only members of the family or intimate friends, and may act at their own discretion in the matter of giving presents.

On the occasion of golden or silver weddings, it is not amiss to have printed at the bottom of the invitation the words "No presents," or to enclose a card announcing—

"It is preferred that no wedding gifts be offered."

INVITATIONS TO ANNIVERSARY WEDDINGS.

The invitations to anniversary weddings may vary something in their wording, according to the fancy of the writer, but they are all similar. They should give the date of the marriage and the anniversary. They

19

may or may not give the name of the husband at the
right-hand side and the maiden name of the wife at the
left.   What the anniversary is should also be indicated.
The following form will serve as a model:

1855=1880.

*The pleasure of your company is
requested at the*

Silver Wedding Reception

of

*Mr and Mrs. Cyrus Jennings,
On Thursday evening, November
13th, at nine o'clock.*

25 Jackson Avenue.

R. S. V. P.

A proper variation will make this form equally suitable for any of the other anniversary weddings.

MARRIAGE CEREMONY AT ANNIVERSARY WEDDINGS.

It is not unusual to have the marriage ceremony repeated at these anniversary weddings, especially at the
silver or golden wedding.   The earliest anniversaries
are almost too trivial occasions upon which to introduce
this ceremony.   The clergyman who officiates may so
change the exact words of the marriage ceremony as to
render them appropriate to the occasion.

CHAPTER XXV.

Births and Christenings.

PON the announcement of the birth of a child, the lady friends of the mother send her their cards, with inquiries after her health. As soon as she is strong enough to permit, the mother returns her own card to all from whom she received cards and inquiries, with "thanks for kind inquiries." Her lady friends then make personal visits, but gentlemen do not call upon the mother on these occasions. If they wish, they may pay their visits to the father, and inquire after the health of the mother and child.

NAMING THE CHILD.

It becomes an all-important matter to the parents, what name they shall give to the newly-born child, and as this is a matter which may also concern the latter at some future day, it becomes an object of solicitude, until a suitable name is settled upon. The custom in

Scotland is to name the first son after the father's father, and the first daughter after the mother's mother, the second son after the father, the second daughter after the mother, and succeeding children after other near relations. This perpetuates family names, and if they are persons whose names are regarded as worthy of perpetuation, it may be considered a good custom to follow. With some it is customary to name children after some renowned person, either living or dead. There are objections to this plan, however, for if the person be still living, he may commit some act which will bring opprobrium to his name, and so cause both the parent and child to be ashamed of bearing such a disgraced name. If the person after whom the child is named be dead, it may be that the child's character may be so entirely different from the person who formerly bore it, that the name shall be made a reproach or satire.

The plan of reviving the old Saxon names has been adopted by some, and it has been claimed that the names of Edgar, Edwin, Arthur, Alfred, Ethel, Maud, Edith, Theresa, and many others of the Saxon names are pleasant sounding and strong, and a desirable contrast to the Fannies, Mamies, Minnies, Lizzies, Sadies, and other petty diminutives which have taken the place of better sounding and stronger names.

THE CHRISTENING.

The christening and the baptism usually occur at the same time, and are regulated according to the practices of the special church where the parents attend worship. As these are quite varied, it will be sufficient only to indicate the forms and customs which society imposes at such times.

GODPARENTS OR SPONSORS.

In the Episcopal Church there are two, and somtimes three, godparents or sponsors. If the child is a boy, there are two godfathers and one godmother. If a girl, two godmothers and one godfather. The persons selected for godparents should be near relatives or friends of long and close standing, and should be members of the same church into which the child is baptized. The maternal grandmother and paternal grandfather usually act as sponsors for the first child, the maternal grandfather and paternal grandmother for the second. A person invited to act as godparent should not refuse without good reason. If the grandparents are not selected, it is an act of courtesy to select the godmother, and allow her to designate the godfather. Young persons should not stand sponsors to an infant; and none should offer to act unless their superior position warrants them in so doing.

PRESENTS FROM GODFATHERS.

The sponsors must make their godchild a present of some sort—a silver mug, a knife, spoon and fork, a handsomely-bound bible, or perhaps a costly piece of lace or embroidery suitable for infants' wear. The godfather may give a cup, with name engraved, and the godmother the christening robe and cap.

THE CHRISTENING CEREMONY.

Upon entering the church the babe is carried first in the arms of its nurse. Next come the sponsors, and after them the father and mother, if she is able to be present. The invited guests follow. In taking their places the sponsors stand, the godfather on the right and the godmother on the left of the child. When the question is asked, " Who are the sponsors for the child ?" the proper persons should merely bow their heads without speaking.

In the Roman Catholic Church baptism takes place at as early a date as possible. If the child does not seem to be strong, a priest is sent for at once, and the ceremony is performed at the mother's bedside. If, on the other hand, the child is healthy, it is taken to the church within a few days after its birth. In Protestant churches the ceremony of baptism is usually deferred until the mother is able to be present. If the ceremony is performed at home, a carriage must be sent for the clergyman, and retained to convey him back again after the ceremony is concluded. A luncheon may follow the christening, though a collation of cake and wine will fill all the requirements of etiquette. It is the duty of the godfather to propose the health of the infant.

PRESENTS FROM GUESTS.

Friends invited to a christening should remember the babe in whose honor they convene, by some trifling gift.

Gentlemen may present an article or silver, ladies something of their own manufacture.

THE HERO OF THE OCCASION.

It should be remembered that the baby is the person of the greatest importance on these occasions, and the guests should give it a large share of attention and praise. The parents, however, must not make this duty too onerous to their guests by keeping a tired, fretful child on exhibition. It is better to send it at once to the care of the nurse as soon as the ceremony is over.

FEES TO THE CLERGYMAN.

Though the Church performs the ceremony of baptism gratuitously, the parents should, if they are able, make a present to the officiating clergyman, or, through him a donation to the poor of the neighborhood.

CHAPTER XXVI.

𝔉𝔲𝔫𝔢𝔯𝔞𝔩𝔰.

HE saddest of all ceremonies is that attendant upon the death of relatives and friends, and it becomes us to show, in every possible way, the utmost consideration for the feelings of the bereaved, and the deepest respect for the melancholy occasion. Of late the forms of ostentation at funerals are gradually diminishing, and by some people of intelligence, even mourning habiliments are rejected in whole or in part.

INVITATION TO A FUNERAL.

It is customary in cities to give the notice of death and announcement of a funeral through the daily newspapers, though sometimes when such announcement may not reach all friends in time, invitations to the funeral are sent to personal and family friends of the deceased. In villages where there is no daily paper, such invitations are often issued.

Private invitations are usually printed on fine small note paper, with a heavy black border, and in such form as the following:

Yourself and family are respect-fully invited to attend the funeral of Mr. James B. Southey, from his late residence, No. 897 Williams avenue, on Friday, October 18, at 8 o'clock P. M. (or from St. Paul's Episcopal Church), *to proceed to Woodland Cemetery.*

When an announcement of a death is sent to a friend or relative at a distant point, it is usual to telegraph or to write the notice of death, time and place of funeral, to allow the friend an opportunity to arrive before the services.

It is a breach of good manners not to accept an invitation to a funeral, when one is sent.

ARRANGEMENTS FOR THE FUNERAL.

It is customary to trust the details of the arrangements for the funeral to some relative or friend of the family, and if there be no friend who can perform this duty, it can be safely left with the undertaker to perform the painful duties of master of ceremonies. It is prudent to name a limit for the expenses of the funeral, and the means of the family should always govern these. Pomp and display should always be avoided, as they are out of keeping with the solemn occasion, and inconsistent with real grief. At the funeral some one should act as usher to seat the friends who attend.

THE HOUSE OF MOURNING.

Upon entering the house of mourning, a gentleman should always remove his hat in the hall, and not replace it until he is about to depart. No calls of condolence should be made upon the bereaved family while the dead remains in the house, and members of the family may be excused from receiving any but their most intimate friends at that time.

There should be no loud talking or confusion while the body remains in the house. All differences and quarrels must be forgotten in the house of mourning, and personal enemies who meet at a funeral must treat each other with respect and dignity. The bell knob or door handle is draped with black crape, with a black ribbon tied on, if the deceased is married or advanced in years, and with a white ribbon, if young or unmarried.

THE FUNERAL SERVICES.

If the services are held at the house, some near friend or relative will receive the guests. The immediate members of the family and near relatives should take a final view of the corpse just before the arrival of the guests, and should not make their appearance again until the services are about to commence. It is becoming customary now to reserve a room of the house adjoining that in which the services are held, for the exclusive use of the near relatives and members of the family during the services. Then the clergyman takes his position at the door between the two rooms while conducting the services. As guests arrive, they are requested to take a last look at the corpse before seating themselves, and upon the conclusion of the services the coffin lid is closed, and the remains are borne to the hearse. The custom of opening the coffin at the church to allow all who attend to take a final look at the corpse, is rapidly coming into disfavor. The friends who desire it are requested to view the corpse at the house, before it is taken to the church.

If, however, the deceased is a person of great prominence in the community, and the house is not able to accommodate the large numbers who desire to take a last look at the face of the deceased, then, perhaps, it may be well that the coffin should be opened at the church.

THE PALL-BEARERS.

The pall-bearers, usually six, but sometimes eight, when the deceased is a person of considerable prominence, are generally chosen from the intimate acquaintances of the deceased, and of nearly the same age. If they walk to the cemetery, they take their position in equal numbers on either side of the hearse. If they ride, their carriage or carriages precede the hearse.

ORDER OF THE PROCESSION.

The carriages containing the clergyman and pall-bearers precede the hearse, immediately following which are the carriages of the nearest relatives, more distant relatives and friends respectively. When societies or masonic bodies take part in the procession they precede the hearse.

The horse of a deceased mounted military officer, fully equipped and draped in mourning, will be led immediately after the hearse. As the mourners pass out to enter the carriage, the guests stand with uncovered heads. No salutations are given or received. The person who officiates as master of ceremonies, assists the mourners to enter and alight from the carriages. At the cemetery the clergyman or priest walks in advance of the coffin. In towns and villages where the cemetery is near at hand and the procession goes on foot, the men should go with uncovered heads, if the weather permit, the hat being held in the right hand. Guests return to their respective homes after the services at the grave.

FLORAL DECORATIONS.

The usual decorations of the coffin are flowers, tastefully arranged in a beautiful wreath for a child or young person, and a cross for a married person, which are placed upon the coffin. These flowers should mostly be white. Near friends of the deceased may send beautiful floral devices, if they wish, as a mark of their esteem for the deceased, which should be sent in time to be used for decorative purposes.

OTHER DECORATIONS.

A person of rank generally bears some insignia upon his coffin. Thus a deceased army or naval officer will have his coffin covered with the national flag, and his hat, epaulettes, sword and sash laid upon the lid. The regalia of a deceased officer of the Masonic or Odd Fellows' fraternity is often placed upon the coffin.

CALLS UPON THE BEREAVED FAMILY.

About a week after the funeral, friends call upon the bereaved family, and acquaintances call within a month. The calls of the latter are not repeated until cards of acknowledgment have been received by the family, the leaving of which announces that they are ready to see their friends. It is the custom for friends to wear no bright colors when making their calls of condolence. In making first calls of condolence, none but most intimate friends ask to see the family. Short notes of condolence, expressing the deepest sympathy, are usually accepted, and help to comfort stricken hearts. Formal notes of condolence are no longer sent. Those who have known anything of the unsounded depths of sorrow do not attempt consolation. All that they attempt to do is to find words wherein to express their deep sympathy with the grief-stricken ones.

SECLUSION OF THE BEREAVED FAMILY.

No member of the immediate family of the deceased will leave the house between the time of the death and the funeral. A lady friend will be commissioned to make all necessary purchases, engage seamstresses, etc. It is not desirable to enshroud ourselves in gloom after a bereavement, however great it may be, and consequently no prescribed period of seclusion can be given. Real grief needs no appointed time for seclusion. It is the duty of every one to interest himself or herself in accustomed objects of care as soon as it is possible to make the exertion; for, in fulfilling our duties to the living, we best show the strength of our affection for the dead, as well as our submission to the will of Him who knows what is better for our dear ones than we can know or dream.

CHAPTER XXVII.

Washington Etiquette.

ERTAIN local rules have been recognized in society at Washington, from the fact that a gentleman's social position is acquired by virtue of certain offices which he holds, and the social status of woman is also determined by the official rank of her husband.

THE PRESIDENT.

As the President of the United States holds the highest official rank in political life, so is he also by virtue of that office, awarded precedence in social life. There is no necessity of special formalities to form his acquaintance, and he receives calls without being under any obligation to return them. He may be addressed either as "Mr. President," or "Your Excellency." Sometimes he gives up the morning hours to receiving calls, and at such times precedence is given to such people as have business with him, over parties who go to make a formal call. In either case, the caller is shown to the room occupied by the President's secretaries, presents his card and waits his turn to be admitted. If the caller has no business, but goes out of curiosity, he pays his respects and withdraws to make room for others. It is better in making a private call, to secure the company of some official or some friend of the President to introduce you.

RECEPTIONS AT THE WHITE HOUSE.

Stated receptions are given at the White House by the President during sessions of congress, and all are at liberty to attend them. Sometimes these are morning, and sometimes evening, receptions. Upon entering the reception room, the caller gives his name to the usher, who announces it, and upon approaching the President is introduced, by some official to whom the duty is assigned, both to the President and to the members of his family who receive with him. The callers pass on, after being introduced, mingle in social intercourse and view the various rooms until ready to depart. If a caller wishes he may leave his card.

The same rules of etiquette prevail at state dinners given by the President as at any formal dinner, precedence being given to guests according to official rank and dignity. An invitation by the President must be accepted, and it is admissible to break any other engagement already made; however, it is necessary to explain the cause, in order to avoid giving offense. It is not regarded as discourteous to break an engagement for this reason.

The wife of the President is not under obligation to return calls, though she may visit those whom she wishes to favor with such attentions. Other members of the President's family may receive and return calls.

NEW-YEAR'S RECEPTIONS AT THE WHITE HOUSE.

As the New-Year's receptions at the White House are the most ceremonious occasions of the executive mansion, it is the custom of the ladies who attend them to appear in the most elegant toilets suited to a morning reception. Members of foreign legations appear in the court dresses of their respective countries on this occasion, in paying their respects to the President of the United States.

ORDER OF OFFICIAL RANK.

Next in rank to the President come the Chief Justice, the Vice-President and the Speaker of the House of Representatives. These receive first visits from all others. The General of the army and the Admiral of the navy come next in the order of official rank. Members of the House of Representatives call first on all the officials named. The wife of any official is entitled to the same social precedence as her husband. Among officers of the army and navy, the Lieutenant-General corresponds to the Vice-Admiral, the Major-General to Rear-Admiral, Brigadier-General to Commodore, Colonel to Captain in the navy, and so on through the lower grades.

THE CABINET OFFICERS.

The officers of the cabinet, comprising the Secretaries of State, the Treasury, the War, the Navy, the

Postmaster-General, the Secretary of the Interior and Attorney-General, expect to receive calls, aud as all the officers are of the same rank and dignity, it is only on occasions of State ceremonies that an order of preference is observed, which is as above given. The wives of the cabinet officers, or the ladies of their household, have onerous social duties to perform. They hold receptions every Wednesday during the season, which lasts from the first of January to Lent, when their houses are open to all who choose to favor them with a call, and on these occasions refreshments are served. The ladies of the family are expected to return these calls, at which time they leave the card of the cabinet officer, and an invitation to an evening reception. The cabinet officers are expected to entertain Senators, Representatives, Justices of the Supreme Court, members of the diplomatic corps and distinguished visitors at Washington, as well as the ladies of their respective families. The visiting hours at the capital are usually from two until half-past five. The labor and fatigue which social duties require of the ladies of the family of a cabinet officer are fairly appalling. To stand for hours during receptions at her own house, to stand at a series of entertainments at the houses of others, whose invitation courtesy requires should be accepted, and to return in person calls made upon her, are a few of the duties of the wife of a cabinet officer.

HOW TO ADDRESS THE OFFICIALS.

When writing to the different officials, the President is addressed "His Excellency, the President of the

United States;" the members of the cabinet "The Honorable, the Secretary of State," etc., giving each his proper title; the Vice-President, "The Honorable, the Vice-President of the United States." In a ceremonious note, words must not be abbreviated. In conversation the Speaker of the House of Representatives is addressed as "Mr. Speaker;" a member of the cabinet as "Mr. Secretary;" a senator as "Mr. Senator;" a member of the House of Representatives as "Mister," unless he has some other title; but he is introduced as "The Honorable Mr. Burrows, of Michigan." The custom is becoming prevalent of addressing the wives of officials with the prefixed titles of their husbands, as "Mrs. General Sherman," "Mrs. Senator Thurman," "Mrs. Secretary Evarts."

THE FIRST TO VISIT.

The custom of first visits or calls at the capital is that residents shall make the first call on strangers, and among the latter those arriving first upon those coming later. Foreign ministers, however, in order to make themselves known, call first upon the members of the cabinet, which is returned.

SENATORS AND REPRESENTATIVES.

It is entirely optional with Senators, Representatives and all other officials except the President and members of his cabinet, whether they entertain. They act upon their own pleasure in the matter.

CHAPTER XXVIII.

Foreign Titles.

N this country, where everybody possesses one and the same title, that of a citizen of this Republic, no one can claim a superiority of rank and title. Not so in European countries, where the right of birth entitles a person to honor, rank and title. And as our citizens are constantly visiting foreign countries, it is well to understand something of titles and ranks and their order of precedence.

ROYALTY.

In England, the king and queen are placed at the top of the social structure. The mode by which they are addressed is in the form "Your Majesty."

The Prince of Wales, the heir-apparent to the throne, stands second in dignity. The other children are all known during their minority as princes and princesses. The eldest princess is called the crown princess. Upon their majority the younger sons have the title of duke bestowed upon them, and the daughters retain that of princesses, adding to it the title of their husbands. They are all designated as "Their Royal Highnesses."

THE NOBILITY.

A duke who inherits the title from his father, stands one grade below a royal duke. The wife of a duke is known as a duchess. They are both addressed as "Your Grace. The eldest son is a marquis until he inherits the higher title of his father. His wife is a marchioness. The younger sons are lords by courtesy, and the daughters are distinguished by having "Lady" prefixed to their Christian names. Earls and barons are both spoken of as lords and their wives as ladies, though the latter are by right respectively countesses and baronesses. The daughters of the former are "ladies," the younger sons of both "honorables." The earl occupies the higher position of the two in the peerage.

These complete the list of nobility, unless we include bishops, who are lords in right of their ecclesiastical office, but whose title is not hereditary.

All these are entitled to seats in the upper House of Parliament.

THE GENTRY.

Baronets are known as "Sirs," and their wives receive the title of "Lady;" but they are only commoners of a higher degree, though there are families who have borne their title for many successive generations who would not exchange it for a recently created peerage.

A clergyman, by right of his calling, stands on an equality with all commoners, a bishop with all peers.

ESQUIRE.

The title of Esquire, which is only an empty compliment in this country, has special significance in England. The following in that country have a legal right to the title:

The sons of peers, whether known in common conversation as lords or honorables.

The eldest sons of peers' sons, and their eldest sons in perpetual succession.

All the sons of baronets.

All esquires of the Knights of the Bath.

Lords of manors, chiefs of clans and other tenants of the crown *in capite* are esquires by prescription.

Esquires created to that rank by patent, and their eldest sons in perpetual succession.

Esquires by office, such as justices of the peace while on the roll, mayors of towns during mayoralty, and sheriffs of counties (who retain the title for life).

Members of the House of Commons.

Barristers-at-law.

Bachelors of divinity, law and physic.

All who in commissions signed by the sovereign, are ever styled esquires retain that designation for life.

IMPERIAL RANK.

Emperors and empresses rank higher than kings. The sons and daughters of the emperor of Austria are called archdukes and archduchesses, the names being handed down from the time when the ruler of that country claimed for himself no higher title than that of archduke. The emperor of Russia is known as the czar, the name being identical with the Roman cæsar and the German kaiser. The heir-apparent to the Russian throne is the czarowitch.

EUROPEAN TITLES.

Titles in continental Europe are so common and so frequently unsustained by landed and moneyed interests, that they have not that significance which they hold in England. A count may be a penniless scamp, depending upon the gambling-table for a precarious subsistence, and looking out for the chance of making a wealthy marriage.

A German baron may be a good, substantial, unpretending man, something after the manner of an American farmer. A German prince or duke, since the absorption of the smaller principalities of Germany by Prussia, may have nothing left him but a barren title and a meagre rent-roll. The Italian prince is even of less account than the German one, since his rent-roll is too frequently lacking altogether, and his only inheritance may be a grand but decayed palace, without means sufficient to keep it in repair or furnish it properly.

PRESENTATION AT THE COURT OF ST JAMES.

It is frequently a satisfaction to an American to be presented to the Queen during a sojourn in England, and

as the Queen is really an excellent woman, worthy of all
honor, not only can there be no valid cause for objection to such presentation, but it may well be looked
upon as an honor to be sought for.

THOSE ELIGIBLE TO PRESENTATION AT COURT.

The nobility, with their wives and daughters, are eligible to presentation at court, unless there be some grave
moral objection, in which case, as it has ever been the
aim of the good and virtuous Queen to maintain a high
standard of morality within her court, the objectionable
parties are rigidly excluded. The clergy, naval and
military officers, physicians and barristers and the
squirearchy, with their wives and daughters, have also
the right to pay their personal respects to their queen.
Those of more democratic professions, such as solici-
tors, merchants and mechanics, have not, as a rule, that
right, though wealth and connection have recently
proven an open sesame at the gates of St. James. Any
person who has been presented at court may present a
friend in his or her turn. A person wishing to be presented, must beg the favor from the friend or relative
of the highest rank he or she may possess.

PRELIMINARIES TO PRESENTATION.

Any nobleman or gentleman who proposes to be presented to the queen, must leave at the lord chamberlain's
office before twelve o'clock, two days before the levee,
a card with his name written thereon, and with the
name of the nobleman or gentleman by whom he is to

be presented. In order to carry out the existing regulation that no presentation can be made at a levee except by a person actually attending that levee, it is also necessary that a letter from the nobleman or gentleman who is to make the presentation, stating it to be his intention to be present, should accompany the presentation card above referred to, which will be submitted to the queen for Her Majesty's approbation. These regulations of the lord chamberlain must be implicitly obeyed.

Directions at what gate to enter and where the carriages are to stop are always printed in the newspapers. These directions apply with equal force to ladies and to gentlemen.

The person to be presented must provide himself or herself with a court costume, which for men consists partly of knee-breeches and hose, for women of an ample court train. These costumes are indispensable, and can be hired for the occasion.

THE PRESENTATION.

It is desirable to be early to escape the crowd. When the lady leaves her carriage, she must leave everything in the shape of a cloak or scarf behind her. Her train must be carefully folded over her left arm as she enters the long gallery of St. James, where she waits her turn for presentation.

The lady is at length ushered into the presence-chamber, which is entered by two doors. She goes in at the one indicated to her, dropping her train as she passes the threshold, which train is instantly spread out by the wands of the lords-in-waiting. The lady then walks forward towards the sovereign or the person who represents the sovereign. The card on which her name is inscribed is then handed to another lord-in-waiting, who reads the name aloud. When she arrives just before His or Her Majesty, she should courtesy as low as possible, so as to almost kneel.

If the lady presented be a peeress or a peer's daughter, the queen kisses her on the forehead. If only a commoner, then the queen extends her hand to be kissed by the lady presented, who, having done so, rises, courtesies to each of the other members of the royal family present, and then passes on. She must keep her face turned toward the sovereign as she passes to and through the door leading from the presence-chamber.

CHAPTER XXIX.

𝔅usiness.

N the chapter on "Our Manners," we have spoken of the importance of civility and politeness as a means of success to the business and professional man. It is in the ordinary walks of life, in the most trivial affairs that a man's real charater is shown, and consequently every man, whatever may be his calling, will do well to give due attention to those trivial affairs which, in his daily association with men of the world, will give him a reputation of being cold, austere, and unapproachable, or warm-hearted, genial, and sympathetic.

FORM GOOD HABITS.

It is important for the young man learning business, or just getting a start in business, to form correct habits, and especially of forming the habit of being polite to all with whom he has business relations, showing the same courteous treatment to men or women, poorly or plainly dressed, as though they were attired in the most costly of garments. A man who forms habits of politeness and gentlemanly treatment of everybody in early life, has acquired the good-will of all with whom he has ever been brought into social or business relations. He should also guard against such habits as profanity, the use of tobacco and intoxicating liquors, if he would gain and retain the respect of the best portion of the community, and should, if possible, cultivate the habit of being cheerful at all times and in all places.

KEEP YOUR TEMPER.

In discussing business matters, never lose your temper, even though your opponent in a controversy should become angry, and in the heat of discussion make rude and disagreeable remarks and charges. By a calm and dignified bearing and courteous treatment you will conquer his rudeness.

HONESTY THE BEST POLICY.

"Honesty is the best policy," is a maxim which merchants and tradesmen will find as true as it is trite, and no tradesman who wishes to retain his customers and his reputation will knowingly misrepresent the quality of his goods. It is not good policy for a merchant or clerk, in selling goods, to tell the customer what they cost, as, in a majority of cases, he will not be believed.

THE EXAMPLE OF A MERCHANT PRINCE.

The value of politeness to a merchant is nowhere more clearly shown than in the case of the late A. T. Stewart, the merchant prince of New York. He not only treated every customer he waited upon with the utmost courtesy, but he demanded it of every employe, and sought for men possessing every quality of character tending to secure this suavity of manner, in the selection of his salesmen and clerks. He required them to observe rigidly all rules and forms of politeness, and would allow no partiality shown to people on account of their dress, those clad in humble apparel being treated with the same affability and politeness as those richly dressed. Everybody who entered his store was sure of receiving kind and courteous treatment. This may, or may not, have been his secret of success, but it certainly gained and retained for him a large custom, and was one element in his character which can be highly commended. And every merchant will be judged of by his customers in proportion to the courteous treatment they receive from him, or from clerks in his store. The lawyer or the doctor will also acquire popularity and patronage as he exhibits courteous and kind treatment to all with whom he comes into social or business relations.

BREAKING AN APPOINTMENT.

Do not break an appointment with a business man, if possible to avoid it, for if you do, the party with whom you made it may have reason to think that you are not a man of your word, and it may also cause him great annoyance, and loss of time. If, however, it becomes absolutely necessary to do so, you should inform him beforehand, either by a note or by a special messenger, giving reasons for its non-fulfillment.

PROMPTLY MEETING NOTES AND DRAFTS.

Every business man knows the importance of meeting promptly his notes and drafts, for to neglect it is disastrous to his reputation as a prompt business man. He should consider, also, apart from this, that he is under a moral obligation to meet these payments promptly when due. If circumstances which you cannot control prevent this, write at once to your creditor, stating plainly and frankly the reason why you are unable to pay him, and when you will be able. He will accommodate you if he has reason to believe your statements.

PROMPT PAYMENT OF BILLS.

If a bill is presented to you for payment, you should, if it is correct, pay it as promptly as though it were a note at the bank already due. The party who presents the bill may be in need of money, and should receive what is his due when he demands it. On the other hand, do not treat a man who calls upon you to pay a bill, or to whom you send to collect a bill, as though you were under no obligation to him. While you have a right to expect him to pay it, still its prompt payment may have so inconvenienced him as to deserve your thanks.

GENERAL RULES.

If you chance to see a merchant's books or papers left open before you, it is not good manners to look over them, to ascertain their contents.

If you write a letter asking for information, you should always enclose an envelope, addressed and stamped for the answer.

Courtesy demands that you reply to all letters immediately.

If you are in a company of men where two or more are talking over business matters, do not listen to the conversation which it was not intended you should hear.

In calling upon a man during business hours, transact your business rapidly and make your call as short as is consistent with the matters on hand. As a rule, men have but little time to visit during business hours.

If an employer has occasion to reprove any of his clerks or employes, he will find that by speaking kindly he will accomplish the desired object much better than by harsher means.

In paying out a large sum of money, insist that the person to whom it is paid shall count it in your presence, and on the other hand, never receive a sum of money without counting it in the presence of the party who pays it to you. In this way mistakes may be avoided.

CHAPTER XXX.

Dress.

O dress well requires good taste, good sense and refinement. A woman of good sense will neither make dress her first nor her last object in life. No sensible wife will betray that total indifference for her husband which is implied in the neglect of her appearance, and she will remember that to dress consistently and tastefully is one of the duties which she owes to society. Every lady, however insignificant her social position may appear to herself, must exercise a certain influence on the feelings and opinions of others. An attention to dress is useful as retaining, in the minds of sensible men, that pride in a wife's appearance, which is so agreeable to her, as well as that due influence which cannot be obtained without it. But a love of dress has its perils for weak minds. Uncontrolled by good sense, and stimulated by personal vanity it becomes a temptation at first, and then a curse. When it is indulged

in to the detriment of better enployments, and beyond
the compass of means, it cannot be too severely con-
demned. It then becomes criminal.

CONSISTENCY IN DRESS.

Consistency in regard to station and fortune is the
first matter to be considered. A woman of good sense
will not wish to expend in unnecessary extravagances
money wrung from an anxious, laborious husband; or
if her husband be a man of fortune, she will not, even
then, encroach upon her allowance. In the early years
of married life, when the income is moderate, it should
be the pride of a woman to see how little she can spend
upon her dress, and yet present that tasteful and credit-
able appearance which is desirable. Much depends
upon management, and upon the care taken of garments. She should turn everything to account, and be
careful of her clothing when wearing it.

EXTRAVAGANCE IN DRESS.

Dress, to be in perfect taste, need not be costly. It
is unfortunate that in the United States, too much
attention is paid to dress by those who have neither the
excuse of ample means nor of social culture. The wife
of a poorly paid clerk, or of a young man just starting
in business, aims at dressing as stylishly as does the
wealthiest among her acquaintances. The sewing girl,
the shop girl, the chambermaid, and even the cook,
must have their elegantly trimmed silk dresses and
velvet cloaks for Sunday and holiday wear, and the

injury done by this state of things to the morals and manners of the poorer classes is incalculable.

As fashions are constantly changing, those who do not adopt the extremes, as there are so many of the prevailing modes at present, can find something to suit every form and face.

INDIFFERENCE TO DRESS.

Indifference and inattention to dress is a defect of character rather than virtue, and often denotes indolence and slovenliness. Every woman should aim to make herself look as well as possible with the means at her command. Among the rich, a fondness for dress promotes exertion and activity of the mental powers, cultivates a correct taste and fosters industry and ingenuity among those who seek to procure for them the material and designs for dress. Among the middle classes it encourages diligence, contrivance, planning and deftness of handiwork, and among the poorer classes it promotes industry and economy. A fondness for dress, when it does not degenerate into vain show, has an elevating and refining influence on society.

APPROPRIATE DRESS.

To dress appropriately is another important matter to be considered. Due regard must be paid to the physical appearance of the person, and the dress must be made to harmonize throughout. An appropriate dress is that which so harmonizes with the figure as to make the apparel unnoticeable. Thin ladies can wear delicate

colors, while stout persons look best in black or dark
grey. For young and old the question of appropriate
color must be determined by the figure and complexion.
Rich colors harmonize with brunette complexions or
dark hair, and delicate colors with persons of light hair
and blonde complexions.

GLOVES.

Gloves are worn by gentlemen as well as ladies in
the street, at an evening party, at the opera or theatre,
at receptions, at church, when paying a call, riding or
driving; but not in the country or at dinner. White
should be worn at balls; the palest colors at evening
parties and neutral shades at church.

EVENING DRESS FOR GENTLEMEN.

The evening or full dress for gentlemen is a black
dress-suit—a "swallow-tail" coat, the vest cut low, the
cravat white, and kid gloves of the palest hue or white.
The shirt front should be white and plain; the studs
and cuff-buttons simple. Especial attention should be
given to the hair, which should be neither short nor
long. It is better to err upon the too short side, as too
long hair savors of affectation, destroys the shape of the
physiognomy, and has a touch of vulgarity about it.
Evening dress is the same for a large dinner party, a
ball or an opera. In some circles, however, evening
dress is considered an affectation, and it is as well to do
as others do. On Sunday, morning dress is worn, and
on that day of the week no gentleman is expected to

appear in evening dress, either at church, at home or away from home. Gloves are dispensed with at dinner parties, and pale colors are preferred to white for evening wear.

MORNING DRESS FOR GENTLEMEN.

The morning dress for gentlemen is a black frock-coat, or a black cut-away, white or black vest, according to the season, gray or colored pants, plaid or stripes, according to the fashion, a high silk (stove-pipe) hat, and a black scarf or necktie. A black frock coat with black pants is not considered a good combination, nor is a dress coat and colored or light pants. The morning dress is suitable for garden parties, Sundays, social teas, informal calls, morning calls and receptions.

It will be seen that morning and evening dress for gentlemen varies as much as it does for ladies. It is decidedly out of place for a gentleman to wear a dress coat and white tie in the day-time, and when evening dress is desired on ceremonious occasions, the shutters should be closed and the gas or lamps lighted. The true evening costume or full dress suit, accepted as such throughout the world, has firmly established itself in this country; yet there is still a considerable amount of ignorance displayed as to the occasions when it should be worn, and it is not uncommon for the average American, even high officials and dignified people, to wear the full evening costume at a morning reception or some midday ceremony. A dress coat at a morning or afternoon reception or luncheon, is entirely out of place, while the frock-coat or cut-away and gray pants, make a becoming costume for such an occasion.

It is not considered in good taste for men to wear much jewelry. They may with propriety wear one gold ring, studs and cuff-buttons, and a watch chain, not too massive, with a modest pendant, or none at all. Anything more looks like a superabundance of ornament.

Evening dress for ladies may be as rich, elegant and gay as one chooses to make it. It is everywhere the custom to wear full evening dress in brilliant evening assemblages. It may be cut either high or low at the neck, yet no lady should wear her dress so low as to make it quite noticeable or a special subject of remark. Evening dress is what is comonly known as " full dress," and will serve for a large evening party, ball or dinner. No directions will be laid down with reference to it, as fashion devises how it is to be made and what material used.

Ball dressing requires less art than the nice gradations of costume in the dinner dress, and the dress for evening parties. For a ball, everything should be light and diaphanous, somewhat fanciful and airy. The heavy, richly trimmed silk is only appropriate to those who do not dance. The richest velvets, the brightest and most delicate tints in silk, the most expensive laces, elaborate

coiffures, a large display of diamonds, artificial flowers
for the head-dress and natural flowers for hand bouquets,
all belong, more or less, to the costume for a large ball.

THE FULL DINNER DRESS.

The full dinner dress for guests admits of great splendor. It may be of any thick texture of silk or velvet
for winter, or light rich goods for summer, and should
be long and sweeping. Every trifle in a lady's costume
should be, as far as she can afford it, faultless. The
fan should be perfect in its way, and the gloves should
be quite fresh. Diamonds are used in broaches, pend-
ants, ear-rings and bracelets. If artificial flowers are
worn in the hair, they should be of the choicest descrip-
tion. All the light neutral tints, and black, dark blue,
purple, dark green, garnet, brown and fawn are suited
for dinner wear.

DRESS OF HOSTESS AT A DINNER PARTY.

The dress of a hostess at a dinner party should be
rich in material, but subdued in tone, so as not to
eclipse any of her guests. A young hostess should wear
a dress of rich silk, black or dark in color, with collar
and cuffs of fine lace, and if the dinner be by daylight,
plain jewelry, but by gaslight diamonds.

SHOWY DRESS.

The glaring colors and "loud" costumes, once so common, have given place to sober grays, and browns and

olives; black predominating over all. The light, show-ily-trimmed dresses, which were once displayed in the streets and fashionable promenades, are now only worn in carriages. This display of showy dress and glaring colors is generally confined to those who love ostentation more than comfort.

DRESS FOR RECEIVING CALLS.

If a lady has a special day for the reception of calls, her dress must be of silk, or other goods suitable to the season, or to her position, but must be of quiet colors and plainly worn. Lace collars and cuffs should be worn with this dress, and a certain amount of jewelry is also admissible. A lady whose mornings are devoted to the superintendence of her domestic affairs, may receive a casual caller in her ordinary morning dress, which must be neat, yet plain, with white plain linen collars and cuffs. For New Year's, or other calls of special significance, the dress should be rich, and may be elaborately trimmed. If the parlors are closed and the gas lighted, full evening dress is required.

CARRIAGE DRESS.

The material for a dress for a drive through the public streets of a city, or along a fashionable drive or park, cannot be too rich. Silks, velvets and laces, are all appropriate, with rich jewelry and costly furs in cold weather. If the fashion require it, the carriage dress may be long enough to trail, or it may be of the length of a walking dress, which many prefer. For driving in the country, a different style of dress is required, as the dust and mud would soil rich material.

Visiting costumes, or those worn at a funeral or informal calls, are of richer material than walking suits. The bonnet is either simple or rich, according to the taste of the wearer. A jacket of velvet, or shawl, or fur-trimmed mantle are the concomitants of the carriage dress for winter. In summer all should be bright, cool, agreeable to wear and pleasant to look at.

DRESS FOR MORNING CALLS.

Morning calls may be made either in walking or carriage dress, provided the latter is justified by the presence of the carriage. The dress should be of silk; collar and cuffs of the finest lace; light gloves; a full dress bonnet and jewelry of gold, either dead, burnished or enameled, or of cameo or coral. Diamonds are not usually worn in daylight. A dress of black or neutral tint, in which light colors are introduced only in small quantities, is the most appropriate for a morning call.

MORNING DRESS FOR STREET.

The morning dress for the street should be quiet in color, plainly made and of serviceable material. It should be short enough to clear the ground without collecting mud and garbage. Lisle-thread gloves in midsummer, thick gloves in midwinter, are more comfortable for street wear than kid ones. Linen collars and cuffs are most suitable for morning street dress. The bonnet and hat should be quiet and inexpressive, matching the dress as nearly as possible. In stormy weather a large waterproof with hood is more convenient and less troublesome than an umbrella. The morning dress for visiting or breakfasting in public may be, in winter, of woolen goods, simply made and quietly trimmed, and in summer, of cambric, pique, marseilles or other wash goods, either white or figured. For morning wear at home the dress may be still simpler. The hair should be plainly arranged without ornament.

THE PROMENADE DRESS.

The dress for the promenade should be in perfect harmony with itself. All the colors worn should harmonize if they are not strictly identical. The bonnet should not be of one color, and parasol of another, the dress of a third and the gloves of a fourth. Nor should one article be new and another shabby. The collars and cuffs should be of lace; the kid gloves should be selected to harmonize with the color of the dress, a perfect fit. The jewelry worn should be bracelets, cuff-buttons, plain gold ear-rings, a watch chain and brooch.

OPERA DRESS.

Opera dress for matinees may be as elegant as for morning calls. A bonnet is always worn even by those who occupy boxes, but it may be as dressy as one chooses to make it. In the evening, ladies are at liberty to wear evening dresses, with ornaments in their hair, instead of a bonnet, and as the effect of light colors is much better than dark in a well-lighted opera house, they should predominate.

THE RIDING DRESS.

A lady's riding habit should fit perfectly without being tight. The skirt must be full, and long enongh to cover the feet, but not of extreme length. The boots must be stout and the gloves gauntleted. Broadcloth is regarded as the more dressy cloth, though waterproof is the more serviceable. Something lighter may be worn for summer, and in the lighter costumes a row of shot must be stitched at the bottom of the breadths of the left side to prevent the skirts from being blown by the wind. The riding dress is made to fit the waist closely, and button nearly to the throat. Above a small collar or reverse of the waist is shown a plain linen collar, fastened at the throat with a bright or black necktie. Coat sleeves should come to the wrist with linen cuffs beneath them. No lace or embroidery is allowable in a riding costume. It is well to have the waist attached to a skirt of the usual length, and the long skirt fastened over it, so that if any accident occurs obliging the lady to dismount, she may easily remove the long overskirt and still be properly dressed.

The hair should be put up compactly, and no veil should be allowed to stream in the wind. The shape of the hat will vary with the fashion, but it should always be plainly trimmed, and if feathers are worn they must be fastened so that the wind cannot blow them over the wearer's eyes.

A WALKING SUIT.

The material for a walking suit may e either rich or plain to suit the taste and means of the wearer. It should always be well made and never appear shabby. Bright colors appear best only as trimmings. Black has generally been adopted for street dresses as the most becoming. For the country, walking dresses are made tasteful, solid and strong, more for service than display, and what would be perfectly appropriate for the streets of a city would be entirely out of place on the muddy, unpaved walks of a small town or in a country neighborhood. The walking or promenade dress is always made short enough to clear the ground. Thick boots are worn with the walking suit.

DRESS FOR LADIES OF BUSINESS.

For women who are engaged in some daily employment such as teachers, saleswomen and those who are occupied in literature, art or business of some sort, the dress should be somewhat different from the ordinary walking costume. Its material should be more serviceable, better fitted to endure the vicissitudes of the weather, and of quiet colors, such as brown or gray, and not easily soiled. While the costume should not be of the simplest nature, it should dispense with all superfluities in the way of trimming. It should be made with special reference to a free use of the arms, and to easy locomotion. Linen cuffs and collars are best suited to this kind of dress, gloves which can be easily removed, street walking boots, and for jewelry, plain cuff-buttons, brooch and watch chain. The hat or bonnet should be neat and tasty, with but few flowers or feathers. For winter wear, waterproof, tastefully made up, is the best material for a business woman's outer garment.

ORDINARY EVENING DRESS.

The ordinary evening house dress should be tasteful and becoming, with a certain amount of ornament, and worn with jewelry. Silks are the most appropriate for this dress, but all the heavy woolen dress fabrics for winter, and the lighter lawns and organdies for summer, elegantly made, are suitable. For winter, the colors should be rich and warm, and knots of bright ribbon of a becoming color, should be worn at the throat and in the hair. The latter should be plainly dressed. Artificial flowers and diamonds are out of place. This is both a suitable dress in which to receive or make a casual evening call. If a hood is worn, it must be removed during the call. Otherwise a full dress bonnet must be worn.

DRESS FOR SOCIAL PARTY.

For the social evening party, more latitude is allowed in the choice of colors, material, trimmings, etc., than for the ordinary evening dress. Dresses should cover the arms and shoulder; but if cut low in the neck, and with short sleeves, puffed illusion waists or some similar device should be employed to cover the neck and arms.

Gloves may or may not be worn, but if they are they should be of some light color.

DRESS FOR CHURCH.

The dress for church should be plain, of dark, quiet colors, with no superfluous trimming or jewelry. It should, in fact, be the plainest of promenade dresses, as church is not the place for display of fine clothes.

THE DRESS FOR THE THEATRE.

The promenade dress with the addition of a handsome cloak or shawl, which may be thrown aside if it is uncomfortable, is suitable for a theatre. The dress should be quiet and plain without any attempt at display. Either a bonnet or hat may be worn. Gloves should be dark, harmonizing with the dress.

DRESS FOR LECTURE AND CONCERT.

For the lecture or concert, silk is an appropriate dress, and should be worn with lace collars and cuffs and jewelry. A rich shawl or velvet promenade cloak, or opera cloak for a concert is an appropriate outer garment. The latter may or may not be kept on the shoulders during the evening. White or light kid gloves should be worn.

CROQUET, ARCHERY AND SKATING COSTUMES.

Croquet and archery costumes may be similar, and they admit of more brilliancy in coloring than any of the out-of-door costumes. They should be short, dis-

playing a handsomely fitting but stout boot, and should
be so arranged as to leave the arms perfectly free.   The
gloves should be soft and washable.   Kid is not suitable
for either occasion.   The hat should have a broad brim,
so as to shield the face from the sun, and render a parasol unnecessary.   The trimming for archery costumes is
usually of green.

An elegant skating costume may be of velvet,
trimmed with fur, with fur bordered gloves and boots.
Any of the warm, bright colored wool fabrics, however,
are suitable for the dress.   If blue or green are worn,
they should be relieved with trimmings of dark furs.
Silk is not suitable for skating costume.   To avoid suffering from cold feet, the boot should be amply loose.

BATHING COSTUME.

Flannel is the best material for a bathing costume,
and gray is regarded as the most suitable color.   It may
be trimmed with bright worsted braid.   The best form
is the loose sacque, or the yoke waist, both of them to
be belted in, and falling about midway between the knee
and ankle; an oilskin cap to protect the hair from the
water, and merino socks to match the dress, complete
the costume.

TRAVELING DRESS.

Comfort and protection from dust and dirt are the
requirements of a traveling dress.   When a lady is
about making an extensive journey, a traveling suit is
a great convenience, but for a short journey, a large
linen overdress or duster may be put on over the ordinary

dress in summer, and in winter a waterproof cloak may be used in the same way. For traveling costumes a variety of materials may be used, of soft, neutral tints, and smooth surface which does not retain the dust. These should be made up plainly and quite short. The underskirts should be colored, woolen in winter and linen in summer. The hat or bonnet must be plainly trimmed and completely protected by a large veil. Velvet is unfit for a traveling hat, as it catches and retains the dust; collars and cuffs of plain linen. The hair should be put up in the plainest manner. A waterproof and warm woolen shawl are indispensible, and may be rolled in a shawl strap when not needed. A satchel should be carried, in which may be kept a change of collars, cuffs, gloves, handkerchiefs, toilet articles, and towels. A traveling dress should be well supplied with pockets. The waterproof should have large pockets, and there should be one in the underskirt in which to carry such money and valuables as are not needed for immediate use.

THE WEDDING DRESS.

A full bridal costume should be white from head to foot. The dress may be of silk, heavily corded, moire antique, satin or plain silk, merino, alpaca, crape, lawn or muslin. The veil may be of lace, tulle or illusion, but it must be long and full. It may or may not descend over the face. Orange blossoms or other white flowers and maiden blush roses should form the bridal wreath and bouquet. The dress is high and the arms covered. Slippers of white satin and white kid gloves complete the dress.

The dress of the bridegroom and ushers is given in the chapter treating of the etiquette of weddings.

DRESS OF BRIDEMAIDS.

The dresses of bridemaids are not so elaborate as that of the bride. They should also be of white, but may be trimmed with delicately colored flowers and ribbons. White tulle, worn over pale pink or blue silk and caught up with blush roses or forget-me-nots, with *bouquet de corsage* and hand bouquet of the same, makes a beautiful costume for the bridemaids. The latter, may or may not, wear veils, but if they do, they should be shorter than that of the bride.

TRAVELING DRESS OF A BRIDE.

This should be of silk, or any of the fine fabrics for walking dresses; should be of some neutral tint; and bonnet and gloves should match in color. It may be more elaborately trimmed than an ordinary traveling dress, but if the bride wishes to attract as little attention as possible, she will not make herself conspicuous by a too showy dress. In private weddings the bride is sometimes married in traveling costume, and the bridal pair at once set out upon their journey.

DRESS AT WEDDING RECEPTIONS.

At wedding receptions in the evening, guests should wear full evening dress. No one should attend in black or mourning dress, which should give place to grey or lavender. At a morning reception of the wedded couple, guests should wear the richest street costume with white gloves.

MOURNING.

The people of the United States have settled upon no prescribed periods for the wearing of mourning garments. Some wear them long after their hearts have ceased to mourn. Where there is profound grief, no rules are needed, but where the sorrow is not so great, there is need of observance of fixed periods for wearing mourning.

Deep mourning requires the heaviest black of serge, bombazine, lustreless alpaca, delaine, merino or similar heavily clinging material, with collar and cuffs of crape. Mourning garments should have little or no trimming; no flounces, ruffles or bows are allowable. If the dress is not made *en suite,* then a long or square shawl of barege or cashmere with crape border is worn. The bonnet is of black crape; a hat is inadmissible. The veil is of crape or barege with heavy border; black gloves and black-bordered handkerchief. In winter dark furs may be worn with the deepest mourning. Jewelry is strictly forbidden, and all pins, buckles, etc., must be of jet. Lustreless alpaca and black silk trimmed with crape may be worn in second mourning, with white collars and cuffs. The crape veil is laid aside for net or tulle, but the jet jewelry is still retained. A still less degree of mourning is indicated by black and white, purple and gray, or a combination of these colors,

22

Crape is still retained in bonnet trimming, and crape flowers may be added. Light gray, white and black, and light shades of lilac, indicate a slight mourning. Black lace bonnet, with white or violet flowers, supercedes crape, and jet and gold jewelry is worn.

PERIODS OF WEARING MOURNING.

The following rules have been given by an authority competent to speak on these matters regarding the degree of mourning and the length of time it should be worn:

"The deepest mourning is that worn by a widow for her husband. It is worn two years, sometimes longer. Widow's mourning for the first year consists of solid black woolen goods, collar and cuffs of folded untrimmed crape, a simple crape bonnet, and a long, thick, black crape veil. The second year, silk trimmed with crape, black lace collar and cuffs, and a shorter veil may be worn, and in the last six months gray, violet and white are permitted. A widow should wear the hair perfectly plain if she does not wear a cap, and should always wear a bonnet, never a hat.

"The mourning for a father or mother is worn for one year. The first six months the proper dress is of solid black woolen goods trimmed with crape, black crape bonnet with black crape facings and black strings, black crape veil, collar and cuffs of black crape. Three months, black silk with crape trimming, white or black lace collar and cuffs, veil of tulle and white bonnet-facings; and the last three months in gray, purple and violet. Mourning worn for a child is the same as that worn for a parent.

"Mourning for a grandparent is worn for six months, three months black woolen goods, white collar and cuffs, short crape veil and bonnet of crape trimmed with black silk or ribbon; six weeks in black silk trimmed with crape, lace collar and cuffs, short tulle veil ; and six weeks in gray, purple, white and violet.

"Mourning worn for a friend who leaves you an inheritance, is the same as that worn for a grandparent.

"Mourning for a brother or sister is worn six months, two months in solid black trimmed with crape, white linen collar and cuffs, bonnet of black with white facing and black strings; two months in black silk, with white lace collar and cuffs; and two months in gray, purple, white and violet.

"Mourning for an uncle or aunt is worn for three months, and is the second mourning named above, tulle, white linen and white bonnet facings being worn at once. For a nephew or niece, the same is worn for the same length of time.

"The deepest mourning excludes kid gloves; they should be of cloth, silk or thread; and no jewelry is permitted during the first month of close mourning. Embroidery, jet trimmings, puffs, plaits—in fact, trimming of any kind—is forbidden in deep mourning, but worn when it is lightened.

"Mourning handkerchiefs should be of very sheer fine linen, with a border of black, very wide for close mourning, narrower as the black is lightened.

"Mourning silks should be perfectly lusterless, and the ribbons worn without any gloss.

"Ladies invited to funeral ceremonies should always wear a black dress, even if they are not in mourning; and it is bad taste to appear with a gay bonnet or shawl, as if for a festive occasion.

"The mourning for children under twelve years of age is white in summer and gray in winter, with black trimmings, belt, sleeve ruffles and bonnet ribbons."

CHAPTER XXXI.

Harmony of Colors in Dress.

THE selection and proper arrangement of colors, so that they will produce the most pleasant harmony, is one of the most desirable requisites in dress. Sir Joshua Reynolds says: "Color is the last attainment of excellence in every school of painting." The same may also be said in regard to the art of using colors in dress. Nevertheless, it is the first thing to which we should give our attention and study.

We put bright colors upon our little children; we dress our young girls in light and delicate shades; the blooming matron is justified in adopting the warm, rich hues which we see in the autumn leaf, while black and neutral tints are declared appropriate to the old.

One color should predominate in the dress; and if another is adopted, it should be in a limited quantity and only by way of contrast or harmony. Some colors may never, under any circumstances, be worn together, because they produce positive discord to the eye. If the dress be blue, red should never be introduced by way of trimming, or *vice versa.* Red and blue, red and yellow, blue and yellow, and scarlet and crimson may never be united in the same costume. If the dress be red, green may be introduced in a minute quantity; if blue, orange; if green, crimson. Scarlet and solferino are deadly enemies, each killing the other whenever they meet.

Two contrasting colors, such as red and green, may not be used in equal quantities in the dress, as they are both so positive in tone that they divide and distract the attention. When two colors are worn in any quantity, one must approach a neutral tint, such as gray or drab. Black may be worn with any color, though it looks best with the lighter shades of the different colors. White may also be worn with any color, though it looks best with the darker tones. Thus white and crimson, black and pink, each contrast better and have a richer effect than though the black were united with the crimson and the white with the pink. Drab, being a shade of no color between black and white, may be worn with equal effect with all.

A person of very fair, delicate complexion, should always wear the most delicate of tints, such as light blue, mauve and pea-green. A brunette requires bright colors, such as scarlet and orange, to bring out the brilliant tints in her complexion. A florid face and auburn hair call for blue.

Black hair has its color and depth enhanced by scarlet, orange or white, and will bear diamonds, pearls or lustreless gold.

Dark brown hair will bear light blue, or dark blue in a lesser quantity.

If the hair has no richness of coloring, a pale yellowish green will by reflection produce the lacking warm tint.

Light brown hair requires blue, which sets off to advantage the golden tint.

Pure golden or yellow hair needs blue, and its beauty is also increased by the addition of pearls or white flowers.

Auburn hair, if verging on the red, needs scarlet to tone it down. If of a golden red, blue, green, purple or black will bring out the richness of its tints.

Flaxen hair requires blue.

MATERIAL FOR DRESS.

The material for dress must be selected with reference to the purpose which it is to serve. No one buys a yellow satin dress for the promenade, yet a yellow satin seen by gaslight is beautiful, as an evening-dress. Neither would one buy a heavy serge of neutral tint for an opera-dress.

SIZE IN RELATION TO DRESS AND COLORS.

A small person may dress in light colors which would be simply ridiculous on a person of larger proportions. So a lady of majestic appearance should never wear white, but will be seen to the best advantage in black or dark tints. A lady of diminutive stature is dressed in bad taste when she appears in a garment with large

figures, plaids or stripes. Neither should a lady of large
proportions be seen in similar garments, because, united
with her size, they give her a "loud" appearance. Indeed, pronounced figures and broad stripes and plaids
are never in perfect taste.

Heavy, rich materials suit a tall figure, while light,
full draperies should only be worn by those of slender
proportions and not too short. The very short and
stout must be content with meagre drapery and quiet
colors.

Tall and slim persons should avoid stripes; short,
chunky ones, flounces, or any horizontal trimming of
the dress which, by breaking the outline from the waist
to the feet, produces an effect of shortening.

HOW COLORS HARMONIZE.

Colors may form a harmony either by contrast or by
analogy. When two remote shades of one color are
associated, such as very light blue and a very dark blue,
they harmonize by contrast, though the harmony may
be neither striking nor perfect. When two colors which
are similar to each other are grouped, such as orange
and scarlet, crimson and orange, they harmonize by
analogy. A harmony of contrast is characterized by
brilliancy and decision, and a harmony of analogy by a
quiet and pleasing association of colors.

When a color is chosen which is favorable to the complexion, it is well to associate with it the tints which
will harmonize by analogy, as to use contrasting colors
would diminish its favorable effect. When a color is

used in dress, not suitable to the complexion, it should
be associated with contrasting colors, as they have the
power to neutralize its objectionable influence.

Colors of similar power which contrast with each

other, mutually intensify each other's brilliancy, as blue
and orange, scarlet and green; but dark and light colors
associated do not intensify each other to the same degree, the dark appearing darker and the light appearing

lighter, as dark blue and straw color. Colors which
harmonize with each other by analogy, reduce each
other's brilliancy to a greater or less degree, as white
and yellow, blue and purple, black and brown.

The various shades of purple and lilac, dark blues
and dark greens, lose much of their brilliancy by gaslight, while orange, scarlet, crimson, the light browns
and light greens, gain brilliancy by a strong artificial
light.

Below the reader will find a list of colors that harmonize, forming most agreeable combinations, in which
are included all the latest and most fashionable shades
and colors:

Black and pink.
Black and lilac.
Black and scarlet.
Black and maize.
Black and slate color.
Black and orange, a rich harmony.
Black and white, a perfect harmony.
Black and brown, a dull harmony.
Black and drab or buff.
Black, white or yellow and crimson.
Black, orange, blue and scarlet.
Black and chocolate brown.
Black and shaded cardinal.
Black and cardinal.
Black, yellow, bronze and light blue.
Black, cardinal, blue and old gold.
Blue and brown.
Blue and black.
Blue and gold, a rich harmony.
Blue and orange, a perfect harmony.
Blue and chestnut (or chocolate).
Blue and maize.

Blue and straw color.
Blue and white.
Blue and fawn color, weak harmony.
Blue and stone color.
Blue and drab.
Blue and lilac, weak harmony.
Blue and crimson, imperfectly.
Blue and pink, poor harmony.
Blue and salmon color.
Blue, scarlet and purple (or lilac).
Blue, orange and black.
Blue, orange and green.
Blue, brown, crimson and gold (or yellow).
Blue, orange, black and white.
Blue, pink and bronze green.
Blue, cardinal and old gold.
Blue, yellow, chocolate-brown and gold.
Blue, mulberry and yellow.
Bronze and old gold.
Bronze, pink and light blue.
Bronze, black, blue, pink and gold.
Bronze, cardinal and peacock blue.
Brown, blue, green, cardinal and yellow.
Brown, yellow, cardinal and peacock blue.
Crimson and gold, rich harmony.
Crimson and orange, rich harmony.
Crimson and brown, dull harmony.
Crimson and black, dull harmony.
Crimson and drab.
Crimson and maize.
Crimson and purple.
Cardinal and old gold.
Cardinal, brown and black.
Cardinal and navy blue.
Chocolate, blue, pink and gold.
Claret and old gold.
Dark green, white and cardinal.
Ecrue, bronze and peacock.
Ecrue and light blue.

Garnet, bronze and pink.
Gensd'arme and cardinal.
Gensd'arme and bronze.
Gensd'arme and myrtle.
Gensd'arme and old gold.
Gensd'arme, yellow and cardinal.
Gensd'arme, pink, cardinal and lavender.
Green and gold, or gold color.
Green and scarlet.
Green and orange.
Green and yellow.
Green, crimson, blue and gold, or yellow.
Green, blue and scarlet.
Green, gold and mulberry
Green and cardinal.
Lilac and white, poor.
Lilac and gray, poor.
Lilac and maize.
Lilac and cherry.
Lilac and gold, or gold color.
Lilac and scarlet.
Lilac and crimson.
Lilac, scarlet and white or black.
Lilac, gold color and crimson.
Lilac, yellow or gold, scarlet and white.
Light pink and garnet.
Light drab, pine, yellow and white.
Myrtle and old gold.
Myrtle and bronze.
Myrtle, red, blue and yellow.
Myrtle, mulberry, cardinal, gold and light green
Mulberry and old gold.
Mulberry and gold.
Mulberry and bronze.
Mulberry, bronze and gold.
Mulberry and pearl.
Mode, pearl and mulberry.
Maroon, yellow, silvery gray and light green.
Navy blue, light blue and gold.

Navy blue, gensd'arme and pearl.
Navy blue, maize, cardinal and yellow.
Orange and bronze, agreeable.
Orange and chestnut.
Orange, lilac and crimson.
Orange, red and green.
Orange, purple and scarlet.
Orange, blue, scarlet and purple.
Orange, blue, scarlet and claret.
Orange, blue, scarlet, white and green.
Orange, blue and crimson.
Pearl, light blue and peacock blue.
Peacock blue and light gold.
Peacock blue and old gold.
Peacock blue and cardinal.
Peacock blue, pearl, gold and cardinal.
Purple and maize.
Purple and blue.
Purple and gold, or gold color, rich.
Purple and orange, rich.
Purple and black, heavy.
Purple and white, cold.
Purple, scarlet and gold color.
Purple, scarlet and white.
Purple, scarlet, blue and orange.
Purple, scarlet, blue, yellow and black.
Red and white, or gray.
Red and gold, or gold color.
Red, orange and green.
Red, yellow or gold color and black.
Red, gold color, black and white.
Seal brown, gold and cardinal.
Sapphire and bronze.
Sapphire and old gold.
Sapphire and cardinal.
Sapphire and light blue.
Sapphire and light pink.
Sapphire and corn.
Sapphire and garnet.

Sapphire and mulberry.
Shaded blue and black.
Scarlet and blue.
Scarlet and slate color.
Scarlet and orange.
Scarlet, blue and white.
Scarlet, blue and yellow.
Scarlet, black and white.
Scarlet, blue, black and yellow.
Shaded blue, shaded garnet and shaded gold.
Shaded blue and black.
White and cherry.
White and crimson.
White and brown.
White and pink.
White and scarlet.
White and gold color, poor.
Yellow and black.
Yellow and brown.
Yellow and red.
Yellow and chestnut or chocolate.
Yellow and white, poor.
Yellow and purple, agreeable.
Yellow and violet.
Yellow and lilac, weak.
Yellow and blue, cold.
Yellow and crimson.
Yellow, purple and crimson.
Yellow, purple, scarlet and blue.
Yellow, cardinal and peacock blue.
Yellow, pink, maroon and light blue.

CHAPTER XXXII.

The Toilet.

TO appear at all times neat, clean and tidy, is demanded of every well-bred person. The dress may be plain, rich or extravagant, but there must be a neatness and cleanliness of the person. Whether a lady is possessed of few or many personal attractions, it is her duty at all times to appear tidy and clean, and to make herself as comely and attractive as circumstances and surroundings will permit. The same may be said of a gentleman. If a gentleman calls upon a lady, his duty and his respect for her demand that he shall appear not only in good clothes, but with well combed hair, exquisitely clean hands, well trimmed beard or cleanly shaven face, while the lady will not show herself in an untidy dress, or disheveled hair. They should appear at their best.

Upon the minor details of the toilet depend, in a great degree, the health, not to say the beauty, of the individual. In fact the highest state of health is equivalent to the highest degree of beauty of which the individual is capable.

PERFUMES.

Perfumes, if used at all, should be used in the strictest moderation, and be of the most *recherche* kind. Musk and patchouli should always be avoided, as, to many people of sensitive temperament, their odor is exceedingly disagreeable. Cologne water of the best quality is never offensive.

THE BATH.

Cleanliness is the outward sign of inward purity. Cleanliness of the person is health, and health is beauty. The bath is consequently a very important means of preserving the health and enhancing the beauty. It is not to be supposed that we bathe simply to become clean, but because we wish to remain clean. Cold water refreshes and invigorates, but does not cleanse, and persons who daily use a sponge bath in the morning, should frequently use a warm one, of from ninety-six to one hundred degrees Fahrenheit for cleansing purposes. When a plunge bath is taken, the safest temperature is from eighty to ninety degrees, which answers the purposes of both cleansing and refreshing. Soap should be plentifully used, and the fleshbrush applied vigorously, drying with a coarse Turkish towel. Nothing improves the complexion like the daily use of the fleshbrush, with early rising and exercise in the open air.

In many houses, in large cities, there is a separate bath-room, with hot and cold water, but in smaller places and country houses this convenience is not to be found. A substitute for the bath-room is a large piece of oil-cloth, which can be laid upon the floor of an ordinary dressing-room. Upon this may be placed the bath tub or basin, or a person may use it to stand upon while taking a sponge bath. The various kinds of baths, both hot and cold, are the shower bath, the douche, the hip bath and the sponge bath.

The shower bath can only be endured by the most vigorous constitutions, and therefore cannot be recommended for indiscriminate use.

A douche or hip bath may be taken every morning, with the temperature of the water suited to the endurance of the individual. In summer a sponge bath may be taken upon retiring. Once a week a warm bath, at from ninety to one hundred degrees, may be taken, with plenty of soap, in order to thoroughly cleanse the pores of the skin. Rough towels should be vigorously used after these baths, not only to remove the impurities of the skin but for the beneficial friction which will send a glow over the whole body. The hair glove or flesh brush may be used to advantage in the bath before the towel is applied.

THE TEETH.

The teeth should be carefully brushed with a hard brush after each meal, and also on retiring at night. Use the brush so that not only the outside of the teeth

23

becomes white, but the inside also. After the brush is used plunge it two or three times into a glass of water, then rub it quite dry on a towel.

Use tooth-washes or powders very sparingly. Castile soap used once a day, with frequent brushings with pure water and a brush, cannot fail to keep the teeth clean and white, unless they are disfigured and destroyed by other bad habits, such as the use of tobacco, or too hot or too cold drinks.

DECAYED TEETH.

On the slightest appearance of decay or tendency to accumulate tartar, go at once to the dentist. If a dark spot appearing under the enamel is neglected, it will eat in until the tooth is eventually destroyed. A dentist seeing the tooth in its first stage, will remove the decayed part and plug the cavity in a proper manner.

TARTAR ON THE TEETH.

Tartar is not so easily dealt with, but it requires equally early attention. It results from an impaired state of the general health, and assumes the form of a yellowish concretion on the teeth and gums. At first it is possible to keep it down by a repeated and vigorous use of the tooth brush; but if a firm, solid mass accumulates, it is necessary to have it chipped off by a dentist. Unfortunately, too, by that time it will probably have begun to loosen and destroy the teeth on which it fixes, and is pretty certain to have produced one obnoxious effect—that of tainting the breath. Washing the teeth with vinegar when the brush is used has been recommended as a means of removing tartar.

Tenderness of the gums, to which some persons are subject, may sometimes be met by the use of salt and water. but it is well to rinse the mouth frequently with water with a few drops of tincture of myrrh in it.

FOUL BREATH.

Foul breath, unless caused by neglected teeth, indicates a deranged state of the system. When it is occasioned by the teeth or other local case, use a gargle consisting of a spoonful of solution of chloride of lime in half a tumbler of water. Gentlemen smoking, and thus tainting the breath, may be glad to know that the common parsley has a peculiar effect in removing the odor of tobacco.

THE SKIN.

Beauty and health of the skin can only be obtained by perfect cleanliness of the entire person, an avoidance of all cosmetics, added to proper diet, correct habits and early habits of rising and exercise. The skin must be thoroughly washed, occasionally with warm water and soap, to remove the oily exudations on its surface. If any unpleasant sensations are experienced after the use of soap, they may be immediately removed by rinsing the surface with water to which a little lemon juice or vinegar has been added.

PRESERVING A YOUTHFUL COMPLEXION.

The following rules may be given for the preservation of a youthful complexion· Rise early and go to bed early. Take plenty of exercise. Use plenty of cold water and good soap frequently. Be moderate in eating and drinking. Do not lace. Avoid as much as possible the vitiated atmosphere of crowded assemblies. Shun cosmetics and washes for the skin. The latter dry the skin, and only defeat the end they are supposed to have in view.

MOLES.

Moles are frequently a great disfigurement to the face, but they should not be tampered with in any way. The only safe and certain mode of getting rid of moles is by a surgical operation.

FRECKLES.

Freckles are of two kinds. Those occasioned by exposure to the sunshine, and consequently evanescent, are denominated " summer freckles;" those which are constitutional and permanent are called " cold freckles." With regard to the latter, it is impossible to give any advice which will be of value. They result from causes not to be affected by mere external applications. Summer freckles are not so difficult to deal with, and with a little care the skin may be kept free from this cause of disfigurement. Some skins are so delicate that they become freckled on the slightest exposure to open air in summer. The cause assigned for this is that the iron in the blood, forming a junction with the oxygen, leaves a rusty mark where the junction takes place. We give in their appropriate places some recipes for removing these latter freckles from the face.

OTHER DISCOLORATIONS.

There are various other discolorations of the skin, proceeding frequently from derangement of the system. The cause should always be discovered before attempting a remedy; otherwise you may aggravate the com plaint rather than cure it.

THE EYES.

Beautiful eyes are the gift of Nature, and can owe little to the toilet. As in the eye consists much of the expression of the face, therefore it should be borne in mind that those who would have their eyes bear a pleasing expression must cultivate pleasing traits of character and beautify the soul, and then this beautiful soul will look through its natural windows.

Never tamper with the eyes. There is danger of destroying them. All daubing or dyeing of the lids is foolish and vulgar.

SHORT-SIGHTEDNESS.

Short-sightedness is not always a natural defect. It may be acquired by bad habits in youth. A short-sighted person should supply himself with glasses exactly adapted to his wants; but it is well not to use these glasses too constantly, as, even when they perfectly fit the eye, they really tend to shorten the sight. Unless one is very short-sighted, it is best to keep the glasses for occasional use, and trust ordinarily to the unaided eye. Parents and teachers should watch their children and see that they do not acquire the habit of holding their books too close to their eyes, and thus injure their sight.

SQUINT-EYES AND CROSS-EYES.

Parents should also be careful that their children do not become squint or cross-eyed through any carelessness. A child's hair hanging down loosely over its eyes, or a bonnet projecting too far over them, or a loose ribbon or tape fluttering over the forehead, is sometimes sufficient to direct the sight irregularly until it becomes permanently crossed.

THE EYELASHES AND EYEBROWS.

A beautiful eyelash is an important adjunct to the eye. The lashes may be lengthened by trimming them occasionally in childhood. Care should be taken that this trimming is done neatly and evenly, and especially that the points of the scissors do not penetrate the eye. The eyebrows may be brushed carefully in the direction in which they should lie. In general, it is in exceeding bad taste to dye either lashes or brows, for it usually brings them into disharmony with the hair and features. There are cases, however, when the beauty of an otherwise fine countenance is utterly ruined by white lashes and brows. In such cases one can hardly be blamed if

India ink is resorted to to give them the desired color. Never shave the brows. It adds to their beauty in no way, and may result in an irregular growth of new hair.

TAKE CARE OF THE EYES.

The utmost care should be taken of the eyes. They should never be strained in an imperfect light, whether that of shrouded daylight, twilight or flickering lamp or candle-light. Many persons have an idea that an habitually dark room is best for the eyes. On the contrary, it weakens them and renders them permanently unable to bear the light of the sun. Our eyes were naturally designed to endure the broad light of day, and the nearer we approach to this in our houses, the stronger will be our eyes and the longer will we retain our sight.

EYEBROWS MEETING.

Some persons have the eyebrows meeting over the nose. This is usually considered a disfigurement, but there is no remedy for it. It may be a consolation for such people to know that the ancients admired this style of eyebrows, and that Michael Angelo possessed it. It is useless to pluck out the uniting hairs; and if a depilatory is applied, a mark like that of a scar left from a burn remains, and is more disfiguring than the hair.

INFLAMED EYES.

If the lids of the eyes become inflamed and scaly, do not seek to remove the scales roughly, for they will bring the lashes with them. Apply at night a little cold cream to the edges of the closed eyelids, and wash them in the morning with lukewarm milk and water. It is well to have on the toilet-table a remedy for inflamed eyes. Spermaceti ointment is simple and well adapted to this purpose. Apply at night, and wash off with rose-water in the morning. There is a simple lotion made by dissolving a very small piece of alum and a piece of lump-sugar of the same size in a quart of water; put the ingredients into the water cold and let them simmer. Bathe the eyes frequently with it.

THE STY.

A sty in the eye is irritating and disfiguring. Bathe with warm water; at night apply a bread-and-milk poultice. When a white head forms, prick it with a fine needle. Should the inflammation be obstinate, a little citrine ointment may be applied, care being taken that it does not get into the eye.

THE HAIR.

There is nothing that so adds to the charm of an individual, especially a lady, as a good head of hair. The skin of the head requires even more tenderness and cleanliness than any other portion of the body, and is capable of being irritated by disease. The hair should be brushed carefully. The brush should be of moderate hardness, not too hard. The hair should be separated, in order that the head itself may be well brushed, as by doing so the scurf is removed, and that is most essential,

as it is not only unpleasant and unsightly, but if suffered
to remain it becomes saturated with perspiration, and
tends to weaken the roots of the hair, so that it is easily
pulled out. In brushing or combing, begin at the extreme points, and in combing, hold the portion of hair
just above that through which the comb is passing,
firmly between the first and second fingers, so that if it
is entangled it may drag from that point, and not from
the roots. The finest head of hair may be spoiled by
the practice of plunging the comb into it high up and
dragging it in a reckless manner. Short, loose, broken
hairs are thus created, and become very troublesome.

THE USE OF HAIR OILS.

Do not plaster the hair with oil or pomatum. A
white, concrete oil pertains naturally to the covering of
the human head, but some persons have it in more
abundance than others. Those whose hair is glossy and
shining need nothing to render it so; but when the hair
is harsh, poor and dry, artificial lubrication is necessary.
Persons who perspire freely, or who accumulate scurf
rapidly, require it also. Nothing is simpler or better in
the way of oil than pure, unscented salad oil, and in the
way of a pomatum, bear's grease is as pleasant as anything. Apply either with the hands, or keep a soft
brush for the purpose, but take care not to use the oil
too freely. An overoiled head of hair is vulgar and
offensive. So are scents of any kind in the oil applied
to the hair. It is well also to keep a piece of flannel
with which to rub the hair at night after brushing it, in

order to remove the oil before laying the head upon the pillow.

Vinegar and water form a good wash for the roots of the hair. Ammonia diluted in water is still better.

The hair-brush should be frequently washed in diluted ammonia.

For removing scurf, glycerine, diluted with a little rose-water, will be found of service. Any preparation of rosemary forms an agreeable and highly cleansing wash. The yolk of an egg beaten up in warm water is an excellent application to the scalp. Many heads of hair require nothing more in the way of wash than soap and water. Beware of letting the hair grow too long, as the points are apt to weaken and split. It is well to have the ends clipped off once a month.

Young girls should wear their hair cut short until they are grown up, if they would have it then in its best condition.

DYEING THE HAIR.

A serious objection to dyeing the hair is that it is almost impossible to give the hair a tint which harmonizes with the complexion. If the hair begins to change early, and the color goes in patches, procure from the druggist's a preparation of the husk of the walnut water of *eau crayon*. This will, by daily application, darken the tint of the hair without actually dyeing it. When the change of color has gone on to any great extent, it is better to abandon the application and put up with the change, which, in nine cases out of ten, will be in accordance with the change of the face. Indeed, there is nothing more beautiful than soft, white hair worn in bands or clustering curls about the face. The walnut water may be used for toning down too red hair.

BALDNESS.

Gentlemen are more liable to baldness than ladies, owing, no doubt, to the use of the close hat, which confines and overheats the head. If the hair is found to be falling out, the first thing to do is to look to the hat and see that it is light and thoroughly ventilated. There is no greater enemy to the hair than the silk dress-hat. It is best to lay this hat aside altogether and adopt a light felt or straw in its place.

Long, flowing hair on a man is not in good taste, and will indicate him to the observer as a person of unbalanced mind and unpleasantly erratic character—a man, in brief, who seeks to impress others with the fact that he is eccentric, something which a really eccentric person never attempts.

THE BEARD.

Those who shave should be careful to do so every morning. Nothing looks worse than a shabby beard. Some persons whose beards are strong should shave twice a day, especially if they are going to a party in the evening.

The style of the growth of the beard should be governed by the character of the face. But whatever the style be, the great point is to keep it well brushed and trimmed, and to avoid any appearance of wildness or inattention. The full, flowing beard of course requires more looking after in the way of cleanliness, than any other. It should be thoroughly washed and brushed at least twice a day, as dust is sure to accumulate in it, and it is very easy to suffer it to become objectionable to one's self as well as to others. If it is naturally glossy, it is better to avoid the use of oil or pomatum. The moustache should be worn neatly and not over-large. There is nothing that so adds to native manliness as the full beard if carefully and neatly kept.

THE HAND.

The beautiful hand is long and slender, with tapering fingers and pink, filbert-shaped nails. The hand to be in proper proportion to the rest of the body, should be as long as from the point of the chin to the edge of the hair on the forehead.

The hands should be kept scrupulously clean, and therefore should be very frequently washed—not merely rinsed in soap and water, but thoroughly lathered, and scrubbed with a soft nail-brush. In cold weather the use of lukewarm water is unobjectionable, after which the hands should be dipped into cold water and very carefully dried on a fine towel.

Be careful always to dry the hands thoroughly, and rub them briskly for some time afterward. When this is not sufficiently attended to in cold weather, the hands chap and crack. When this occurs, rub a few drops of honey over them when dry, or anoint them with cold cream or glycerine before going to bed.

CHAPPED HANDS.

As cold weather is the usual cause of chapped hands, so the winter season brings with it a cure for them. A thorough washing in snow and soap will cure the worst case of chapped hands, and leave them beautifully soft.

TO MAKE THE HANDS WHITE AND DELICATE.

Should you wish to make your hands white and delicate, you might wash them in milk and water for a day or two. On retiring to rest, rub them well over with some palm oil and put on a pair of woolen gloves. The hands should be thoroughly washed with hot water and soap the next morning, and a pair of soft leather gloves worn during the day. They should be frequently rubbed together to promote circulation. Sunburnt hands may be washed in lime-water or lemon-juice.

TREATMENT OF WARTS.

Warts, which are more common with young people than with adults, are very unsightly, and are sometimes very difficult to get rid of. The best plan is to buy a stick of lunar caustic, which is sold in a holder and case at the druggist's for the purpose, dip it in water, and touch the wart every morning and evening, care being taken to cut away the withered skin before repeating the operation. A still better plan is to apply acetic acid gently once a day with a camel's hair pencil to the summit of the wart. Care should be taken not to allow this acid to touch any of the surrounding skin; to prevent this the finger or hand at the base of the wart may be covered with wax during the operation.

THE NAILS.

Nothing is so repulsive as to see a lady or gentleman, however well dressed they may otherwise be, with unclean nails. It always results from carelessness and inattention to the minor details of the toilet, which is most reprehensible. The nails should be cut about once a week—certainly not oftener. This should be accomplished just after washing, the nail being softer at such a time. Care should be taken not to cut them too short, though, if they are left too long, they will frequently get torn and broken. They should be nicely rounded at the corners. Recollect the filbert-shaped nail is considered the most beautiful. Never bite the nails; it not only is a most disagreeable habit, but tends to make the nails jagged, deformed and difficult to clean, besides gives a red and stumpy appearance to the finger-tips.

Some persons are troubled by the cuticle adhering to the nail as it grows. This may be pressed down by the towel after washing; or should that not prove efficacious, it must be loosened round the edge with some blunt instrument. On no account scrape the nails with a view to polishing their surface. Such an operation only tends to make them wrinkled.

Absolute smallness of hand is not essential to beauty, which requires that the proper proportions should be observed in the human figure. With proper care the hand may be retained beautiful, soft and shapely, and yet perform its fair share of labor. The hands should always be protected by gloves when engaged in work calculated to injure them. Gloves are imperatively required for garden-work. The hands should always be washed carefully and dried thoroughly after such labor. If they are roughened by soap, rinse them in a little vinegar or lemon-juice, and they will become soft and smooth at once.

REMEDY FOR MOIST HANDS.

People afflicted with moist hands should revolutionize their habits, take more out-door exercise and more frequent baths. They should adopt a nutritious but not over-stimulating diet, and perhaps take a tonic of some sort. Local applications of starch-powder and the juice of lemon may be used to advantage.

THE FEET.

A well formed foot is broad at the sole, the toes well spread, each separate toe perfect and rounded in form. The nails are regular and perfect in shape as those of the fingers. The second toe projects a little beyond the others, and the first, or big toe, stands slightly apart from the rest and is slightly lifted. The feet, from the circumstance of their being so much confined by boots and shoes, require more care in washing than the rest of the body. Yet they do not always get this care. The hands receive frequent washings every day. Once a week is quite as often as many people can bestow the same attention upon their feet. A tepid bath at about

80 or 90 degrees, should be used. The feet may remain in the water about five minutes, and the instant they are taken out they should be rapidly and thoroughly dried by being well rubbed with a coarse towel. Sometimes bran is used in the water. Few things are more invigorating and refreshing after a long walk, or getting wet in the feet, than a tepid foot-bath, clean stockings and a pair of easy shoes. After the bath is the time for pairing the toe-nails, as they are so much softer and more pliant after having been immersed in warm water.

TREATMENT FOR MOIST OR DAMP FEET.

Some persons are troubled with moist or damp feet. This complaint arises more particularly during the hot weather in summer-time, and the greatest care and cleanliness should be exercised in respect to it. Persons so afflicted should wash their feet twice a day in soap and warm water, after which they should put on clean socks. Should this fail to cure, they may, after being washed as above, be rinsed, and then thoroughly rubbed with a mixture consisting of half a pint of warm water and three tablespoonfuls of concentrated solution of chloride of soda.

BLISTERS ON THE FEET.

People who walk much are frequently afflicted with blisters. The best preventative of these is to have easy, well-fitting boots and woolen socks. Should blisters occur, a very good plan is to pass a large darning-needle threaded with worsted through the blister lengthwise, leaving an inch or so of the thread outside at each end. This keeps the scurf-skin close to the true skin, and prevents any grit or dirt entering. The thread absorbs the matter, and the old skin remains until the new one grows. A blister should not be punctured save in this manner, as it may degenerate into a sore and become very troublesome.

CHILBLAINS.

To avoid chilblains on the feet it is necessary to observe three rules: 1. Avoid getting the feet wet; if they become so, change the shoes and stockings at once. 2. Wear lamb's wool socks or stockings. 3. Never under any circumstances "toast your toes" before the fire, especially if you are very cold. Frequent bathing of the feet in a strong solution of alum is useful in preventing the coming of chilblains. On the first indication of any redness of the toes and sensation of itching it would be well to rub them carefully with warm spirits of rosemary, to which a little turpentine has been added. Then a piece of lint soaked in camphorated spirits, opodeldoc or camphor liniment may be applied and retained on the part. Should the chilblain break, dress it twice daily with a plaster of equal parts of lard and beeswax, with half the quantity in weight of oil of turpentine.

THE TOE NAILS.

The toe-nails do not grow so fast as the finger-nails, but they should be looked after and trimmed at least once a fortnight. They are much more subject to irregularity of growth than the finger-nails, owing to their confined position. If the nails show a tendency to grow in at the sides, the feet should be bathed in hot water, pieces of lint introduced beneath the parts with an inward tendency, and the nail itself scraped longitudinally.

Pare the toe-nails squarer than those of the fingers. Keep them a moderate length—long enough to protect the toe, but not so long as to cut holes in the stockings. Always cut the nails; never tear them, as is too frequently the practice. Be careful not to destroy the spongy substance below the nails, as that is the great guard to prevent them going into the quick.

CORNS.

It is tolerably safe to say that those who wear loose, easy-fitting shoes and boots will never be troubled with corns. Some people are more liable to corns than others, and some will persist in the use of tightly-fitting shoes in spite of corns.

HOW TO HAVE SHOES MADE.

The great fault with modern shoes is that their soles are made too narrow. If one would secure perfect healthfulness of the feet, he should go to the shoemaker and step with his stockinged feet on a sheet of paper. Let the shoemaker mark with a pencil upon the paper the exact size of his foot, and then make him a shoe whose sole shall be as broad as this outlined foot.

Still more destructive of the beauty and symmetry of our women's feet have been the high, narrow heels so

much worn lately. They make it difficult to walk, and
even in some cases permanently cripple the feet. A
shoe, to be comfortable, should have a broad sole and a
heel of moderate height, say one-half an inch, as broad
at the bottom as at the top.

CHAPTER XXXIII.

Toilet Recipes.

TO REMOVE FRECKLES.

BRUISE and squeeze the juice out of common chick-weed, and to this juice add three times its quantity of soft water. Bathe the skin with this for five or ten minutes morning and evening, and wash afterwards with clean water.

Elder flowers treated and applied exactly in the same manner as above. When the flowers are not to be had, the distilled water from them, which may be procured from any druggist, will answer the purpose.

A good freckle lotion is made of honey, one ounce, mixed with one pint of luke-warm water. Apply when cold.

Carbonate of potassa, twenty grains; milk of almonds, three ounces; oil of sassafras, three drops. Mix and apply two or three times a day.

One ounce of alcohol; half a dram salts tartar; one dram oil bitter almonds. Let stand for one day and apply every second day.

FOR PIMPLES ON THE FACE.

Wash the face in a solution composed of one teaspoonful of carbolic acid to a pint of water. This is an excellent purifying lotion, and may be used on the most delicate skin. Be careful not to get any of it in the eyes as it will weaken them.

One tablespoonful of borax to half a pint of water is an excellent remedy for cutaneous eruptions, canker, ringworm, etc.

Pulverize a piece of alum the size of a walnut, dissolve it in one ounce of lemon juice, and add one ounce of alcohol. Apply once or twice a day.

Mix two ounces of rose-water with one dram of sulphate of zinc. Wet the face gently and let it dry. Then touch the affected part with cream.

WASH FOR THE COMPLEXION.

A teaspoonful of the flour of sulphur and a wine-glassful of lime-water, well shaken and mixed; half a wineglass of glycerine and a wine-glass of rose water. Rub it on the face every night before going to bed. Shake well before using.

Another prescription, used by hunters to keep away the black flies and mosquitoes, is said to leave the skin very clear and fair, and is as follows: Mix one spoonful of the best tar in a pint of pure olive oil or almond oil, by heating the two together in a tin cup set in boiling water. Stir till completely mixed and smooth, putting in more oil if the compound is too thick to run

easily. Rub this on the face when going to bed, and
lay patches of soft cloth on the cheeks and forehead to
keep the tar from rubbing off. The bed linen must
be protected by cloth folded and thrown over the
pillows.

The whites of four eggs boiled in rose-water; half an
ounce of alum; half an ounce of sweet almonds; beat
the whole together until it assumes the consistency of
paste. Spread upon a silk or muslin mask, to be worn
at night.

Take a small piece of the gum benzoin and boil it in
spirits of wine till it becomes a rich tincture. In using
it pour fifteen drops into a glass of water, wash the face
and hands and allow it to dry.

BORACIC ACID FOR SKIN DISEASES.

Boracic acid has been used with great success as an
external application in the treatment of vegetable para-
sitic diseases of the skin. A solution of a dram of the
acid to an ounce of water, or as much of the acid as the
water will take up, is found to meet the requirements of
the case satisfactorily. The affected parts should be
well bathed in the solution twice a day and well rubbed.

TO SOFTEN THE SKIN.

Mix half an ounce of glycerine with half an ounce of
alcohol, and add four ounces of rose-water. Shake well
together and it is ready for use. This is a splendid
remedy for chapped hands.

REMEDY FOR RINGWORM.

Apply a solution of the root of common narrow-leafed dock, which belongs to the botanical genus of *Rumex.* Use vinegar for the solvent.

Dissolve a piece of sulphate of potash, the size of a walnut, in one ounce of water. Apply night and morning for a couple of days, and it will disappear.

TO REMOVE SUNBURN.

Take two drams of borax, one dram of alum, one dram of camphor, half an ounce of sugar-candy, and a pound of ox-gall. Mix and stir well for ten minutes, and stir it three or four times a fortnight. When clear and transparent, strain through a blotting paper and bottle for use.

TO PREVENT HAIR FALLING OUT.

Ammonia one ounce, rosemary one ounce, cantharides four drams, rose-water four ounces, glycerine one ounce. First wet the head with cold water, then apply the mixture, rubbing briskly.

Vinegar of cantharides half an ounce, eau-de-cologne one ounce, rose-water one ounce. The scalp should be brushed briskly until it becomes red, and the lotion should then be applied to the roots of the hair twice a day.

TO BEAUTIFY THE HAIR.

Take two ounces of olive oil, four ounces of good bay rum, and one dram of the oil of almonds; mix and shake well. This will darken the hair.

HAIR OILS.

Mix two ounce of castor oil with three ounces of alcohol, and add two ounces of olive oil. Perfume to liking.

TO MAKE POMADES FOR THE HAIR.

Take the marrow out of a beef shank bone, melt it in a vessel placed over or in boiling water, then strain and scent to liking, with ottar of roses or other perfume.

Unsalted lard five ounces, olive oil two and a half ounces, castor oil one-quarter ounce, yellow wax and spermaceti one-quarter ounce. These ingredients are to be liquified over a warm bath, and when cool, perfume to liking.

Fresh beef marrow, boiled with a little almond oil or sweet oil, and scented with ottar of roses or other mild perfume.

A transparent hair pomade is made as follows: Take half a pint of fine castor oil and an ounce of white wax. Stir until it gets cool enough to thicken, when perfume may be stirred in; geranium, bergamot or lemon oil may be used.

GERMAN METHOD OF TREATING THE HAIR.

The women of Germany have remarkably fine and luxuriant hair. The following is their method of managing it: About once in two or three weeks, boil for half an hour or more a large handful of bran in a quart of soft water; strain into a basin, and when tepid, rub into the water a little white soap. With this wash the head thoroughly, using a soft linen cloth or towel, thoroughly dividing the hair so as to reach the roots. Then take the yolk of an egg, slightly beaten in a saucer, and with the fingers rub it into the roots of the hair. Let it remain a few minutes, and then wash it off entirely with a cloth dipped in pure water. Rinse the head well till the yolk of the egg has disappeared from it, then wipe and rub it dry with a towel, and comb the hair from the head, parting it with the fingers, then apply some soft pomatum. In winter it is best to do all this in a warm room.

TO KEEP THE HAIR FROM TURNING GREY.

Take the hulls of butternuts, about four ounces, and infuse in a quart of water, and to this add half an ounce of copperas. Apply with a soft brush every two or three days. This preparation is harmless, and is far better than those dyes made of nitrate of silver.

Oxide of bismuth four drams, spermaceti four drams, pure hog's lard four ounces. Melt the two last and add the first.

TO CLEANSE THE HAIR AND SCALP.

Beat up a fresh egg and rub it well into the hair, or if more convenient, rub it into the hair without beating. Rub the egg in until a lather is formed, occasionally wetting the hands in warm water softened by borax. By the time a lather is formed, the scalp is clean, then rinse the egg all out in a basin of warm water, containing a tablespoonful of powdered borax: after that rinse in a basin of clean water.

HAIR WASH.

Bay rum six ounces, aromatic spirits of ammonia half
an ounce, bergamot oil six drops.   Mix.

TO MAKE THE HAIR GROW.

If the head be perfectly bald, nothing will ever cause
the hair to grow again.   If the scalp be glossy, and no
small hairs are discernible, the roots or follicles are
dead, and can not be resuscitated.   However if small
hairs are to be seen, there is hope.   Brush well, and
bathe the bald spot three or four times a week with
cold, soft water; carbonate of ammonia one dram, tincture of cantharides four drams, bay rum four ounces,
castor oil two ounces.   Mix well and use it every day.

SEA FOAM OR DRY SHAMPOO.

Take a pint of alcohol, half pint of bay rum, and half
an ounce of spirits of ammonia, and one dram of salts
tartar.   Shake well together and it is ready for use.
Pour a quantity on the head, rub well with the palm
of the hand.   It will produce a thick foam, and will
cleanse the scalp.   This is used generally by first-class
barbers.

BARBER'S SHAMPOO.

To one pint of warm water add half an ounce of salts
tartar.   Cut up very fine a piece of castile soap, the size
of two crackers, and mix it, shaking the mixture well,
and it is ready for use.

CLEANING GOLD JEWELRY.

Gold ornaments may be kept bright and clean with soap and warm water, scrubbing them well with a soft nail brush. They may be dried in sawdust of box-wood. Imitation jewelry may be treated in the same way.

TO LOOSEN STOPPERS OF TOILET BOTTLES.

Let a drop of pure oil flow round the stopper and let the bottle stand a foot or two from the fire. After a time tap the stopper smartly, but not too hard, with the handle of a hair brush. If this is not effectual, use a fresh drop of oil and repeat the process. It is almost sure to succeed.

TO MAKE BANDOLINE.

Half a pint of water, rectified spirits with an equal quantity of water three ounces, gum tragacanth one and a half drams. Add perfume, let the mixture stand for a day or two and then strain.

Simmer an ounce of quince seed in a quart of water for forty minutes, strain, cool, add a few drops of scent, and bottle, corking tightly.

Iceland moss one-fourth of on ounce, boiled in a quart of water, and a little rectified spirit added, so that it will keep.

TO MAKE LIP-SALVE.

Melt in a jar placed in a basin of boiling water a quarter of an ounce each of white wax and spermaceti, flour of benzoin fifteen grains, and half an ounce of the oil of almonds. Stir till the mixture is cool. Color red with alkanet root.

TO CLEAN KID BOOTS.

Mix a little white of egg and ink in a bottle, so that the composition may be well shaken up when required for use. Apply to the kid with a piece of sponge and rub dry. The best thing to rub dry with is the palm of the hand. When the kid shows symptoms of cracking, rub in a few drops of sweet oil. The soles and heels should be polished with common blacking.

TO CLEAN PATENT-LEATHER BOOTS.

In cleaning patent-leather boots, first remove all the dirt upon them with a sponge or flannel; then the boot should be rubbed lightly over with a paste consisting of two spoonfuls of cream and one of linseed oil, both of which require to be warmed before being mixed. Polish with a soft cloth.

TO REMOVE STAINS AND SPOTS FROM SILK.

Boil five ounces of soft water and six ounces of powdered alum for a short time, and pour it into a vessel to cool. Warm it for use, and wash the stained part with it and leave dry.

Wash the soiled part with ether, and the grease will disappear.

We often find that lemon-juice, vinegar, oil of vitriol and other sharp corrosives stain dyed garments. Sometimes, by adding a little pearlash to a soap-lather and passing the silks through these, the faded color will be restored. Pearlash and warm water will sometimes do alone, but it is the most efficacious to use the soap-lather and pearlash together.

TOOTHACHE PREVENTIVE.

Use flower of sulphur as a tooth powder every night, rubbing the teeth and gums with a rather hard tooth-brush. If done after dinner, too, all the better. It preserves the teeth and does not communicate any smell whatever to the mouth.

HOW TO WHITEN LINEN.

Stains occasioned by fruit, iron rust and other similar causes may be removed by applying to the parts injured a weak solution of the chloride of lime, the cloth having been previously well washed. The parts subjected to this operation should be subsequently rinsed in soft, clear, warm water, without soap, and be immediately dried in the sun.

Oxalic acid diluted with water will accomplish the same end.

TO TAKE STAINS OUT OF SILK.

Mix together in a vial two ounces of essence of lemon and one ounce of oil of turpentine. Grease and other spots in silk must be rubbed gently with a linen rag dipped in the above composition. To remove acid stains from silks, apply with a soft rag, spirits of ammonia.

TO REMOVE STAINS FROM WHITE COTTON GOODS.

For mildew, rub in salt and some buttermilk, and expose it to the influence of a hot sun. Chalk and soap or lemon juice and salt are also good. As fast as the spots become dry, more should be rubbed on, and the garment should be kept in the sun until the spots disappear. Some one of the preceding things will extract most kinds of stains, but a hot sun is necessary to render any one of them effectual.

Scalding water will remove fruit stains. So also will hartshorn diluted with warm water, but it will be necessary to apply it several times.

Common salt rubbed on fruit stains before they become dry will extract them.

Colored cotton goods that have ink spilled on them, should be soaked in lukewarm sour milk.

TO REMOVE SPOTS OF PITCH OR TAR.

Scrape off all the pitch or tar you can, then saturate the spots with sweet oil or lard; rub it in well, and let it remain in a warm place for an hour.

TO EXTRACT PAINT FROM GARMENTS.

Saturate the spot with spirits of turpentine, let it remain a number of hours, then rub it between the hands; it will crumble away without injury either to the texture or color of any kind of woolen, cotton or silk goods.

TO CLEAN SILKS AND RIBBONS.

Take equal quantities of soft lye-soap, alcohol or gin, and molasses. Put the silk on a clean table without creasing; rub on the mixture with a flannel cloth. Rinse the silk well in cold, clear water, and hang it up to dry without wringing. Iron it before it gets dry, on the wrong side. Silks and ribbons treated in this way will look very nicely.

Camphene will extract grease and clean ribbons without changing the color of most things. They should be dried in the open air and ironed when pretty dry.

The water in which pared potatoes have been boiled is very good to wash black silks in; it stiffens and makes them glossy and black.

Soap-suds answer very well. They should be washed in two suds and not rinsed in clean water.

REMEDY FOR BURNT KID OR LEATHER SHOES.

If a lady has had the misfortune to put her shoes or slippers too near the stove, and thus had them burned, she can make them nearly as good as ever by spreading soft-soap upon them while they are still hot, and then, when they are cold, washing it off. It softens the leather and prevents it drawing up.

REMEDY FOR CORNS.

Soak the feet for half an hour two or three nights successively in a pretty strong solution of common soda. The alkali dissolves the indurated cuticle and the corn comes away, leaving a little cavity which, however, soon fills up.

Corns between the toes are generally more painful than others, and are frequently so situated as to be almost inaccessible to the usual remedies. They may be cured by wetting them several times a day with spirits of ammonia.

INFLAMED EYELIDS.

Take a slice of stale bread, cut as thin as possible, toast both sides well, but do not burn it; when cold soak it in cold water, then put it between a piece of old linen and apply, changing when it gets warm.

TO MAKE COLD CREAM.

Melt in a jar two ounces of white wax, half an ounce of spermaceti, and mix with a pint of sweet oil. Add perfume to suit.

Melt together an ounce of white wax, half an ounce of spermaceti, and mix with a pint of oil of sweet almonds and half a pint of rose-water. Beat to a paste.

TO MAKE ROSE-WATER.

Take half an ounce of powdered white sugar and two drams of magnesia. With these mix twelve drops of ottar of roses. Add a quart of water, two ounces of alcohol, mix in a gradual manner, and filter through blotting paper.

HOW TO WASH LACES.

Take a quart bottle and cover it over with the leg of a soft, firm stocking, sew it tightly above and below. Then wind the collar or lace smoothly around the covered bottle; take a fine needle and thread and sew very carefully around the outer edge of the collar or lace, catching every loop fast to the stocking. Then shake the bottle up and down in a pailful of warm soap-suds, occasionally rubbing the soiled places with a soft sponge. It must be rinsed well after the same manner in clean water. When the lace is clean, apply a very weak solution of gum arabic and stand the bottle in the sunshine to dry. Take off the lace very carefully when perfectly dry. Instead of ironing, lay it between the white leaves of a heavy book; or, if you are in a hurry, iron on flannel between a few thicknesses of fine muslin. Done up in this way, lace collars will wear longer, stay clean longer, and have a rich, new, lacy look that they will not have otherwise.

HOW TO DARKEN FADED FALSE HAIR.

The switches, curls and frizzes which fashion demands should be worn, will fade in course of time; and though they matched the natural hair perfectly at first, they will finally present a lighter tint. If the hair is brown this can be remedied. Obtain a yard of dark brown calico. Boil it until the color has well come out into the water. Then into this water dip the hair, and take

25

it out and dry it. Repeat the operation until it shall be of the required depth of shade.

PUTTING AWAY FURS FOR THE SUMMER.

When you are ready to put away furs and woolens, and want to guard against the depredations of moths, pack them securely in paper flour sacks and tie them up well. This is better than camphor or tobacco or snuff scattered among them in chests and drawers. Before putting your muffs away for the summer, twirl them by the cord at the ends, so that every hair will straighten. Put them in their boxes and paste a strip of paper where the lid fits on.

TO KEEP THE HAIR IN CURL.

To keep the hair in curl take a few quince-seed, boil them in water, and add perfumery if you like; wet the hair with this and it will keep in curl longer than from the use of any other preparation. It is also good to keep the hair in place on the forehead on going out in the wind.

PROTECTION AGAINST MOTHS.

Dissolve two ounces of camphor in half a pint each of alcohol and spirits of turpentine; keep in a stone bottle and shake before using. Dip blotting paper in the liquid, and place in the box with the articles to be preserved.

TO TAKE MILDEW OUT OF LINEN.

Wet the linen in soft water, rub it well with white soap, then scrape some fine chalk to powder, and rub it well into the linen; lay it out on the grass in the sunshine, watching to keep it damp with soft water. Repeat the process the next day, and in a few hours the mildew will entirely disappear.

CURE FOR INGROWING NAILS ON TOES.

Take a little tallow and put it into a spoon, and heat it over a lamp until it becomes very hot; then pour it on the sore or granulation. The effect will be almost magical. The pain and tenderness will at once be relieved. The operation causes very little pain if the tallow is perfectly heated. Perhaps a repetition may be necessary in some cases.

TO REMOVE GREASE-SPOTS FROM WOOLEN CLOTH.

Take one quart of spirits of wine or alcohol, twelve drops of winter green, one gill of beef-gall and six cents' worth of lavendar. A little alkanet to color if you wish. Mix.

TO CLEAN WOOLEN CLOTH.

Take equal parts of spirits hartshorn and ether. Oxgall mixed with it makes it better.

TO TAKE INK-SPOTS FROM LINEN.

Take a piece of mould candle of the finest kind, melt it, and dip the spotted part of the linen in the melted tallow: Then throw the linen into the wash.

TO REMOVE FRUIT-STAINS.

Moisten the parts stained with cold water; then hold it over the smoke of burning brimstone, and the stain will disappear. This will remove iron mould also.

CLEANING SILVER.

For cleaning silver, either articles of personal wear or those pertaining to the toilet-table or dressing-case, there is nothing better than a spoonful of common whiting, carefully pounded so as to be without lumps, reduced to a paste with gin.

TO REMOVE GREASE SPOTS.

French chalk is useful for removing grease-spots from clothing. Spots on silk will sometimes yield if a piece of blotting-paper is placed over them and the blade of a knife is heated (not too much) and passed over the paper.

TO REMOVE A TIGHT RING.

When a ring happens to get so tight on a finger that it cannot be removed, a piece of string, well soaped, may be wound tightly round the finger, commencing at the end of the finger and continued until the ring is reached. Then force the end of the twine between the ring and finger, and as the string is unwound, the ring will be gradually forced off.

MOSQUITOES WARDED OFF.

To ward off mosquitoes, apply to the skin a solution made of fifty drops of carbolic acid to an ounce of glycerine. Mosquito bites may be instantly cured by touching them with the solution. Add two or three drops of the ottar of roses to disguise the smell. The pure, crystalized form of the acid has a less powerful odor than the common preparation.

LINIMENT FOR THE FACE AFTER SHAVING.

One ounce of lime water, one ounce of sweet oil, one drop oil of roses, is a good liniment for the face after shaving. Shake well before using. Apply with the forefinger.

TO REMOVE SUNBURN.

Wash thoroughly with milk of almonds, which can be obtained at the drug store.

TO WHITEN THE FINGER NAILS.

Take two drams of dilute sulphuric acid, one dram of the tincture of myrrh, four ounces of spring water, and mix in a bottle. After washing the hands, dip the fingers in a little of the mixture. Rings with stones or pearls in them should be removed before using this mixture.

TO REMOVE TAN.

Tan can be removed from the face by dissolving magnesia in soft water. Beat it to a thick mass, spread it on the face, and let it remain a minute or two. Then wash off with castile soapsuds and rinse with soft water.

TO CURE WARTS.

Take a piece of raw beef steeped in vinegar for twenty-four hours, tie it on the part affected. Apply each night for two weeks.

REMEDY FOR IN-GROWING TOE-NAILS.

The best remedy for in-growing toe-nails is to cut a notch about the shape of a V in the end of the nail, about one-quarter the width of the nail from the in-growing side. Cut down as nearly to the quick as possible, and one-third the length of the nail. The pressure of the boot or shoe will tend to close the opening you have made in the nail, and this soon affords relief. Allow the in-growing portion of the nail to grow without cutting it, until it gets beyond the flesh.

TO REMOVE WRINKLES.

Melt one ounce of white wax, add two ounces of juice of lily-bulbs, two ounces of honey, two drams of rose-water, and a drop or two of ottar of roses. Use it twice a day.

Put powder of best myrrh upon an iron plate sufficiently hot to melt the gum gently, and when it liquefies, cover over your head with a napkin, and hold your face over the fumes at a distance that will cause you no inconvenience. If it produces headache, discontinue its use.

In washing, use warm instead of cold water.

REMEDY FOR CHAPPED HANDS.

After washing with soap, rinse the hands in fresh water and dry them thoroughly, by applying Indian meal or rice flour.

Lemon-juice three ounces, white wine vinegar three ounces, and white brandy half a pint.

Add ten drops of carbolic acid to one ounce of glycerine, and apply freely at night.

TO CURE CHILBLAINS.

Two tablespoonfuls of lime water mixed with enough sweet oil to make it as thick as lard. Rub the chilblains with the mixture and dry it in, then wrap up in linen.

Bathe the chilblains in strong alum water, as hot as it can be borne.

When indications of the chilblains first present themselves, take vinegar three ounces and camphorated spirits of wine one ounce; mix and rub on the parts affected.

Bathe the feet in warm water, in which two or three handsful of common salt have been dissolved.

Rub with a raw onion dipped in salt.

HAIR RESTORATIVE.

The oil of mace one-half ounce, mixed with a pint of deodorized alcohol, is a powerful stimulant for the hair. To apply it, pour a spoonful or two into a saucer, dip a stiff brush into it and brush the hair and head smartly.

On bald heads, if hair will start at all, it may be stimulated by friction with a piece of flannel till the skin becomes red. Repeat this process three times a day, until the hair begins to grow, when the tincture may be applied but once a day, till the growth is well established. The head should be bathed in cold water every morning, and briskly brushed to bring the blood to the surface.

WASH FOR THE TEETH.

Dissolve two ounces of borax in three pints of warm water. Before the water is quite cold, add one teaspoonful of spirits of camphor. Bottle the mixture for use. One wine-glass of the mixture, added to half a pint of tepid water, is sufficient for each application. This solution used daily, beautifies and preserves the teeth.

FOR WHITENING THE HANDS.

A wine-glass of cologne and one of lemon-juice strained clear. Scrape two cakes of brown Windsor soap to a powder and mix well in a mould. When hard, it is fit for use, and will be found excellent for whitening the hands.

Wear during the night, large cloth mittens filled with wet bran or oatmeal, and tied closely at the wrist. Persons who have a great deal of house-work to do, may keep their hands soft and white by wearing bran or oatmeal mittens.

TO REDUCE THE FLESH.

A strong decoction of sassafras, drank frequently, will reduce the flesh as rapidly as any remedy known. A strong infusion is made at the rate of an ounce of sassafras to a quart of water. Boil it half an hour very slowly, and let it stand till cold, heating again if desired. Keep it from the air.

SMOOTH AND SOFT HANDS.

A few drops of glycerine thoroughly rubbed over the hands, after washing them, will keep them smooth and soft.

TO MAKE TINCTURE OF ROSES.

Take the leaves of the common rose and place, without pressing them, in a glass bottle, then pour some spirits of wine on them, close the bottle and let it stand till required for use. Its perfume is nearly equal to that of ottar of roses.

SOFT CORNS.

A weak solution of carbolic acid will heal soft corns between the toes.

BURNED EYEBROWS.

Five grains sulphate of quinine dissolved in an ounce of alcohol, will, if applied, cause eyebrows to grow when burned off by the fire.

TO RESTORE GRAY HAIR.

A recipe for restoring gray hair to its natural color, said to be very effective when the hair is changing color, is as follows: One pint of water, one ounce tincture of acetate of iron, half an ounce of glycerine, and five grains sulphuret potassium. Mix and let the bottle stand open until the smell of the potassium has disappeared, then add a few drops of ottar of roses. Rub a little into the hair daily, and it will restore its color and benefit the health.

Bathing the head in a strong solution of rock salt, is said to restore gray hair in some cases. Make the solution two heaping tablespoonfuls of salt to a quart of boiling water, and let it stand until cold before using.

A solution made of a tablespoonful of carbonate of ammonia to a quart of water is also recommended. wash the head thoroughly with the solution and brush the hair while wet.

TO TAKE STAINS OUT OF SILKS.

Make a solution of two ounces of essence of lemon, and one ounce oil of turpentine. Rub the silk gently with linen cloth, dipped in the solution.

To remove acid stains from silk, apply spirits of ammonia with a soft rag.

TO TAKE INKSPOTS FROM LINEN.

Dip the spotted part of the linen in clean, pure melted tallow, before being washed.

TO REMOVE DISCOLORATION BY BRUISING.

Apply to the bruise a cloth wrung out of very hot water, and renew frequently until the pain ceases.

TO CLEAN KID GLOVES.

Make a solution of one quart of distilled benzine with one-fourth of an ounce of carbonate of ammonia, one-fourth of an ounce of fluid chloroform, one-fourth of an ounce of sulphuric ether. Pour a small quantity into a saucer, put on the gloves, and wash, as if washing the hands, changing the solution until the gloves are clean. Rub them clean and as dry as possible with a clean dry cloth, and take them off and hang them where there is a good current of air to dry. This solution is also excellent for cleaning ribbons, silks, etc., and is perfectly harmless to the most delicate tints. Do not get near the fire when using, as the benzine is very inflammable.

Washing the gloves in turpentine, the same as above, is also a good means of cleaning them.

PERSPIRATION.

To remove the unpleasant odor produced by perspiration, put two tablespoonfuls of the compound spirit of ammonia in a basin of water, and use it for bathing. It leaves the skin clear, sweet and fresh as one could wish. It is perfectly harmless, very cheap, and is recommended on the authority of an experienced physician.

TO REMOVE FLESH WORMS.

Flesh worms, or little black specks, which appear on the nose, may be removed by washing in warm water, drying with a towel, and applying a wash of cologne and liquor of potash, made of three ounces of the former to one ounce of the latter.

CHAPPED LIPS.

Oil of roses four ounces, white wax one ounce, spermaceti half an ounce, melt in a glass vessel, stirring with a wooden spoon, and pour into a china or glass cup.

RECIPES FOR THE CARE OF THE TEETH.

A remedy for unsound gums, is a gargle made of one ounce of coarsely powdered Peruvian bark steeped in half a pint of brandy for two weeks. Put a teaspoonful of this into a tablespoonful of water, and gargle the mouth twice a day.

The ashes of stale bread, thoroughly burned, is said to make a good dentifrice.

The teeth should be carefully brushed after every meal, as a means of preserving a sweet breath. In addition, a small piece of licorice may be dissolved in the mouth, which corrects the effects of indigestion. Licorice has no smell, but simply corrects ill-flavored odor.

A good way to clean teeth is to dip the brush in water, rub it over white castile soap, then dip it in prepared chalk, and brush the teeth briskly.

To beautify the teeth, dissolve two ounces of borax in three pints of boiling water, and before it is cold, add one teaspoonful of spirits of camphor; bottle for use. Use a teaspoonful of this with an equal quantity of warm water.

TO MAKE COLD CREAM.

Five ounces oil of sweet almonds, three ounces spermaceti, half an ounce of white wax, and three to five drops ottar of roses. Melt together in a shallow dish over hot water. Strain through a piece of muslin when melted, and as it begins to cool, beat it with a silver spoon until cold and snowy white. For the hair use seven ounces of oil of almonds instead of five.

REMEDY FOR BLACK TEETH.

Take equal parts of cream of tartar and salt, pulverize it and mix it well. Wash the teeth in the morning and rub them well with the powder.

TO CLEANSE THE TEETH AND GUMS.

Take an ounce of myrrh in fine powder, two tablespoonfuls of honey, and a little green sage in very fine powder; mix them well together, and wet the teeth and gums with a little, twice a day.

CHAPTER XXXIV.

𝔖𝔭𝔬𝔯𝔱𝔰, 𝔊𝔞𝔪𝔢𝔰, 𝔄𝔪𝔲𝔰𝔢𝔪𝔢𝔫𝔱𝔰.

THERE is a great variety of games, sports and amusements for both out-door and in-door entertainment, in which both sexes mingle for pleasure, and brief mention is here made of some of these.

ARCHERY.

The interest that has been recently awakened in this country in archery, is worthy of mention. As a graceful, healthful and innocent sport, it has no equal among any of the games that have been introduced, where both sexes participate. Our young and middle aged ladies too often neglect out-door physical exertion, which is essential to acquiring strength of limbs and muscle, and a gracefulness of carriage which is dependent thereon. It is a mistaken idea that with youth all indulgence in physical recreation should cease. On the contrary, such exercises as are most conducive to health, and are attended with pleasure, might with propriety be kept up by young women as well as by young men, as a means of retaining strength and elasticity of the muscles; and, instead of weak, trembling frames and broken down constitutions, in the prime of life, a bright, vigorous old age would be the reward. The pursuit of archery is recommended to both young and old, male and female, as having advantages far superior to any of the out-door games and exercises, as a graceful and invigorating pastime, developing in ladies a strong constitution, perfection of sight at long range, and above all, imparting to the figure a graceful appearance and perfect action of the limbs and chest. Let the women of this country devote some of their spare hours to this pleasant, health-giving sport, and their reward will be bright, ruddy faces, elasticity of movement, and strong and vigorous constitutions.

IMPLEMENTS FOR ARCHERY.

For the purposes of archery, the implements required are the bow, arrows, targets, a quiver pouch and belt, an arm-guard or brace, a shooting glove or finger tip, and a scoring card.

The bow is from five to six feet long, made of lance-wood or locust. Spanish yew is considered the choicest, next comes the Italian, then the English yew; lance-wood and lancewood backed with hickory are used more than any other. In choosing a bow, get the best you can afford, it will prove the cheapest in the end. Men should use bows six feet long, pulling from forty to sixty pounds, and ladies bows of five feet or five feet six inches in length, and pulling from twenty-five to forty pounds. The arrows are generally of uniform thickness throughout, and are made of pine; the finest grades being made of white deal, with sharp points of iron or brass. They are from 25 to 30 inches in length. The quiver belt is worn round the waist, and contains the arrows which are being used. The arm is protected from the blow of the string by the "arm-guard," a broad guard of strong leather buckled on the left wrist by two straps. A shooting-glove is worn on the right hand to protect the fingers from soreness in drawing the string of the bow.

The target consists of a circular, thick mat of straw, from two to four feet in diameter, covered with canvas, painted in a series of circles. The inner circle is a gold color, then comes red, white, black, and the outer circle white. The score for a gold hit is nine; the red 7; the inner white 5; the black 3, and the outer white 1.

The use of the bow and arrows, the proper manner of holding them, and directions for shooting are to be found in pamphlets of instruction, which often accompany the implements.

ARCHERY CLUBS AND PRACTICE.

In many cities and villages throughout the country, clubs have been formed, and regular days for practice and prize shooting are appointed. Each member of the the club is expected to furnish his or her own implements, and to attend all the practice meetings and prize shootings. The clubs are about equally divided as to ladies and gentlemen, as both sexes participate equally in the sport. The officers are such as are usually chosen in all organizations, with the addition of a Lady Paramount, a scorer, and a Field Marshal. The lady paramount is the highest office of honor in the club. She is expected to act as an umpire or judge in all matters of dispute that may come up in the club, and her decisions must be regarded as final. She is also expected to do all in her power to further the interests of the organization. A field marshal has been appointed by some clubs, and his duties are to place the targets, measure the shooting distances, and have general supervision of the field on practice days. The scorer keeps a score of each individual member of the club.

In meeting for practice, it is customary to have one target for every six, eight or ten persons, the latter number being sufficient for any one target. The targets are placed at any distance required, from thirty to one hundred yards; ladies being allowed an advantage of about one-fourth the distance in shooting. To beginners, a distance of from twenty-five to forty yards for gentlemen, and twenty to thirty for ladies, is sufficient, and this distance may be increased as practice is acquired. An equal number of ladies and gentlemen usually occupy one target, and each shoots a certain number of arrows as agreed upon, usually from three to six, a score being kept as the target is hit. After each person has shot the alloted number of arrows, it is re-

26

garded as an "end," and a certain number of ends, as agreed upon, constitute a "round." For prize shooting, the National Archery Association has established three rounds, known as the "York Round," the "American Round," and the "Columbia Round" (for ladies). The "York Round" consists of 72 arrows at 100 yards, 48 at 80 yards, and 24 at 60 yards. The "American Round" consists of 30 arrows, each at 60, 50 and 40 yards respectively, and the "Columbia Round" (for ladies), 24 arrows, each at 50, 40 and 30 yards respectively. A captain is appointed for each target, who designates a target scorer, and the gentleman who makes the largest score, is appointed captain of the target at the succeeding meeting. The target scorer, at the close of the round, hands the score to the official scorer, who announces the result at the next meeting of the club. Some clubs have adopted the plan of having every alternate meeting for prize shooting, awarding some small token to the lady and gentleman who makes the highest scores.

Ladies' costume for archery may be more brilliant than for an ordinary walking dress, and are usually trimmed with green and gold color, and in many cases a green jacket is worn. The costumes are short enough for convenience in movement, and made so as to give free and easy movement of the arms.

LAWN-TENNIS.

Amongst all games, none, perhaps can so justly lay claim to the honor of antiquity as tennis. The ancient

Greeks played it, the Romans knew it as *pila*, and ever since those days, with little intermission, the game has been played in many European countries. After a long season of rest, the game has now re-appeared in all the freshness of renewed youth. There are many points to be said to commend tennis. Both ladies and gentlemen can join in the game, and often the palm will be borne off by the "weaker, yet fairer" sex. The exercise required to enjoy the game is not in any way of an exhausting character, and affords ladies a training in graceful and charming movements. Lawn-tennis may be played either in summer or winter, and in cold weather, if the ground be dry, is a very agreeable out-door recreation. At a croquet or garden party it is certainly a desideratum.

The requisites for playing lawn-tennis, are a lawn or level surface about 45 by 100 feet, as the "court" upon which the playing is done is 27 by 78 feet. A net four or five feet in height and 27 feet long, divides the court. A ball made of india rubber and covered with cloth, and a "racket" for each player are the implements needed for playing. The racket is used for handling the ball, and is about two feet in length, with net work at the outer end, by means of which the ball is tossed from one place to another. Rules for playing the game are obtained with the implements needed, which can be procured from dealers in such lines of goods.

CROQUET.

The game of croquet is played by opposite parties, of one or more on a side, each player being provided with a mallet and her own ball which are distinguished by their color.

The players in their turn place their ball a mallet's length from the starting stake, and strike it with the mallet, the object being to pass it through the first one or two hoops. The turning or upper stake must be struck with the ball before the player can pass her ball through the returning hoops, and on returning to the starting point the ball must hit the starting stake before the player is the winner. The one who passes through all the hoops and gets her ball to the starting stake first is the winner. We do not give the rules of the game as each croquet set is accompanied by a complete set of rules.

Where four are playing, two of whom are gentlemen, one lady and gentleman usually play as partners. As it is the height of ill-manners to display any rudeness, no lady or gentleman will be so far forgetful as to become angry should the opposing parties be found "cheating."

Invitations to a croquet party may be of the same form as invitations to any other party.

BOATING.

Where there is a sufficiently large body or stream of water to admit of it, boating is a very enjoyable recreation, which may be pursued by both ladies and gentle-

men. There is much danger in sailing, and the proper
management of a sail-boat requires considerable tact
and experience. Rowing is safer, but caution should be
observed in not over-loading the boat. A gentleman
should not invite ladies to ride on the water unless he is
thoroughly capable of managing the boat. Rowing is
a healthful and delightful recreation, and many ladies
become expert and skillful at it. Every gentleman
should have some knowledge of rowing, as it is easily
acquired. If a gentleman who is inexperienced in rowing, goes out with other gentlemen in a boat, he should
refrain from any attempt to row, as he will only display
his awkwardness, and render the ride uncomfortable to
his companions.

In rowing with a friend, it is polite to offer him the
"stroke" oar, which is the post of honor.

When two gentlemen take a party of ladies out for a
row, one stands in the boat to steady it and offer assistance to the ladies in getting seated, and the other aids
from the wharf.

A lady's dress for rowing should be one which will
give perfect freedom to her arm; a short skirt, stout
boots, and hat with sufficient brim to protect her face
from the sun.

PICNICS.

While ladies and gentlemen never forget their good
manners, and are always polite and courteous, yet at
picnics they are privileged to relax many of the forms
and ceremonies required by strict etiquette. Here men

and women mingle for a day of pleasure in the woods or fields, or on the water, and it is the part of all who attend to do what they can for their own and their neighbor's enjoyment. Hence, formal introductions and other ceremonies need not stand in the way of enjoyment either by ladies or gentlemen, and at the same time no act of rudeness should occur to mar the pleasure of the occasion. It is the duty of gentlemen to do all they can to make the occasion enjoyable and even mirthful. They should also look to providing the means of conveyance to and from the spot selected for the festivities, make such arrangements as are necessary in the way of providing music, games, boats, and whatever else is needed to enhance the pleasure of the day. The ladies provide the luncheon or dinner, which is spread upon the grass or eaten out of their baskets, and at which the restraints of the table are withdrawn. At picnics, gentlemen become the servants as well as the escorts and guides of the ladies, and perform such services for ladies in the way of procuring flowers, carrying baskets, climbing trees, baiting their fish-hooks, and many other things as are requested of them.

PRIVATE THEATRICALS.

Private theatricals may be made very pleasing and instructive entertainments for fall or winter evenings, among either young or married people. They include charades, proverbs, tableaux, dramatic readings, and the presentation of a short dramatical piece, and may successfully be given in the parlor or drawing room. The hostess seeks the aid of friends in the preparation of her arrangements, and if a drama has been determined upon, she assigns the various parts to each. Her friends should aid her in her efforts by giving her all the assistance they can, and by willingly and good-naturedly complying with any request she may make, accepting the parts allotted to them, even if they are obscure or distasteful. They should endeavor to perform their part in any dramatical piece, tableau or charade as well as possible, and the success they achieve will determine how conspicuous a part they may be called upon to perform at a subsequent time. The hostess should consult each performer before alloting a part, and endeavor to suit each one. The host or hostess should not have any conspicuous part assigned them, unless it is urged by all the other performers. Those who are to participate, should not only learn their parts, but endeavor to imbue themselves with the spirit of the character they personate, so as to afford pleasure to all who are invited to witness its performance. When persons have consented to participate in any such entertainment, only sickness or some very grave cause should prevent them from undertaking their part. Supper or refreshments usually follow private theatricals, of which both the performers and invited guests are invited to partake, and the remainder of the evening is spent in social intercourse.

ETIQUETTE OF CARD PLAYING.

Never urge any one who seems to be unwilling to play a game of cards. They may have conscientious scruples in the matter, which must be respected.

If you have no scruples of conscience, it is not courteous to refuse, when a game cannot be made up without you.

You may refuse to play if you do not understand the game thoroughly. If, however, you are urged to try, and your partner and opponents offer to instruct you, you may accede to their requests, for in so doing, you will acquire a better knowledge of the game.

Married and elderly people take precedence over young and unmarried people, in a game of cards.

It is the privilege of the host and hostess to suggest cards as a means of amusement for the guests. The latter should never call for them.

"Whist" is a game of cards so-called, because it requires silence and close attention. Therefore in playing this game, you must give your whole attention to the cards, and secure at least comparative silence. Do not suggest or keep up any conversation during a game, which will distract your own mind or the mind of others from the game.

Never hurry any one who is playing. In endeavoring to play their best, they should take their own time, without interruption.

Betting at cards is vulgar, partakes of the nature of gambling, and should at all times be avoided.

Never finger the cards while they are being dealt, nor take up any of them until all are dealt out, when you may take your own cards and proceed to play.

In large assemblies it is best to furnish the cards and tables, and allow guests to play or not, at their option, the host and hostess giving their assistance in seeking for people disposed to play, and in making up a game. In giving card parties, new cards should be provided on every occasion.

CHAPTER XXXV.

The Language of Flowers.

HOW beautiful and yet how cheap are flowers! Not exotics, but what are called common flowers. A rose, for instance, is among the most beautiful of the smiles of nature. The "laughing flowers," exclaims the poet. But there is more than gayety in blooming flowers, though it takes a wise man to see the beauty, the love, and the adaptation of which they are full.

What should we think of one who had *invented* flowers, supposing that, before him, flowers were unknown? Would he not be regarded as the opener-up of a paradise of new delight? Should we not hail the inventor as a genius, as a god? And yet these lovely offsprings of the earth have been speaking to man from the first dawn of his existence until now, telling him of the goodness and wisdom of the Creative Power, which bid the earth bring forth, not only that which was useful as food, but also flowers, the bright consummate flowers to clothe it in beauty and joy!

FLOWERS.

"The meanest flower that blows can give
Thoughts that do often lie too deep for tears."

Bring one of the commonest field-flowers into a room, place it on a table, or chimney-piece, and you seem to have brought a ray of sunshine into the place. There is a cheerfulness about flowers. What a delight are they to the drooping invalid! They are a sweet enjoyment, coming as messengers from the country, and seeming to say, "Come and see the place where we grow, and let your heart be glad in our presence."

There is a sentiment attached to flowers, and this sentiment has been expressed in language by giving names to various flowers, shrubs and plants. These names constitute a language, which may be made the medium of pleasant and amusing interchange of thought between men and women. A bouquet of flowers and leaves may be selected and arranged so as to express much depth of feeling—to be truly a poem. We present herewith a list of many flowers and plants, to which, by universal consent, a sentiment has become attached.

Acacia—Concealed love.
Acacia, Rose—Friendship.
Acanthus—Arts.
Adonis Vernalis—Bitter memories.
Agnus Casus—Coldness.
Agrimony—Thankfulness.
Almond—Hope.
Aloe—Superstition.
Althea—Consumed by love.
Alyssum, Sweet—Worth beyond beauty.
Amaranth—Immortality.
Amaryllis—Splendid beauty.
Ambrosia—Love returned.
Anemone—Expectation.

Anemone, Garden—Forsaken.
Angelica—Inspiration.
Apocynum (Dogbane)—Inspiration.
Apple—Temptation.
Apple Blossom—Preference.
Arbor vitæ—Unchanging friendship.
Arbutus, Trailing—Welcome.
Arum—Ardor.
Ash—Grandeur.
Ash, Mountain—Prudence.
Aspen Tree—Lamentation.
Asphodel—Regrets beyond the grave.
Aurilica—Avarice.
Azalea—Romance.
Bachelor's Button—Hope in love.
Balm—Sympathy.
Balm of Gilead—Healing.
Balsam—Impatience.
Barberry—Sharpness, satire.
Basil—Hatred.
Bay Leaf—No change till death.
Beech—Prosperity.
Bee Ophrys—Error.
Bee Orchis—Industry.
Bell Flower—Gratitude.
Belvidere, Wild (Licorice)—I declare against you.
Bilberry—Treachery.
Birch Tree—Meekness.
Black Bryony—Be my support.
Bladder-Nut Tree—Frivolous amusements
Blue Bottle—Delicacy.
Borage—Bluntness.
Box—Constancy.
Briers—Envy.
Broken Straw—Constancy.
Broom—Neatness.
Buckbean—Calm repose.
Bugloss—Falsehood.
Burdock—Importunity.

Buttercup—Riches.
Cactus—Thou leavest me.
Calla Lilly—Feminine beauty.
Calycanthus—Benevolence.
Camelia—Pity.
Camomile—Energy in action.
Candytuft—Indifference.
Canterbury Bell—Gratitude.
Cape Jasmine Gardenia—Transport, ecstasy.
Cardinal Flower—Distinction.
Carnation, Yellow—Disdain.
Catchfly (Silene), Red—Youthful love.
Catchfly, White—I fall a victim.
Cedar—I live for thee.
Cedar of Lebanon—Incorruptible.
Celandine—Future joy.
Cherry Tree—Good education.
Chickweed—I cling to thee.
Chickory—Frugality.
China Aster—I will think of thee.
China, Pink—Aversion.
Chrysanthemum, Rose—In love.
Chrysanthemum, White—Truth.
Chrysanthemum, Yellow—Slighted love.
Cinquefoil—Beloved child.
Clematis—Artifice.
Clover, Red—Industry.
Cobœa—Gossip.
Coxcomb—Foppery.
Colchium—My best days fled.
Coltsfoot—Justice shall be done you.
Columbine—Folly.
Columbine, Purple—Resolved to win.
Columbine, Red—Anxious.
Convolvulus Major—Dead hope.
Convolvulus Minor—Uncertainty.
Corchorus—Impatience of happiness.
Coreopsis—Love at first sight.
Coriander—Hidden merit.

Corn—Riches.
Cornelian Cherry Tree—Durability.
Coronilla—Success to you.
Cowslip—Pensiveness.
Cowslip, American—My divinity.
Crocus—Cheerfulness.
Crown Imperial—Majesty.
Currants—You please me.
Cypress—Mourning.
Cypress and Marigold—Despair.
Daffodil—Chivalry.
Dahlia—Forever thine.
Daisy, Garden—I share your feelings.
Daisy, Michaelmas—Farewell.
Daisy, Red— Beauty unknown to possessor
Daisy, White—Innocence.
Daisy, Wild—I will think of it.
Dandelion—Coquetry.
Daphne Mezereon—I desire to please.
Daphne Odora—I would not have you otherwise.
Deadleaves—Sadness.
Diosma—Usefulness.
Dittany—Birth.
Dock—Patience.
Dodder—Meanness.
Dogwood Flowering (Cornus)—Am I indifferent to
    you?
Ebony—Hypocrisy.
Eglantine—I wound to heal.
Elder—Compassion.
Elm—Dignity.
Endine—Frugality.
Epigæa, Repens (Mayflower)—Budding beauty
Eupatorium—Delay.
Evening Primrose—Inconstancy.
Evergreen—Poverty.
Everlasting (Graphalium)—Never ceasing memory.
Filbert—Reconciliation.
Fir Tree—Elevation

Flax—I feel your kindness.
Flora's Bell—Without pretension.
Flowering Reed—Confide in heaven.
Forget-me-not—True love.
Foxglove—Insincerity.
Fraxinella—Fire.
Fritilaria (Guinea-hen Flower)—Persecution.
Furze—Anger.
Fuchsia—The ambition of my love thus plagues itself.
Fuchsia, Scarlet—Taste.
Gardenia—Transport; Ecstasy.
Gentian, Fringed—Intrinsic worth.
Geranium, Apple—Present preference.
Geranium, Ivy—Your hand for next dance.
Geranium, Nutmeg—I expect a meeting.
Geranium, Oak—Lady, deign to smile.
Geranium, Rose—Preference.
Geranium, Silver-leaf—Recall.
Gillyflower—Lasting beauty.
Gladiolus—Ready armed.
Golden Rod—Encouragement.
Gooseberry—Anticipation.
Goosefoot—Goodness.
Gorse—Endearing affection.
Grape—Charity.
Grass—Utility.
Guelder Rose (Snowball)—Winter.
Harebell—Grief.
Hawthorn—Hope.
Heart's Ease—Think of me.
Heart's Ease, Purple—You occupy my thoughts.
Hazel—Reconciliation.
Heath—Solitude.
Helenium—Tears.
Heliotrope, Peruvian—I love; devotion.
Hellebore—Scandal.
Henbane—Blemish.
Hepatica—Confidence.
Hibiscus—Delicate Beauty.

Holly—Foresight.
Hollyhock—Fruitfulness.
Hollyhock, White—Female ambition.
Honesty (Lunaria)—Sincerity.
Honeysuckle—The bond of love.
Honeysuckle, Coral—The color of my fate.
Honeysuckle, Monthly—I will not answer hastily
Hop—Injustice.
Hornbeam—Ornament.
Horse-Chestnut—Luxury.
House-Leek—Domestic Economy.
Houstonia—Content.
Hoya (Wax Plant)—Sculpture.
Hyacinth—Jealousy.
Hyacinth, Blue—Constancy.
Hyacinth, Purple—Sorrow.
Hydrangea—Heartlessness.
Ice Plant—Your looks freeze me.
Indian Cress—Resignation.
Ipomaca—I attach myself to you.
Iris—Message.
Iris, German—Flame.
Ivy—Friendship; matrimony.
Jessamine, Cape—Transient joy.
Jessamine, White—Amiability.
Jessamine, Yellow—Grace; elegance.
Jonquil—Return my affection.
Judas-Tree—Betrayed.
Juniper—Perfect Loveliness.
Kalmia (Mountain Laurel)—Treachery.
Kennedia—Intellectual beauty.
Laburnum—Pensive Beauty.
Lady's Slipper—Capricious beauty.
Lagerstroema (Cape Myrtle)—Eloquence.
Lantana—Rigor.
Larch—Boldness.
Larkspur—Fickleness.
Laurel—Glory.
Laurestinus—I die if neglected.

Lavender—Distrust.
Lemon Blossom—Discretion.
Lettuce—Cold-hearted.
Lilac—First emotion of love.
Lilac, White—Youth.
Lily—Purity; modesty.
Lily of the Valey—Return of happiness.
Lily, Day—Coquetry.
Lily, Water—Eloquence.
Lily, Yellow—Falsehood.
Linden Tree—Conjugal love.
Live Oak—Liberty.
Liverwort—Confidence.
Locust—Affection beyond the grave.
London Pride—Frivolity.
Lotus—Forgetful of the past.
Love in a Mist—You puzzle me.
Love Lies Bleeding—Hopeless, not heartless.
Lucerne—Life.
Lungwort (Pulmonaria)—Thou art my life.
Lupine—Imagination.
Lychnis—Religious Enthusiasm.
Lythrum—Pretension.
Madder—Calumny.
Maiden's Hair—Discretion.
Magnolia, Chinese—Love of Nature.
Magnolia, Grandiflora—Peerless and Proud.
Magnolia, Swamp—Perseverance.
Mallow—Sweetness.
Mandrake—Horror.
Maple—Reserve.
Marigold—Cruelty.
Marigold, African—Vulgar-minded.
Marigold, French—Jealousy.
Marjoram—Blushes.
Marshmallow—Beneficence.
Marvel of Peru (Four o'clock)—Timidity.
Meadow Saffron—My best days gone.
Meadow Sweet—Usefulness.

27

Mignonette—Your qualities surpass your charms.
Mimosa—Sensitiveness.
Mint—Virtue.
Mistletoe—I surmount all difficulties.
Mock Orange (Syringia)—Counterfeit.
Monkshood—A deadly foe is near.
Moonwort—Forgetfulness.
Morning Glory—Coquetry.
Moss—Maternal love.
Motherwort—Secret Love.
Mourning Bride (Scabious)—Unfortunate attachment.
Mouse-ear Chickweed—Simplicity.
Mulberry, Black—I will not survive you.
Mulberry, White—Wisdom.
Mullein—Good nature.
Mushroom—Suspicion.
Mush Plant—Weakness.
Mustard Seed—Indifference.
Myosotis—Forget me not.
Myrtle—Love.
Narcissus—Egotism.
Nasturtium—Patriotism.
Nettle—Cruelty; Slander.
Night Blooming Cereus—Transient beauty.
Nightshade—Bitter truth.
Oak—Hospitality.
Oats—Music.
Oleander—Beware.
Orange—Generosity.
Orange Flower—Chastity.
Orchis—Beauty.
Osier—Frankness.
Osmunda—Dreams.
Pansy—Think of me.
Parsley—Entertainment.
Pasque Flower—Unpretentious.
Passion Flower—Religious Fervor.
Pea—Appointed meeting.
Pea, Everlasting—Wilt go with me?

Pea, Sweet—Departure.
Peach Blossom—My heart is thine.
Pear Tree—Affection.
Peony—Anger.
Pennyroyal—Flee away.
Periwinkle—Sweet memories.
Persimmon—Bury me amid nature's beauties.
Petunica—Am not proud.
Pheasant's Eye—Sorrowful memories.
Phlox—Our souls united.
Pimpernel—Change.
Pine—Time.
Pine Apple—You are perfect.
Pine, Spruce—Farewell.
Pink—Pure affection.
Pink, Clove—Dignity.
Pink, Double-red—Pure, ardent love.
Pink, Indian—Aversion.
Pink, Mountain—You are aspiring.
Pink, Variegated—Refusal.
Pink, White—You are fair.
Pink, Yellow—Disdain.
Plane Tree—Genius.
Pleurisy Root (Asclopias)—Heartache cure.
Plum Tree—Keep promise.
Plum Tree, Wild—Independence.
Polyanthus—Confidence.
Poplar, Black—Courage.
Poplar, White—Time.
Poppy—Consolation.
Poppy, White—Sleep of the heart.
Pomegranate—Foolishness.
Pomegranate Flower—Elegance.
Potato—Beneficence.
Pride of China (Melia)—Dissension.
Primrose—Early youth.
Primrose, Evening—Inconstancy.
Privet—Mildness.
Pumpkin—Coarseness.

Quince—Temptation.
Ragged-robin (Lychnis)—Wit.
Ranunculus—Radiant with charms.
Reeds—Music.
Rhododendron—Agitation.
Rose—Beauty.
Rose, Austrian—Thou art all that is lovely.
Rose, Bridal—Happy love.
Rose, Burgundy—Unconscious beauty.
Rose, Cabbage—Love's Ambassador.
Rose, Campion—Only deserve my love.
Rose, Carolina—Love is dangerous.
Rose, China—Grace.
Rose, Daily—That smile I would aspire to.
Rose, Damask—Freshness.
Rose, Dog—Pleasure and pain.
Rose, Hundred Leaf—Pride.
Rose, Inermis—Ingratitude.
Rose, Maiden's Blush—If you do love me you will
    find me out.
Rose, Moss—Superior merit.
Rosebud, Moss—Confessed love.
Rose, Multiflora—Grace.
Rose, Musk-cluster—Charming.
Rose, Sweetbriar—Sympathy.
Rose, Tea—Always lovely.
Rose, Unique—Call me not beautiful.
Rose, White—I am worthy of you.
Rose, White (withered)—Transient impression.
Rose, Wild—Simplicity.
Rose, Yellow—Decrease of love.
Rose, York and Lancaster—War.
Roses, Garland of—Reward of Virtue.
Rosebud—Young girl.
Rosebud, White—The heart that knows not love.
Rosemary—Your presence revives me.
Rue—Disdain.
Rush—Docility.
Saffron—Excess is dangerous.

Sage—Esteem.
Sardonia—Irony.
Satin-flower (Lunaria)—Sincerity.
Scabious, Mourning Bride—Widowhood.
Sensitive Plant—Timidity.
Service Tree—Prudence.
Snapdragon—Presumption.
Snowball—Thoughts of heaven.
Snowdrop—Consolation.
Sorrel—Wit ill-timed.
Southernwood—Jesting.
Spearmint—Warm feelings.
Speedwell, Veronica—Female fidelity.
Spindle-tree—Your image is engraven on my heart.
Star of Bethlehem—Reconciliation.
Starwort, American—Welcome to a stranger.
St. John's Wort (Hypericum)—Superstition.
Stock, Ten-week—Promptitude.
Stramonium, Common—Disguise.
Strawberry—Perfect excellence.
Strawberry Tree (Arbutus)—Esteemed love.
Sumac—Splendor.
Sunflower, Dwarf—Your devout admirer.
Sunflower, Fall—Pride.
Sweet Sultan—Felicity.
Sweet William—Artifice.
Sycamore—Curiosity.
Syringia—Memory.
Tansy—I declare against you.
Teasel—Misanthropy.
Thistle—Austerity.
Thorn Apple—Deceitful charms.
Thorn, Black—Difficulty.
Thorns—Severity.
Thrift—Sympathy.
Throatwood (Pulmonaria)—Neglected beauty.
Thyme—Activity.
Tiger Flower—May pride befriend thee.
Touch me not, Balsam—Impatience.

Truffle—Surprise.
Trumpet Flower—Separation.
Tuberose—Dangerous pleasures.
Tulip—Declaration of love.
Tulip Tree—Rural happiness.
Tulip, Variegated—Beautiful eyes.
Tulip, Yellow—Hopeless love.
Turnip—Charity.
Valerian—Accommodating disposition.
Venus's Flytrap—Caught at last.
Venus's Looking-glass—Flattery.
Verbena—Sensibility.
Vine—Intoxicating.
Violet, Blue—Love.
Violet, White—Modesty.
Violet, Yellow—Modest worth.
Virgin's Bower—Filial love.
Wall Flower—Fidelity.
Walnut—Stratagem.
Weeping Willow—Forsaken.
Wheat—Prosperity.
Woodbine—Fraternal love.
Wood Sorrel—Joy.
Wormwood—Absence.
Yarrow—Cure for heartache.
Yew—Sorrow.
Zennæ—Absent friends.

CHAPTER XXXVI.

Precious Stones.

SOME of the precious stones and gems have been given a distinct significance by imparting a special meaning or name to them. The ancients besides considered certain months sacred to the different stones, and some people have considered this in making birthday or wedding presents. Below will be found the stones regarded as sacred to the various months, with the meaning given to each.

January—Garnet—Constancy and Fidelity.
February—Amethyst—Sincerity.
March—Bloodstone—Courage.
April—Sapphire—Repentance.
May—Emerald—Success in love.
June—Agate—Health and long life.
July—Ruby—Forgetfulness of, and exemption from vexations caused by friendship and love.
August—Sardonyx—Conjugal Fidelity.
September—Chrysolite—Freedom from evil passions and sadness of mind.
October—Opal—Hope and Faith.
November—Topaz—Fidelity and Friendship.
December—Turquoise—Prosperity.

Of the precious stones not included in the above list,
the language is given below:

Diamond—Innocence.
Pearl—Purity.
Cornelian—Contented mind.
Moonstone—Protects from danger.
Heliotrope—Causing the owner to walk invisible